TONGUED WITH FIRE

W. Gordon Lawrence

TONGUED WITH FIRE
Groups in Experience

W. Gordon Lawrence

Foreword by
Laurence J. Gould

London & New York
KARNAC BOOKS

First published in 2000 by
H. Karnac (Books) Ltd., 58 Gloucester Road, London SW7 4QY

A subsidiary of Other Press LLC, New York

Copyright © 2000 W. Gordon Lawrence

Foreword copyright © 2000 Laurence J. Gould

British Library Cataloguing in Publication Data

A C.I.P. for this book is available from the British Library

ISBN 1 85575 224 7

10 9 8 7 6 5 4 3 2 1

Edited, designed, and produced by Communication Crafts

Printed in Great Britain by Polestar AUP Aberdeen Limited

www.karnacbooks.com

For Ester,
our family of Anthony, Alexander, and David,
their wives, and our grandchildren;
and for Bipin Patel, Brendan Duddy, and Joan Hutten

ACKNOWLEDGEMENTS

I am grateful to the following publishers for permission to reprint, either in whole or in part:

Brunner/Mazel, Inc., New York, and *Group* for "Signals of Transcendence" (chapter four);

Process Press and *Free Associations* for "The Fifth Basic Assumption" (chapter five);

Routledge & Kegan Paul for "Beyond the Frames" (chapter six);

The A. K. Rice Institute for "Emergent Themes in Group Relations Education" (chapter seven);

South Bank University Press for "The Politics of Salvation and Revelation in the Practice of Consultancy" (chapter eight);

Les Conseillers de Synthese (SICS), Paris, for "To Surprise the Soul" [Surprendre l'Ame] (chapter nine);

A. H. Wheeler & Co. (P) Ltd., Allahabad, for "A Psychoanalytic Perspective for Understanding Organizational Life" (chapter ten).

I regret that I have not been able to cite page numbers in all cases. The references are lost. For this I apologize. Needless to say, all errors in the text are mine.

CONTENTS

FOREWORD

Laurence J. Gould

He is known to almost all of us within group relations work through his writings, many of which have become virtual staples in the courses we teach and the programmes we offer. Some that are especially well known are his papers entitled "A Concept for Today: The Management of Oneself in Role", which is the marvellous concluding essay in his important edited volume dedicated to the memory of Pierre Turquet (*Exploring Individual and Organizational Boundaries*, 1979a), and "Signals of Transcendence in Large Groups as Systems" (1993). A smaller number of us have also had the good fortune to attend group relations or social dreaming conferences where he has been present, or to work with him on consultation projects, and experiencing his extraordinary creativity and courage up close.

When I spent a sabbatical year at the Tavistock Institute of Human Relations in the early 1970s, Gordon Lawrence and I were "senior juniors". He had recently come to the Tavistock to take a full-time post at the Centre for Applied Social Research and was rapidly making his presence felt. Since then that early promise has been far exceeded by his considerable accomplishments. To tell you about them all would take a volume itself, so let me simply note that he has published over forty articles and two books, he has produced two television documentaries on groups (*Them and Us* and *Who's in Charge?*) and has a few poems in *No Other Place* (Olson, 1995a), published by Tuckwell Press, all of which reflect his preoccupation with the nature of the relationship between individuals and their organizations. Happily, many of these writings are collected in this volume, so that you can engage his wisdom and insights about group and organizational life directly through your own experience in these contexts.

The collection of Gordon Lawrence's papers, assembled in this volume, spans two-and-a-half decades and address some of the most difficult, complex, and paradoxical aspects of the human condition. These are apprehended by his, in many ways, quite unique rendering of psychoanalysis as a tool of cultural inquiry into the operation of unconscious processes in the social arena. This approach, pioneered at The Tavistock Institute of Human Relations, drew its early psychoanalytic inspiration from the brilliant work of W. R. Bion, whose writings about groups and institutions—done mostly during his tenure at the Tavistock—were subsequently collected in a volume titled *Experiences in Groups* (1961). In this connection it is difficult to think of more than a scant handful of people that are more oft-quoted than Gordon Lawrence, who, as much as anyone in England or abroad, and far more than most, has carried forward and contributed to extending and shaping in far-ranging, unexpected, and novel ways the rhetorical reach of Bion's seminal ideas. An important and apt recent example is his paper titled "The Fifth Basic Assumption" (this volume, chapter five). Put slightly differently, Gordon Lawrence has been a major contributor to establishing the methodology and field of inquiry, research, and practice now commonly referred to as "the Tavistock approach".

Another aspect of Gordon Lawrence's work requires, I believe, some comment. And that is the avowedly spiritual dimension of his thinking. This is most obvious and notable in his use of the idea of the soul and in his preoccupation with the nature of evil. To what are undoubtedly the secular sensibilities of the majority of those reading this volume, such notions will seem either quaint, peculiar, or simply intrusive and out of place in an otherwise rewarding and engaging meeting. However, any of these reactions would be a mistake. They are integral to his thinking, and if "tough-minded spirituality" is not an oxymoron—and I don't believe it is—it does capture something very important about the courage and backbone of this extraordinary social scientist who has often, in his writings, dared to challenge the scepticism of many of his secular colleagues. That we have, in consequence, indulged him at times is certainly true. That this says a great deal more about us, our own anxieties, and our indulgence as a defence against them, is truer still.

Finally, what is especially striking about Gordon Lawrence's work is not simply the brilliance of his ideas and the depth of his commitments, but the elegance of his language and concepts. We have all had the experience of enchantment as he wrote or talked about social dreaming, about the politics of salvation and the politics of revelation, about a memoir of the future, and about the management of oneself in role. In all of these phrases, and the thinking behind them, Gordon Lawrence always seems to capture the deep resonance of our felt experience in a way that does indeed produce new thoughts, as well as the experience of being understood. And, in his inimitable manner, he himself best captures this idea. For example, in describing the guiding hypothesis underlying the "Social Dreaming for the Management of Change" programmes, he writes that "consultancy and action research, when practised at its best, encourages people in the politics of revelation. These are processes that foster the responsible exercise of authority, both individually and collectively, so that people become generative of ideas." I think that even these few words give you a hint of his own enormous generativity, and the pleasures and illumination you will encounter as you read this volume, *Tongued with Fire: Groups in Experience*. One of his themes is that of "surprising the soul", to which there are a range of references throughout this text. He has continually surprised all of ours since we have known him.

New York

INTRODUCTION

Anyone who attempts to write about aspects of contemporary social realities does so against a larger background of pogroms, holocaust, tribal warfare, killing fields, the gulags, terrorism, poverty, and famine and all the other evils of our century. Living in the comparative plenitude of Western societies, such evil seems to be far way. It can be safely located in the continent of Africa, the Far East, South America, or at the edge of Europe in Yugoslavia, or the periphery of Britain in Northern Ireland, until we start to think of the evils around us—bullying at work, poverty, ruthless ambition, unemployment. And one knows about the pollution of the ecosystem and the stress that people experience personally, and one wonders how can goodness, which is definable by any mature human being, triumph in our times.

One way we can try to understand is to persist in the study of the group, organizations, and the place of the individual. It is a beginning to unravel what happens to individuals when they become lost in the unconscious mental world of the group, become mindless, and lose their capacity to discriminate between good and evil. It is the experience of evil that inspires the search for the good, for they are inextricably linked and we cannot know one but for the other.

The study of the group was accelerated because of the events leading to the 1939 war. The phenomenon of Nazism, and other forms of totalitarianism demanded an understanding of what was happening to the people of Germany and to make sense of what had happened in the Spanish Civil War. It is difficult now to comprehend how popular Adolf Hitler's *My Struggle* had been. My copy of the English-language edition published by The Paternoster Library records that the book had been republished fourteen times. From 1933, when Hitler seized political power in Germany, civilization, as it was known, and liberal–democratic ideals were under fire from Nazism as the world witnessed the emergence of the most dedicated authoritarian regime to have existed in modern times.

In 1937 Arnold Zweig published his English edition of *Insulted and Exiled*, and here we read of the persecution of the Jews and also some of the sharpest descriptions of mass psychotic-like behaviour. Previously, little had been written on the group. Only Freud (1921c), McDougall (1920), Trotter (1916), and Le Bon (1896) come to mind.

It was after the war that Wilfred Bion published his papers on groups based on his experiences during the war. Trist (1985) has given a first-hand account of how Bion formulated the bases of the leaderless group for the War Office Selection Boards. Afterwards, when at the Tavistock Clinic, he wrote *Experiences in Groups*, which was published as a book in 1961.

It is this text of Bion's that lies at the heart of all the chapters in this collection. The disadvantage of this collection is that it is a palimpsest of the book that has never been written. The advantage is that because the essays represent a distillation of thought at a particular point in time, they can lead on to new thought at another time in another place by other people. This was demonstrated to me when in 1994 I was presented with a Festschrift, entitled *Discovering Social Meanings*, that had been organized and edited by Burkard Sievers and David Armstrong. I found myself moved, and very much rejoicing that other people with whom I had worked were formulating thought on our common concern. This was the discovery of social meaning through experiencing and thinking, contained in both our conscious and unconscious minds as revealed in our waking and dream lives during our daily existence in groups, institutions, and societies.

Bion's ideas on groups were developed at the Tavistock Institute of Human Relations through what became the Group Relations Training Programme. A version of the history of these Working Conferences has been provided by Miller (1990), which I have no wish to rehearse, except for what appears in this collection.

Groups in experience

I have been ambivalent about groups all my life—but fatefully fascinated by them too. My first recallable dream, when I was between three and four years old, is of being with a family of neighbours, enjoying a tea party with sandwiches and cakes. This was probably the only identifiable group I knew at the time. We were all naked, but very decorous. Readers can have their own associations, but it was a dream of a group and what, I believe, was puzzling to me was how to relate to this group of what were for me very happy people.

The first memories I have that can be named as an identifiable "group experience" happened when I was a member of a Moral Rearmament group as a fifteen-year-old in 1949–51. The members were teachers, doctors, and other professional people in Aberdeen, Scotland. Three of us were schoolboys. It was a small group, which met in the drawing-room of the leader. The routine was the same at each weekly meeting. The leader would read aloud from the New Testament. The idea was to start from Matthew and go through to Revelation. Older members of the group had been through this sequence before.

There would be discussion amongst us as to the meaning of particular texts. The discussion was both didactic and associative. The associations were sometimes of a confessional nature and, on reflection, probably had a therapeutic value for the volunteer. Our leader, after all, was a medical practitioner. The confessions were also a relief for the group, because the hard work of teasing out the meaning of a text was leavened by a glimpse into someone's life, which was far more interesting. One woman could always be relied on if the tone of the group was lethargic. She always started in the same way: "I remember a time in my life of great pain and tribulation." The details of what she would recount are lost to me now, but the feelings I recall. The emotions were an admixture of adolescent, prurient curiosity and wonder at the apparent sadness of being adult.

The purpose of the group was for its members to be "saved". People could give the date, sometimes the hour, when they had chosen for Christ and had attained salvation. I never had this experience, even though I wanted it if only to be a member of the group, like most of the others. Being saved is not something one can lie about. After a year or so I stopped attending. Some weeks afterwards I received a postcard, which had the message, "Are you dead?" with the citation "Ephesians 2, 1" which I checked, and which read, "And you hath he quickened who were dead in trespasses and sins."

The War Office Selection Boards were designed by some of my older colleagues at the Tavistock Institute. But I did not know that in 1958 when I attended. The purpose was clear: to be selected for officer training. The group was all-important at WOSB because one was totally reliant on the other members' good will, particularly in the practical, problem-solving exercises that we each had to solve acting as leader to our peers. Bion, in a paper called "The Leaderless Group Project", outlines this method of selection.

> This was done by a method so simple and obvious, when it has been propounded, that its revolutionary nature can easily be lost sight of. The man found that he was not entered into a free-for-all competition with other candidates. Instead he found himself the member of a group and, apparently, all the tests were test, not of himself, but of the group. In concrete terms, a group of eight or nine candidates, an "eye-full" from the testing officer's point of view, was told to build, say, a bridge. No lead was given about organization or leadership;

these were left to emerge and it was the duty of the observing
officers to watch how any given man was reconciling his personal ambitions, hopes and fears with the requirements
exacted by the group for its success. That, in brief outline, is
the basic principle of all the Leaderless Group Tests. [Bion,
1946, pp. 77–78]

All candidates had to complete such a test. One of us was told by
the selecting officer, as we stared at a wide ditch: "You have to
take your platoon across this river, which is full of crocodiles." We
each imagined swirling waters, dense jungle, and lurking crocodiles, while we shivered in the autumnal cold of Salisbury Plain.
"You have this plank", said the officer. We all looked at the plank,
which was too short to bridge the river. The solution was the
cantilever principle. We rushed around willing our colleague chosen to be leader to get a pass mark. Some of us weighed down the
end of the plank on the near bank so that others could use it as a
springboard to reach the other side. Our colleague ably instructed
us. Two men were left on the original bank. They threw the plank
across the river. Deftly we fielded it and arranged it to suspend
above the river, pinning it down with our combined weight to
receive the two remaining members of our platoon. The first
jumped from the bank, nimbly landed on the plank, and ran to
add his weight to it. Full of our feelings of success, we looked at
the last man. He was the heaviest of us all. Everyone could anticipate the *denouément*, except the young man being tested. Delicately
the last man jumped from the bank to the plank, and we all cata-
pulted into the river.

After Mons Officer Cadet School I served in the Royal Army
Education Corps for three years. It was, at the time, a privileged
life. The style of living was memorable. At one point I was posted
to a rather elitist regiment that was so grand that it was rumoured
that they spelt the commonest four-letter expletive in the British
army with two small "f"s. My time with this regiment was, however, a rare opportunity to observe a group that shared the same
social background, having had the same social origins, and who
observed well-rehearsed mores and customs.

There were also very positive learning experiences in groups
during this time in the army. Through Jimmy Mills, later killed on

Anapurna, I became involved with the Army Mountaineering Association and served for a time on the general committee. Then I organized mountaineering schools for soldiers. I had a firm principle: leaders on a climb were selected on merit, not rank. One young subaltern broke this rule. He fell while leading on the climbing rope, but fortunately on his descent his foot got trapped. We rescued him. Years later I met him when he had become a Prison Governor.

Towards the end of my short service commission, when I began to wonder if the barbed wire perimeter fences were to keep intruders out or me in, I took part in the last group event I was to experience in the army. In the winter of 1960 it was realized by someone in the War office that in the event of a nuclear war the ground forces of the British army had no tactics to deal with it. Consequently every officer's mess in the army was convened for a study day in the summer of 1961.

Every chair was taken in our anteroom. We listened to one of our senior colleagues, a major, describe what he had seen of nuclear explosions at the tests in Australia. He vividly described his experiences, and the horror of the effects of nuclear war began to form in our minds.

Discussion was invited by our kindly commanding officer. It was desultory. We aired our views and finally came to the conclusion that the trick was to lure the enemy into a valley and drop our bomb on them. That would minimize the effects of fall-out for us. Some us recognized that this might be difficult should the terrain be flat, as, say, the Hungarian Plain. Norway or Switzerland would be a perfect venue for a nuclear war. We felt we had achieved a good deal. We had a strategy, of a kind, and the tactics would follow.

In the silence that followed one of us diffidently remarked, "D'you realize that if our chaps are watching when the bomb goes off they will be blinded?" There was consternation in the room. A blind army was unthinkable. Would dogs for the blind help? But they would be blinded also! An army with white sticks? Impossible!

One of our brighter officers gave the answer we were seeking. "There's really no problem. We shall issue the men with black eye patches." We relaxed. Why did I not think of that? Then a more intelligent officer leaned forward and asked, "Which eye? His shooting eye or t' other?"

Subsequently, I had my first introduction to the study of groups as an activity when I attended my first Leicester Conference of the Tavistock Institute of Human Relations in 1965. This came about because of Denis Rice, with whom I had been at Aberdeen University in the mid-1950s. We were both working in Leicester and would meet occasionally. He was warden of Vaughan College of the University of Leicester, and I lectured in the local college of further education. Denis told me about a strange conference he had just attended about groups. It was an experiential conference, and he explained what that meant. I quizzed him about what he had learned, and he told me that the only way I would know about it really was to experience it for myself. To Denis Rice I owe a large debt, for it was he who was instrumental in introducing me to a way of thinking that changed the direction of my life.

The Leicester Conference of 1965 was sponsored by the Tavistock Institute of Human Relations and the University of Leicester. I found the experience bewildering. My memories are of the late Ken Rice and Pierre Turquet working together in the large group, which I found terrifying. I also remember the panic flight at the beginning of the inter-group event, and some of the comments made in the small group are still with me.

In that year of 1964–65 I was a student on the diploma course in sociology and the psychology of education at the University of Leicester School of Education. As part of that course we participated each week in a group experience with Professor Billy Tibble who, along with Professor John Alloway, had been sponsors with representatives of the Tavistock Institute in launching the experiential conference on groups. The two experiences, Tibble's group and the Leicester Conference, brought me to a new realization of the possible nature of social realities.

But I did nothing directly with the experiences. Indirectly, they changed my thinking—or, rather, confirmed my intuition that sociology would deliver no insights into human nature and living as long as it was in the grip of the logico-positivists. Gradually, I learned more about the work of the early practitioners at the Tavistock Institute and became convinced that they were the ones who had the most valuable insights into the realities of the social world because they affirmed the importance of the unconscious mind.

After Leicester University, I had gone to Bede College in Durham. There I taught the sociology of education. About three years later Canon Bill Wright, who was an Industrial Chaplain on Teesside, collected a few of us, and we launched a series of weekend conferences on the experiential study of groups. The Extra-Mural Department of the University was the sponsor. These conferences were for local leaders in the community and ran for quite a number of years. Through the "Sandsend" conferences, named after the seaside village in which they were held, I started to "take" groups.

In 1971 I joined the Tavistock Institute as a project officer in the Centre for Applied Social Research (CASR), which had been founded by the late A. K. Rice when Eric Trist was creating the Human Resources Centre. Inevitably, I took part in a year-long advanced training group in group relations run by the late Pierre Turquet and Isabel Menzies Lyth. And, of course, started my psychoanalysis.

On the death of Turquet in 1975 I became joint director of the Group Relations Training Programme of the Tavistock Institute. In the period that followed I was able to relaunch the male–female conferences that had been brought to Britain by Larry Gould when he was a visiting social scientist in CASR. What excited me was creating in 1978 conferences with the title "Individual and Organization: The Politics of Relatedness".

During these years at the Tavistock I was fortunate to be able to work over ten years or so in group relations education in India with Gouranga Chattopadhyay. Before MundO was created, I worked with Burkard Sievers on the first conferences in Germany. Through collaboration with Georges Gueron I was able to start conferences in France, which, I understand, run to this day. There were a number of conferences in Canada with the now defunct Rosehill Institute of Human Relations. All of these experiences, both good and bad, were essential to my continuing to puzzle out the nature of group life.

In 1982 I left the Tavistock Institute to go to the Shell International Petroleum Company in London. Since then I have worked twice on the staff of working conferences in England. Fortunately for my own development I was able to work in Ireland and other countries. Through Eleanor Dorgan and Gerry French we were able to initiate a series of conferences called "Authority for Faith" in Ireland.

In Australia, the "Authority for Faith" conferences have had considerable success since Alastair Bain invited me to introduce them. It gives me enormous pleasure to hear about their developing ideas and innovative work in the field of group relations training.

What also has given me pleasure is to see the development of this work in Israel since I was invited to direct the first conference on group relations there through the invitation of Vered Amitzi, Hanni Biran, Sandra Halevy, and Judit Trieste. Similarly, I feel hopeful of the growth of this work in Bulgaria through the initiative of Robert Young and Tomar Tomov.

It is to the Israel group that I owe an enormous debt because through them I was able to re-launch Social Dreaming. This is a development of group relations training and owes its existence to what I learned during the Tavistock years. The story of the development of the Social Dreaming Matrix is contained in *Social Dreaming @ Work*, (1998). It has been amazing how it has caught the imagination, and now there are programmes in America through the A. K. Rice Institute in New York and the William Alanson White Institute in the same city. There are also programmes in Germany and Switzerland, in India, and, of course, in Britain. In Australia through Alastair Bain and Suzanne Leigh-Ross there have been the most sedulous developments because they have pioneered not only new ways of having Social Dreaming Matrices but have also introduced Social Dreaming into mainstream group relations training.

In 1982 I met Alan King, who was a participant in the last Leicester Conference I took part in. Alan is a film-maker and we decided that one day we would do some project together. It came about quickly. We designed a working conference for unemployed Canadian citizens. The primary task of the event was to explore the experiences of being employed and unemployed. The large group sessions of the conference were filmed in entirety. Discussion groups were not. There were 30 participants, which represented a cross-section of Canadian society. We worked together for four days. The consultants to the group were Elie Dubbane and Austin Lee, both psychoanalysts who had been members of the Rosehill Institute of Human Relations in Toronto.

The result of this work was the film "Who's in Charge?" which was shown on Canadian television. Subsequently, the film was selected for the 28th London Film Festival and was shown there in 1984. I had contributed to an earlier film, "Them and Us", for BBC Panorama in 1981.

What do I feel now about the years of "taking" groups, begun nearly 30 years ago?

At the International Conference in Australia in 1993 I felt considerable sadness at the paucity of thinking present in some—but by no means all—of the participants, who are mostly reputed to be leaders in this field of work. And the level of malevolence was frightening. If one did not recognize that here was an Establishment under siege, one cannot think that the work of Bion, Rice, and Turquet is now reduced to such "interpretations" as "Take back your projections!" And I feel near-distressed at the continual voicing of narcissistic preoccupations. When I hear statements like, "I am what I am because you have caged me in your projections. The wish in the conference is to preserve me." I am amazed, once again, what people will do to survive. But for what?—I ask myself. Fortunately, the method of group relations education, based on the work of Bion, is such that participants learn irrespective of the quality of the staff.

Should I have listened to Denis Rice 35 years ago? To be sure, if I had chosen not to attend that Leicester Conference in 1965, it would have been a different professional life—whether better or worse, I will never know. Is this what is called *karma*?

To surprise the soul

Emily Dickinson has a line: "We must keep the soul terribly surprised." At the time when I read it in George Steiner's *In Bluebeard's Castle* (1971), it made stunning sense to me, and it still does. This idea of surprising the soul is one leitmotif of this collection of papers, which explores dimensions of conscious and unconscious life in groups, institutions, and society. "Surprise" has connotations of wonder, marvel, epiphany, but also negative ones of shock and bewilderment, for surprises are not always good. But they are always instructive. Soul is a notoriously difficult concept, and one given little credence within the academic community. Does it exist? Certainly, it cannot be located physically. For me, more than anything else, soul is a mental capacity to be available for experiencing, feeling, and thinking. I have the idea of heightened consciousness, which is moral. It is the psychic disposition that enhances our ability to experience our experiences and learn from them. Primitive peoples describe as "loss of soul" a condition when the individual is unable to take part in society, when all the traditions and rituals are dead to him and he to them. He is no longer in communion with others. He has no personal myth, nor is he able to take part in shared myths. A vital element is absent. He is "not there". This means accepting that the soul is the primary principle of life, in that it is not a body but that which actuates a body, to echo St Thomas Aquinas. The soul can never be "operationalized" scientifically, but it remains as an open, suggestive hypothesis.

Although Freud used the term *die Seele,* it was not till Bruno Bettelheim published *Freud and Man's Soul* (1983) that the word "soul" became acceptable in professional psychoanalytic discourse. Jung regularly used it for what we would call the psyche. The existence of the soul enables us to acknowledge and attempt to be in touch with the unconscious, the links between life and death, and what can be called the Other. This, it seems to me, is the stuff of psychoanalysis.

Tongued with fire

In his farewell to poetry, T. S. Eliot wrote in *Little Gidding* (Eliot, 1943) that what the dead say is "tongued with fire". I take it that what he meant is that we imbue the mode of communication of the dead with the pentecostal in a way that the living cannot be. What the dead have to tell us becomes saturated with the eternal in relation to the temporal of daily living. What the dead say is everlasting in its meaning. The "intersection of the timeless moment" is the incarnation of the eternal with the temporal. If the response to reading a poem is the creation of another poem, the response to a dream another dream, the experience of the group construes another group within the participant. The creative/destructive tension between the group in reality and the group in the mind is a perennial challenge.

The phrase "tongued with fire" captures the experience of taking part in any group of any size. There is the idea that beyond the spoken words there is a whole other world peopled by our human ancestors who speak, or think, in our minds from their perspective. Our cultural heritage determines how we think and how we feel. On occasion in a group, we catch a thought that we express with passion and fire because we feel it to be important, indeed essential. The "fire" expressed is about the state of our being and becoming, situated in a long-forgotten history that can evoke itself as a dream, or as something that we know but have never thought of till sparked by the unique environmental conditions of the group, which is the space of the possible.

CHAPTER ONE

Thinking refracted

Groups and thinking

Groups of human beings can be tyrannous, or benign. They are, pre-eminently, the *loci* of experience. It is experience that gives rise to feelings/emotions, which activate our thinking. Thinking is the capacity of human beings to engage with their world. Thinking depends on our ability to experience our experiences as opposed to merely perceiving them as events or happenings that occur, whose import never engages us emotionally.

Thinking I am to liken as a metaphor to light falling on a prism, which is then refracted into colour (wavelengths) on leaving the prism. Furthermore—and here I am beholden to Wilfred Bion—thinking and thought exist in search of a thinker. The thinker catches the thought and breaks it down into its constituents with which the thinker proceeds to "play", creating new thinking and thoughts. The metaphor reaches its limits because thinking is not tangible like light.

I want, at the same time, to capture the idea that thinking can also arise from a thinker. It is as if the prism were initiating light from inside itself, which is then refracted through the prism. Thinking I regard as a two-way interactive process; it can be begun from either the outside or the inside of the individual. How else does one explain the inventiveness of an Einstein, who creates a totally new way of construing the world through quantum mechanics, with incalculable effects on thinking about the natural world in our own century? How else does one explain the work of a poet who captures in a telling image the feeling/emotion that a particular experience evokes, causing the reader to look at similar experiences in a totally new way?

While it is possible for individuals to give added value to what has been thought in the past through the quality of their new thinking, I am persuaded that most thinking arises from the *context* that we inhabit. The idea of "refraction" I will stay with as a metaphor because it captures the notion that thinking is a wave function that goes on all the time, to be realized on occasion as a particle function that consists of actual thoughts, which human beings can then transact. Thinking can be conceptualized as being either a wave or a particle. One can "measure" it (identify its qualities) either in one form or the other, but not at the same time.

This flux of thinking is experienced in groups. Without the experiences of taking part in groups we would be ignorant, or not conscious, of the ill-defined—possibly indefinable—oppositions between: creativity and destruction; chaos and cosmos; the sacred and the profane; immanence and transcendence; love and hate; joy and despair; the life-giving and anti-life tendencies; Eros and Thanatos; ruthlessness and ruth (concern); good and evil; knowing and unknowing; the finite and the infinite; the conscious and the unconscious; integration and disintegration; together with all the other interactive polarities that are necessary conditions for knowing and understanding, which are the quintessence of being a human being. In this long sentence I attempt to capture and express the continuous bombardment on our senses of knowing, and not knowing, that we come to experience in relation to other people in groups. Sometimes the thinking is a wave; at other times it freezes, or coagulates, into a particle.

Group life, no matter how small the configuration, is essential for our survival as a species. We learn to think by responding with our feelings to our experiences in relationships and groups, or in no-relationships or no-groups. The absence of a relationship, or group, can be a powerful experience, resulting in feelings and emotions. Ranging from our very first experiences of relating to mother, or mother-substitute, by whom we are inducted into speech, language, and culture, through to the groups and group-ings we belong to as a child, as an adolescent, and as an adult, we face or confront the issues raised by the complexity of living. Thinking, coupled with the ability to use language to communi-cate, is what distinguishes human beings from any other animals. (Dolphins, for example, can think, but they have a different means of communication.) Thinking is integral to our humanity, but is so routine that it is difficult to comprehend how essential it is for us as humans.

All organizations, as I shall say throughout the following chap-ters, rely on the thinking of the people who take up roles within them. Without thinking, there would be no organization. Thinking is a defining characteristic of the life and work of the people in an organization. And the same can be said for any other social con-figuration.

One psychoanalyst who devoted his intellectual life to the study of thinking, thought, and knowing and how these are ar-rived at was Wilfred Bion. In his Introduction to *Experiences in Groups* (1961), he writes:

> I am impressed, as a practising psycho-analyst, by the fact that the psycho-analytic approach, through the individual and the approach that these papers describe, through the group, are dealing with different facets of the same phenomena. The two methods provide the practitioner with a rudimentary binocu-lar vision. The observations tend to fall into two categories, whose affinity is shown by phenomena which, *when examined by one method, centre on the Oedipal situation, related to the pair-ing group, and when examined by the other, centre on the sphinx, related to problems of knowledge and scientific method.* [Bion, 1961, p. 8, italics added]

Bion was using the myth of the riddle of the Sphinx to express the capability of human beings to ask questions of themselves about their existence and its meaning, which is the basis of knowing and knowledge. The private, personal Oedipal myth, which had been used by Freud to found psychoanalysis, Bion regarded as an "integral part of the human mind . . . that allows the young child to make real contact with his parents" (Bléandonu, 1994, p. 185).

This inherent thrust for fundamental knowledge of self in relation to the environment, this epistemophilic instinct (Klein, 1921, 1928), is what makes us human, though it will be impeded by anxieties and fears and rests at the root of all that we know of the world in which we live. It is the basis of knowledge of—or, rather, our personal knowing of—the world and our place in it. In the context of groups, this exploration into their own lives is represented by the riddle of the Sphinx. As Hanna Biran puts it, the person who takes part in the explorations of a group and its life is exploring

> a hidden world long gone and forgotten, which survives in the form of myths leaving behind some traces and signs, which are in fact powerful enough to compel us to inquire into the meaning of our lives. [Biran, 1997, p. 32]

Bion makes the differentiation, when referring to Freud's division between ego instincts and sexual ones, by advocating that in thinking of groups a better distinction would be "between narcissism on the one hand, and what I shall call socialism on the other" (Bion, 1992, p. 105). [At another point in his text, he writes the term as "social-ism", which captures the root idea. This spelling of the word rids it from its associations with ideologies such as Marxism and political movements like communism.] Here Bion is drawing a distinction between the instincts that are mobilized for the fulfilment of the individual's life as such and the instincts that are brought into being when the political, communal features of life are pre-eminent, which are about knowledge and understanding—that is, the shared concerns and preoccupations of peoples as a totality. What can be mobilized against this understanding is psychosis, which is based on a hatred of reality. Psychosis, to which all human beings are prone, is the process whereby humans defend themselves from understanding the meaning and significance of reality, because they regard such knowing as painful. To do this, they use aspects of their mental functioning to destroy, in various degrees, the very process of thinking that would put them in touch with reality. As Iris Murdoch once said in an interview, "The great task in life is to find reality", having already made the point that we settle for illusion and fantasy. T. S. Eliot anticipated this when he wrote in *Burnt Norton*, in effect, that human beings cannot tolerate too much reality (Lines 42/43). The only way the group member can preserve his/her narcissism (the sense of being an individual) is to destroy common sense, or sense of group pressure, by not becoming available for any kind of understanding of the nature of external reality, through working hypotheses (or interpretation).

This can be experienced at first hand in the context of groups. As I have said, Bion makes the key, fundamental observation that we can interpret the phenomena that occur in a group from two perspectives (binocular vision): that of Oedipus and that of Sphinx. The latter is concerned with the "social-istic", political preoccupation, which is that of knowledge and understanding of us, as a common concern, giving meaning to our existence, or being, finding answers to the basic puzzles of what it is to be human. The significance of the "social-ism" (human beings are group animals) is that it leads to, for instance, the development of economics, religions, political institutions, and psychology. Individuals, each with her/his Oedipus, so to speak, think about common concerns and try to find ways of living together by setting guidelines, or laws, or rules, or principles.

Thought products

We use the word "thinking" in everyday speech. It refers to the activities of reasoning, imagining, and remembering. Here I am concerned with thinking in its widest sense, encompassing fantasy and phantasy, the processes of imagining, dreaming, and dream-work, both awake and sleeping, reasoning and problem solving. The end products of thinking are "thought products", such as "poetry and novels, painting and plays, scientific theories and inventions" (McKellar, 1968, p. 77). My focus in this book is on groups and organizations, which I also see as "thought products". In the case of groups, the people participating in them create a narrative that makes sense to them.

Similarly an organization is a narrative, which, in the case of, say, the Shell International Petroleum Company, may stretch over decades. As new employees are inducted into the company, they are introduced to the thinking and thought process of the organization. As these role holders rise in the organization, they may alter the thinking and so change the "thought product" and the ongoing narrative of the company. When the Planning Group was able to predict *perestroika*, the company was able to change its strategic direction. The thinking from the Planning Group altered the nature of the narrative, which changed the "thought product" that is Shell International (Schwartz, 1991).

Whereas a novel or play or painting is a fixed, tangible "thought product" when completed, a group or a company is a continuous, unfolding one. The dynamic that is associated with a group or organization makes it such that one might rather call it a "thinking product" in order to capture the present continuous feeling of how it continually transforms itself. How this dynamic arises I shall try to disentangle.

Forms of thinking

Pursuing the project of Sphinx, my working hypothesis is that there are four *forms* of thinking, each with its distinguishing subject area. To be sure, these four forms have been thought about previously. All of us, as we participate in groups and groupings, have the possibility of thinking about them afresh for ourselves, even though we know that we shall never achieve truth and that what we think, in the present, may well have been thought about before by someone at some time.

These four *forms* can be viewed as a four-sided pyramid. Thus we have the sense of refracted thinking, for knowledge, derived from experience, is not a body of thinking "out there" that has to be acquired through learning; it is, rather, both out there and in

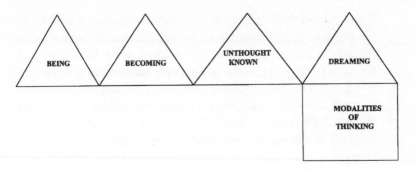

Figure 1.1

here. In a sense, we "make", or construct, knowledge through thinking in our inner world of the mind.

The base of the pyramid, which will be a square, can be allotted to the *modality* of communication. A written text will be different from a dialogue or conversation, or a play, or a novel. The quality of the thinking will be different as it relies on different modalities, which will alter the content of thinking. (See Figure 1.1.)

There is, it can be hypothesized: (1) thinking as BEING; (2) thinking as BECOMING; (3) thinking as DREAMING; and (4) thinking as the "UNTHOUGHT KNOWN" (Bollas, 1987, 1989).

1. THINKING AS BEING is all the thought that has ever been thought and is to do with existing, living, in the world as it is perceived. The substance of this knowledge generated by this type of thinking is the working resolution to the fundamental puzzles of existing, or being, in the world and, I suggest, underlies all architecture, philosophy, ethics, arts, literature, the sciences, and what we know of history, which, in a sense, is continually being re-discovered. There is a real sense in which this approximates the tacit knowledge to which Michael Polanyi refers.

    There is the stream of consciousness with which we are intimately bound up, for it is an expression of how we are continually monitoring the experience of events and happenings as they occur. How we construe this depends on the form of our thinking and on the state of our mental life, which I will argue below, under the headings of *modalities* and *psychic structure*. As we think in the present tense, we are inevitably caught up in thought in the past tense and in the future tense, but the idea of tense, with its rules, is the product of thinking. In groups and groupings one can see this. Organizations would not continue to exist if we did not have access to that thinking which we do practically every second of our lives. Experiencing–feeling–thinking is the process essential to our consciousness and our being.

2. THINKING AS BECOMING is the thinking we engage with as we attempt to alter our state of being. If you will, it is always concerned with the future and arises from a sense of frustration—of wanting things to be different—and from a sense of destiny. To be sure, although I have separated out these two forms of thinking, they interpenetrate each other. As I think of being, I am always thinking of how reality could become. All the advances in the natural sciences, all the creativity associated with the arts of all kinds, have their roots in becoming.

   Imagine the world of business: while businesses can continue as they have in the past, they are always in a state of transition as they transform themselves from what they are into what they are in the process of becoming. In business, for example, we bring markets into being. Markets exist because they have been thought of, but new markets always have to be brought into being. The business environment today exists in the world of information technology, in a global environment, and is in a state of increasingly instant communication. We can have the working hypothesis that the corporate environment is to be "brought into being" by the participation of managers in the environment as an ecosystem.

   Anita Roddick brought into being a market of women who bought her beauty products because they came from natural resources and were not tested on animals. Consequently, all the traditional suppliers of similar products had to re-think their market share and had to change accordingly. But it took one woman to see the potential market.

   Pursuing the idea of thinking as becoming, managers, in particular, have the task of experiencing as directly as possible the business as-a-series-of-events-in-its-environment, through participating in bringing them into being and interpreting the resultant experiences mutatively. (I am using the term "mutatively" to give the sense that interpretation itself leads to new insights and understanding, which, in turn, alters the original interpretation. This is the idea behind the working hypothesis that I will use repeatedly throughout this text, which is that we can only give an approximation of what reality might be. A working hypothesis generates, or stimulates, other working hypotheses from other people as a way of building up as true a picture as possible of what the "truth might be", accepting that we cannot know absolute truth.)

The distinction between thinking as being and thinking as becoming is difficult, but not impossible, to discern. The edges around these two *forms* are fuzzy, in reality. I believe that the concept of future is a useful distinguishing mark. In organizations, when the people in the company start to plan the future, we can see the separation of what the company does now and what the company could become. For example, we can build scenarios of the future, hold these in mind, and alter the company's state of being to fit the nature of reality that is emerging.

Both thinking as being and thinking as becoming are in consciousness, but they do have their origins also in the infinite aspects of mind. They are constructions of what reality is experienced as being and what it could become. As constructions, they owe part of their origin to the Oedipal aspects of the human being in that they are construed through processes of the psyche. Reality is made from the inside world of the individual and exists because of intersubjective agreement. In this, as I shall argue later, the unconscious plays a part. Thinking as becoming owes much to thinking as dreaming.

3. THINKING AS DREAMING. All dreamers are thinkers, according to Bion. Just as we think as total entities, so do we dream. To be sure, dream comes from the unconscious, or the infinite. Dreaming occurs while we are asleep. What the dream does is to set out in images a "flash", a picture, of the state of the relationship between ourselves and the world that often will include significant others. The dream is a metaphor that, once

its meaning is disentangled through association and amplification, can provide a hypothesis of the actual state of our relationship with particular features of our environment. From that can be abstracted statements, or propositions, of our state of relatedness with the world and the cosmos. The dream is a real experience and is always making a synthesis of our state of relationship, and our relatedness, with the environment.

One aspect of dream and dreaming is that, on occasion, we are joined with humanity as a whole. On other occasions we are caught up in our own ego world. The dream comes from the psyche, which can be seen as a "black hole". Once it is put into words, we are beginning the process of wresting its implicate meaning from what was explicate in the dream. And, through the continual process of association and amplification we uncover more and more of the "implicate meaning" (Ullman, 1975, p. 9).

In psychoanalysis the dream is seen primarily as belonging to the domain of Oedipus, and is interpreted in these terms. In this context of thinking, I see the dream as also being a Sphinx project, contributing to the recognition of the epistemophilic drive of being a human being. The content of the dream distinguishes between Oedipus and Sphinx. When a dreamer has a dream as a citizen, we know it is what I have called a "social dream". The best-recorded examples come from Charlotte Beradt (1968), who collected dreams from German citizens during the period of the Third Reich. What people dreamed of were the effects of the totalitarian regime in which they lived, but of which they could say nothing. What comes across vividly is that while people might think that they could alter the political situation consciously, their unconscious, through the dreams, was telling them that they could not.

These ideas are set out in *Social Dreaming @ Work* (1998). There my colleagues and I make a case for using social dreaming as a method of action research in organizations. Our argument runs that everyone dreams while a member of an organization. These dreams will have links with being, becoming, and the unthought known. They offer a different perspective on the organization, tapping into the unconscious life of its members in their roles. They offer insights into being in the organization, and into what it can become. By working on these dreams, using free association, insight can be had into possible ways of development, through offering (very often lateral) insights and so disrupting the rational and logical *gestalt* that everyone shares.

Dreaming is of equal importance to thinking as being and thinking as becoming and, indeed, thinking as the unthought known, yet because of our typical rational–logical perspective on the world, dreaming has become devalued, being seen as tangential to the business of living.

Dreaming plays a role in creative work. Coleridge dreaming *Kubla Khan* is an example, as is Graham Greene, who kept a dream diary, published as *A World of My Own* (1992). Robert Louis Stevenson was inspired by dreams in his writing, as in *Dr Jekyll and Mr Hyde*. In the world of music, too, dreaming has a part to play. Benjamin Britten, when writing *A Midsummer Night's Dream*, was exploring the notion that reality might be better apprehended through the undirected dream state than through the directed state of waking consciousness (Wierzbicki, quoted in Kellogg, 1994).

By claiming dreaming as (a *type* of) thinking, I want to re-affirm the importance of dreaming and to say that dreaming is as important as the other three types. This is contrary to common usage, where the dream is felt to be a kind of aberration of the mind and, as such, not to be taken seriously.

4.   THINKING AS THE UNTHOUGHT KNOWN.   Christopher Bollas (1989) argues a strong case:

> That inherited set of dispositions that constitutes the true self is a form of knowledge which has obviously not been thought, even though it is "there" already at work in the life of the neonate who brings this knowledge with him as he perceives, organizes, remembers, and uses his object world. I have termed this form of knowledge the "unthought known" (Bollas, 1987) to specify, amongst other things, the dispositional knowledge of the true self. [p. 10]

As a psychoanalyst, Bollas is focusing on the individual, which is the proper Oedipal project of his professional life. But I believe that the unthought known also refers to that which we know, say in a group or organization, but of which we have never thought. In this sense, it is that knowledge, which can rarely be acknowledged through thinking. Yet once it is acknowledged, it makes a difference to the life of the organization or the group. I am extending Bollas's usage to the Sphinx project. The reality of a group can be altered once some participant awakens something he or she has not thought about before, even when it is known. The unthought known is the inchoate because it is lost in language and society that would provide the channels for knowing. Bollas writes, "Phantasy is the first representative of the unthought known in mental life. It is a way of thinking that which is there" (Bollas, 1987, p. 279). What is being pointed to is the importance of phantasy in discerning the existence of the unthought known—that is, it postulates the existence of that which is there. The importance of phantasy—essentially imaginatively unconscious in origin—and fantasy—or fanciful invention—is that they are both imagined representation of reality, which exist in fact (if this does not sound too bizarre.) They are forms of thinking, while pointing to the capacity of the mind for imagination, illusion, and hallucination.

What we do know, from using this concept in organizational consultancy, is that once the unthought known is surfaced it makes a difference, forever. For example, in a family business one unthought known could be that a job in management has been made for the son-in-law. Everybody knows that he has been selected on the basis of being sponsored by the family. He does not hold his job because of merit. He never had to enter a contest for the job. This unthought known is never voiced. One result is the fabrication of the Lie. The Lie is about competence and fitness to hold the role on the part of the son-in-law. There is collusion in sustaining the lie by people lower in the hierarchy of the organization who want to survive in the organization of the family firm, and so more and more lies are fabricated. Here, I am pointing to the denial of the unthought known, leading to the stating of untruths. This making of untruths is a collusive process that is based on joint evasion of getting to grips with the uncomfortable, unpalatable, unspeakable aspects of reality. This is in order to avoid whatever discomfort and pain may be associated with the naming of the unthought known.

If thinking as being and thinking as becoming tend to have their origins in conscious thinking (though they are still influenced by the unconscious, or the infinite), thinking as dreaming and as the unthought known arise from the unconscious. To make explicit the meaning of the dream, to articulate what is known but not thought, takes individuals into the realm of the unconscious, or the infinite. Whereas the "unconscious" has tended to be seen negatively, I am arguing for its positive aspects. Both thinking as being and thinking as becoming are enriched and made to be more in touch with reality through the leavening of dream, particularly the social dream, and through the struggle to make the unthought known accessible for thinking and, therefore, becoming part of our consciousness.

Much more could be written on each of these *forms* of thinking. I have no wish to define, merely to suggest, for to define would be to discourage any further thinking in these areas. The relationships among these four *forms* are continuous, and one can slip from one to another in an instant. What has to be held on to is the fact that each is mutually informing of the other, and that, together, they form a powerful dynamic.

I offer this way of approaching the complexity of thinking and thought as I find it useful in the work of consultancy. To be sure, it is an intuition, but I suspect that others have intuited much the same. Certainly, it is the product of the last thirty years of my work and is a statement in simplified form of where I now stand. It is, of course, all much more complex than I am indicating.

Thinking, consciousness, and knowing: enlarging the space of the possible

Thinking is what gives science, art, literature, philosophy, sociology, psychology, psychoanalysis, management science, accounting, music, and, indeed, all other disciplines their substance of knowledge, their scholarly presence. At the same time, thinking is ordinary. We all have a buzzing internal conversation going on "in our heads" about all aspects of living and being in the world. Some of these will be banal or so trite that we do not notice them. Others will be such that they make a difference to what we may think in the future and, more dramatically, may cause, once voiced, others to change their thinking. Thinking and consciousness are intertwined for they are self-reflexive, mutually informing activities.

Thinking is culture-bound in that most of the routine thinking that is passed from generation to generation of human beings tends to be non-genetic. It passes from mouth to mouth, so to say. We belong to the species *Homo symbolificus*. As Walter Percy put it: "You have to accept the fact that man is not simply *Homo sapiens*; he's *Homo symbolificus*—he's someone who makes symbols" (quoted in Kellogg, 1994, pp. 3–4). This fanciful term was invented by Percy to emphasize that culture is the meaning-making capacity through symbols that goes with being human. Thinking is conducted in a *context*. Because of the reductionist orientation of science, we are always taking things to bits in order to find the prime cause of thinking. But what is clearly lost in this endeavour is the idea of *context* that is crucial to the notion of thinking as being interpretative.

All thinking occurs in an ecosystem, and it is forces of information from the external environment interacting with the reality of our inner worlds that enable us to think. Thinking is a product of the symbiosis between human beings and their ecosystem. It is, therefore, not a "thing", or a reification. It occurs at the species level, and thinking is part of the larger emergent phenomenon of life. This, in turn, emerges from chemistry by way of DNA (deoxyribose nucleic acid), which, because of the complexity of its organization, provides the necessary conditions for interacting with its environment.

My postulate is that every living entity, human or otherwise, is engaged in dreaming, or proto-dreaming, as a way of rehearsing, or working through, his/her relationships with the context within which he/she is placed. I suggest that proto-dreaming lies at the heart of evolution. By this I mean that through dream images and through dream work, no matter how vestigial, the organism explores its ecosystemic niche, or whatever aspect of the cosmos it finds itself in. To be sure, the primitive organism has no language, but it is thinking in metaphor of how it can expand what is possible in its niche.

With the development of neurological research into brain and mind, there is a wish to find the causal factors of thinking within the millions of atoms of DNA. Researchers talk confidently of mapping the brain and looking for the connections between brain and mind. This research smacks of explanation based on reductionism, and would deny the role of non-genetic factors and the environmental context. The concept of *context* is crucial to an understanding of thinking.

Thinking is always enlarging the space of the possible. What we know at the end of the millennium has been enlarged from what we knew, say, in terms of science, at the end of 1900. What now constitutes knowledge has been wrested from the infinite. It was unknown, possibly intuited, but then it becomes knowledge that we incorporate into our thinking, and so it becomes finite. The problem for thinking persons is that they are always in a state of being at the limits of their comprehension. Attaining these limits encourages them to draw from the infinite, from what is not known.

In this way culture is formed. In a tribal society knowledge is passed on to subsequent generations through myths that relate to the problem of existence. They are powerful stories, containing ineffable truths, of solutions to the complexities that previous generations encountered. In the industrial societies, or some version of them, in which we live, the culture is also passed on through records, which is possible through the invention of writing. In this way we store knowledge in our cultural artefacts, like libraries and computers, rather than in our brains or memory.

Thinking is so basic, so essential, so taken for granted, so mundane, so elemental, that we never really think about its place in the human sphere. John Wheeler, in an article entitled "Information, Physics, Quantum: The Search for Links" (quoted in Davies & Gribbin), claimed that "the world cannot be a giant machine, ruled by any pre-established continuum physical law". Rather, he suggested, we ought "to think of the physical Universe as a gigantic information-processing system in which the output was as yet un-determined". What does this mean? I may say that I have informa-tion about X. What I mean is that I am privy to thinking about X. I am conscious and able to think further about X because I hold the information, itself the product of thinking. Wheeler coined the phrase "It from bit". "That is to say, every *it*—every particle, every field of force, even space-time itself—is ultimately manifested to us through *bits* (bytes) of information" (Davies & Gribbin, 1991, pp. 300–301). The universe, however, is more than an information-processing system. Because of our cultural fascination with com-puters, we focus almost exclusively on information technology as messages contained in "bit strings" (Cohen & Stewart, 1995, p. 290). This focus on the software tends to overlook the necessity of taking into account the hardware. This is the human being as a total entity. Information is just data until we apply the process of thinking. Then the information has meaning, which makes a dif-ference to our lives. Thus it can be said that the Universe is a gigantic thinking machine whose outcomes are always in the pro-cess of discovery.

People are needed to think thoughts (excluding animals from this discussion), and they have to have an "apparatus", or disposi-tion, to think thoughts. This apparatus is the mind. But what about the brain? "There is no mind without brain, but much of the brain functions without mind. Consciousness is the tip of an iceberg. It emerges through the cortical layers of the brain above a vast and intricate network of highly active but unconscious centres and connections"(de Duve, 1995, p. 245).

So thinking arises from experiences which the mind processes through the use of feeling and emotions to formulate a working hypothesis, which may be in the form of action. Thinking, which is not totally dependent on the brain, occurs when we are in a state of consciousness. We think to experience the physical universe, and by that process bring the universe, with all its diverse fea-tures, into being. Thinking is essential for our being.

Thinking can be conceptualized as both a wave and a particle, as I have said, paraphrasing Heisenberg's discovery about phe-nomena in the context of the quantum world. In its continuous flowing it is a wave function. Even while we are asleep, it continues through dreaming. It is also a particle function in that out of the wave function there are particles of thinking, which we can grasp and of which we are conscious. Particular fields of thinking, like architecture or any recognized science, I see as being produced from waves of thinking that are telescoped in some kind of oscillating density, forming particles that constitute knowledge. The boundaries of knowledge are defined by the extent of the oscillations. New thinking will extend the range of the oscillations.

Thinking as a wave function will often be in the form of a dream. Once it is made explicit through words, it is in the form of a particle, which then can be transacted in conversation to produce meanings. James Joyce captures something of this contrasting flux and stasis of thinking as a wave, together with the apparently chaotic formulation, as a particle, of thinking. He writes in *Finnegan's Wake*:

> every person, place and thing in the chaosmos of Alle anyway connected with the gobblydumped turkery was moving and changing every part of the time: the travelling inkhorn (possibly pot), the hare and turtle pen and paper, the continually more and less intermisunderstanding minds of the anticollaborators, the as time went on as it will variously inflected, differently pronounced, other wise spelled, changeably meaning vocable scriptsigns. [Joyce, 1939, p. 118]

Thinking is chaos, but there are always "pockets" of order. There is the obvious time lag between a conception in the mind and the realization in the form, say, of a painting or a poem. Before that there is a creative process, which is the making of coherent sense and meaning out of the plethora of experiences that have been experienced. Just as real life is not a story but, rather, is a maelstrom of happenings of unimaginable complexity that for a time stumbles into recognizable coherence, so is thinking. These coherent pockets of order, as I am calling them, would be science, art, music, and all the other fields of knowledge to which human beings are privy, if they can make themselves available. At the same time, before an entry can be made to the pocket of order, it has to fulfil the criteria of logic, the rules that humans have developed to have knowledge that is consistent, congruent, and coherent. Another way of putting this is to say that what is newly thought has to fit in with the "narrative" associated with science, and so on. While the syllogism, or any other rule of logic, may be of limited daily value, it is invaluable when judging what is science, and what is not; what is acceptable in art, and what is not; what constitutes harmonious music, and what is cacophony. We take these thinking decisions as we participate in the unceasing crystallizing and fluidity of thinking.

We, as thinking contexts, think as total entities—not with a part of our bodies, or features, or faculties, of our minds and brains. David Bohm's proposal is "that body, emotion, intellect, reflex and artefact are now understood *as one unbroken field of mutually informing thought*" (Lee Nichol, Foreword to Bohm, 1992, xi; italics in original). This mirrors A. N. Whitehead's view expressed in his *Science and the Modern World* (1926) that the universe is pure mind and thought.

Bohm develops his ideas about thinking in his dialogues. The essential point he is making is that most of the time we are dealing with thought. Once a thought is "thinked" (to invent an appalling word), it becomes a thought. Everything that exists in our physical universe is thought embedded in memory. And Bohm argues that what is wrong with what happens in the world arises from our capacity for fragmenting thinking. We make boundaries where there is really a close connection. So we have false divisions and false unification. Fragmentation is the result of thinking and thought being separated from feeling and from the body, and we locate it all in the mind. The mind, in my view, represents the context from and with which we think. The mind itself, which does not exist in physical reality, is an outcome of contextual thinking and the neurophysiological functioning of the brain. We think, or have thought, the mind into being. We think of thinking and the body as being different, and so we come to experience them as different because we think of them as being different.

From this context different kinds of thinking are thought, or we are available for them. In this chapter I aim to conceptualize something of thinking, to bring some order, which itself is the product of thinking, to the process of thinking. There is a complex richness of thinking present in our universe, whether conscious or not, whether it belongs to the finite (the known) or the infinite, which is unknown. And over the millennia since human beings appeared on earth, human beings have forgotten and rediscovered a great deal—a process that never ceases.

If we see the mind as the context—as a kind of summarizing variable representing human beings as a total, holistic entity—we are not devaluing the power of the mind, but trying to get a purchase on the complex reality of thinking as an unbroken field with our bodies and minds. Christian de Duve attempts to capture that complexity in the following passage.

> There is no greater mystery in the known universe, except the universe itself, than the human mind. Born from the brain, critically dependent on the brain at every instant, crippled together with the brain in all sorts of weird fashions directly related to whatever brain area is maimed, the mind is without doubt a product of polyneural functioning.
>
> At the same time, the human mind is, collectively, the creator of the whole of technology, science, art, literature, philosophy, religion, and myth. The mind generates our thoughts, reasonings, intuitions, ponderings, inventions, designs, beliefs, doubts, imaginings, fantasies, desires, intentions, yearnings frustrations, dreams and nightmares. It brings up evocations of our past and it shapes plans for our futures; it weighs, decides, and commands. It is the seat of consciousness, self-awareness, and personhood, the holder of freedom and moral responsibility, the judge of good and bad, the inventor and agent of virtue and sin. It is the focus of all our feelings, emotions, and sensations, of pleasure and pain, love and hate, rapture and despair. The mind is the interface between what we are wont to call the world of matter and the world of spirit. The mind is our window to truth, beauty, charity, and love, to existential mystery, the awareness of death, the poignancy of the human condition. [de Duve, 1995, p. 245]

Out of this plethora of thinking and thought, I have formulated working hypotheses on thinking, using the organizing idea of *forms* of thinking.

Thought is participatory. At one and the same time as we think we take part in whatever it is we are thinking about, we also partake of the phenomenon. It is a two-way process. Thinking and thought have effects on us both inwardly and outwardly. Thinking can lead to suggestions for social change, but as we initiate it we are affected by the results. This we do as we try to impose order on a particular set of experiences, say the health system, which we construe as being in a state of near chaos.

We have the view that the world is in chaos, but we are really saying that both thought and thinking are in chaos. Bohm writes: "That's each one of us. And that is the cause of world being in chaos. Then the chaos of the world comes back and adds to the chaos of thought" (Bohm, 1992, p. 14). Here, I am trying to say that the world is in chaos, and so thinking is. Occasionally we find an order in the chaos that makes sense and, hopefully, satisfies criteria of judgement. The problem is that we can hold on to ordered thinking to the exclusion of making ourselves available for the chaotic thinking that lies behind the apparent order.

Another major aspect of thought is that "thought doesn't know it is doing something and then struggles against what it is doing. It doesn't want to know that it is doing it". It hates the results it is producing. It wants to avoid unpleasant outcomes while it keeps on with that way of thinking. This is what Bohm calls "*sustained* incoherence" (Bohm, 1992, p. 55). I will put forward some hypotheses, derived from psychoanalysis, as to why this sustained incoherence takes place.

What occupies as fundamental a place as matter, energy, space, and number is consciousness. Without consciousness we cannot think or acquire knowledge. Consciousness is of a self-relating, or self-reflexive, character.

> Indeed it is the very subjectivity of consciousness that makes it invisible in a crucial way. *If we try to draw a picture of someone else's consciousness, we just end up drawing the other person* (perhaps with a balloon growing out of his or her head). *If we try to draw our own consciousness, we end up drawing whatever it is we are conscious of*. If consciousness is the rock-bottom epistemic basis for getting at reality, we cannot get at the reality of consciousness in that way. [Searle, 1992, p. 95, quoted in Polkinghorne, 1998, p. 57; italics in original]

The strategy of science has been to see the world and its phenomena as being "out there". This strategy—reality is objective—

has been the fundamental, scientific posture since the Enlightenment. While the mind has to hold a degree of detachment because the results of science (with its measurement) have to be consistent with inter-subjective consensus, it is fatal for philosophy and the mental sciences. As Polkinghorne says, "Consciousness is not the epiphenomenal garnishing of a fundamentally objective and material reality; it is the route of our access to all reality. Refusal to take it seriously subverts the whole metaphysical enterprise" (Polkinghorne, 1998, p. 58). This is not to be condemned to solipsism. There are scientific agreements about the nature of the physical world. There are the creative arts. There is literature that explores the personal world in such a way that others can identify with it. We do, in fact, co-create our worlds from our subjectivity and are able to do so with confidence because we intuit that other minds exist and that we share our world. Objectivity, I am suggesting, is essentially intersubjective agreement (see chapter two). Sorting this out is a major task of research, but it probably will be that mind and matter have to be seen as contrasting poles of the same basic "stuff" of reality.

To summarize to this point: thinking is so basic to our humanity that if we did not think, we would not be human. Thinking provides information that we process to produce outcomes that we cannot predict. The universe is a gigantic system of thinking and thought. Thinking is always surprising. Once we think a thought, it becomes "thought". And thought is the key feature of culture, by which I mean everything that we know, that we are conscious of, everything that is in the realm of the finite. None of the features of our social world environment would exist, except that we inherit a system of thought, which governs and informs our lives. Thinking, in a present continuous sense, arises out of the inherited thought. To think a new thought means that we have totally inside us all the relevant thought that has been thought and are able to make a new thought because we view the phenomena differently and can see a chink in the way that other people have thought to date. Here, I am interested in the thinking, which is socialistic, or socio-centric, that concerns all of us as human beings, to a greater or lesser degree, as it concentrates its focus on the nature and quality of being human.

Thinking is a never-ending, continuous process of participation through interaction between our inner world, which we summarize as "mind", and the outer one of external reality. Thinking always affects us. The thought we have access to is fragmented, imposing boundaries when it should be integrative. This comes about because thinking resists unpleasant results while it continues its own process. We, as humans, cannot bear too much reality, and we come to hate it; as a result, we attack the processes of thinking in order to maintain ourselves by not making links or connections when we should. If one person should be preoccupied with Sphinx issues, others will be affected and may pick it up. They can let it fall into desuetude for reasons that we can locate in Oedipus. This complementarity of perspective is essential for disentangling our experiences of thinking.

Modalities of thinking

I now turn to the *modalities* of thinking and, later in the text, to the deep, *psychic structure* that is inherent to the existence of thinking. The *modality* of thinking that we use in each of the four *forms* (thinking as being, becoming, dreaming, and the unthought known) complicates what looks comparatively straightforward. Although I describe this more fully later (chapters four and eight), for the moment we can see thinking as being done in two ways. This is the distinction made by David Armstrong when he says that there are two forms of thinking: "Thinking 1" and "Thinking 2". In the former, thinking comes out of the process of thinking and owes its existence to a thinker. Epistemologically, thinking is prior to thought. Such thinking, and thought, is capable of being put forward as an exegesis, in a reasoned argument, which demands of the listener or reader that it be justified or falsified. To repeat: epistemologically, thinking is prior to thought. In Thinking 2, on the other hand, thought and thoughts are epistemologically prior to thinking. Bion (1984) expresses the idea as follows: "Thoughts exist without a thinker. . . . The thoughts which have no thinker acquire or are acquired by a thinker" (p. 165). Such thoughts just are; they are neither true nor false. They emerge from the not-known, the infinite, from no-thought, and are experienced as a frustration, a mystery.

This echoes, in some measure, Peter McKellar's idea that there are two kinds of thinking: *A-thinking* and *R-thinking*. The former term he derives from Eugene Bleuler [1857–1939], who coined the term "autism" to refer to the thinking "which is fantasy-dominated, self-generated, and uncorrected by reference to external reality" (McKellar, 1968, p. 78). McKellar uses *A-thinking* to "include fantasy, dreams and nightmares, visionary activity, hypnagogic imaginings, hallucination, and the like" (p. 78). This he contrast, with *R-thinking* to refer to the "thinking of the kind that is prominent in sane, adult wakefulness, in its most logical, realistic and prejudice-free moments . . . (it) is taken to include realistic appraisal in terms of the evidence, critical evaluation, and logical inference of the valid kind" (p. 78).

Each of the four *forms* of thinking (being, becoming, dreaming, and unthought known) can be entertained and pursued through using the *modalities*, which I have just indicated. They overlap, but, at the same time, do contain differences. To each can be applied intelligence, judgement, and inter-subjectively agreed criteria for establishing truth or falsehood since all thoughts are not of the same value.

DNA is the blueprint that each human being carries to replicate itself. It is popularly seen as the information code, contained in a double helix, which contains the information for an eye, a brain, a limb, and the like. The reductionist project would be to analyse the DNA until the source of intelligence, or thinking was found. "The idea of DNA as genetic information also sits uneasily with the phenomenon of convergence. Different causes can produce the same effect" (Cohen & Stewart, 1995, p. 289). The argument is that thinking is the result of the convergence of a whole series of unique factors, not all of which can be identified at present. We think because we are in a particular environment or ecosystem.

My view is that thinking is directed at enlarging the space of the possible. On the basis of the innate, inherited features (intelligence, brain, etc.) of a human being, thinking is produced as the human entity interacts with its environment or ecosystem. It is the challenge of the environmental context that is critical.

Psychic structure
as determining the nature of reality

Taking the complementary perspective to Sphinx, by focusing on Oedipus, we can now regard the place of the deep, *psychic structure* that constructs, or, what I would prefer, refracts thinking. What is thought, whether epistemologically before or after the fact of thinking, depends on the inner world, or life, of the individual and groupings who are engaged in the act of thinking. The thinking of the four *forms* is not always conscious. We know, now, that the unconscious, although always present and rarely named, is decisive in human perception ever since Freud brought it to the world's attention, "into the foreground of modern intellectual concern" (Tarnas, 1991, p. 422). The problem is that as the twentieth century has unfolded, the unconscious has become reified, a thing, an object. People talk of their unconscious as if it were a bounded pocket—"It was my unconscious", or "I know I am projecting!" are examples of thinking in terms of the unconscious as thing. The unconscious becomes concretized in the process of discourse. Bion, following Freud, reformulated this by substituting the infinite for the unconscious because it has no boundary and is limitless.

In this, I follow the ideas of Bion that were made explicit by Joan and Neville Symington. They argue (Symington & Symington, 1996, p. 8) that Bion recast Freud's conception of the unconscious. Bion, I think, catching on to the fundamental meaning of Freud that the unconscious was of no time and place, saw that the polarity of conscious–unconscious needed to be reworked to take account of analytic understanding. Bion believed that this polarity had to be replaced with the finite–infinite—that is: "Won from the void and formless infinite" (Milton).

Each of the four *forms* of thinking has a dynamic existence, in that each is a dynamic process construed on the basis of what is taking place in the internal life of the thinker. As Heraclitus noted, one can never step into the same river twice. Thinking is equally changing and evanescent. Each content is a representation of reality, and a version of potential truth. But these are each made by the individual psyche that constructs outside reality on the basis of the reality that is constructed in the inner world. The inner world will be wrestling with the existence of the finite–infinite, or, more conventionally, the conscious–unconscious. This two-way, participatory process (what is outside is inside and *vice versa*) is the unbroken wholeness. One might say, here, that thinking is an electromagnetic field of which each human being is a part.

Holding the finite–infinite distinction, for the moment, I can represent reality and the thinking that is designed to be in touch with it, with the letters "RT" (by this I mean "thinking to be in touch with reality"). On occasion, we may be in touch with reality (RT+), though in actuality we never are totally so, or "out of touch with reality" (–RT). These have to be seen as a continuum and not as absolute, fixed points, for the nature of reality depends on interpretation.

The identification of the intimacies of making reality outside on the basis of what is inside, in the inner world of the individual, is the fulcrum of psychoanalytic theory on mental functioning. It is postulated that in our mental life we take up different positions psychically. Following the idea that thinking is like light that is refracted through a prism, we are now in the realm of thinking that is initiated by the psyche. To be sure, particularly in the newborn baby, this is the realm of phantasy, which is projected, or refracted, onto reality. As phantasy breaks down into particles, to pursue the metaphor, it is possible to distinguish between phantasy and reality, though this is a life-long process.

As human beings, we live in a dual environment at one and the same time. We are, if you will, a *context* within a *context*. This dual environment can be expressed as

> internal and external, psychic and material, unconscious and deeply rooted in the life of the body and also conscious and deeply influenced by human relationships and all the pressures of the social culture. [Guntrip, 1961, pp. 351–352]

The connection, or links, between inside and outside are made by the psyche, which is always interpreting the reality of experience on a subjective basis. It would be more accurate to say that the psyche tends to be *misinterpreting* reality as it tries to preserve itself from pain and to enhance pleasure. What is meant by this is that the impact of reality could produce unfavourable, or undesired, feelings in us. So human beings tend to find in reality what will give them pleasure and good feelings. This is the root of the sustained incoherence to which Bohm points.

In actuality, reality is not manifested to us through raw sense data. It is mediated through phantasy. (The "ph" spelling is to locate it firmly in the inner world of the psyche, as opposed to the normal spelling "f", which can be a paraphrasing of conscious imagination.) As Joan Riviere succinctly put it:

> The phantasy life of the individual is thus the form in which the real internal and external sensations and perceptions are interpreted and represented to himself [or herself] in his mind under the influence of the pleasure-pain principle. [Riviere, 1936, p. 41]

All thinking as being, in particular, is grounded, in the first instance, in phantasy. Furthermore, it can be said that the elementary and primitive function of the psyche is continually to misinterpret the sensations and perceptions of reality in order to save the psyche from the unpleasurable aspects of reality. This it does to maintain an apparently equable relationship with external reality for the purpose of having a pain-free existence. The sobering thought is that, for the most part, even civilized human beings are always directing their thinking processes to avoiding the unpleasant aspects of reality.

There are two psychic positions, which, I believe, are always directed at being in touch with reality (RT+) in the sense of striving to be cognizant of the true nature of reality. These are the depressive position and the tragic position (postulated by Symington). On the other hand, the remaining position, the paranoid-schizoid one, pulls us to be out of touch, through our thinking, with the state of reality. We are always seduced from being in touch with reality when we are anxious and are seeking pleasurable conclusions. Then we do not want to know the ramifications and complications of knowing what reality would reveal when it promises pain. Here we see that the unconscious, or the infinite, has to be taken into account. The wish not to know that reality takes the form of destroying the very processes of thinking.

We are born possessed of our DNA inheritance, but it tends to operate, for example in producing thinking, only in interaction with the environment. The incidence of these interactions and their nature is a matter of chance. The newly born being comes with a psyche, which it uses to relate to, to experience, feel, and think through its connection to the world of others. This thinking of the connections, or the nature of the links, may be done through dreaming and will be intuited because there are no words. It will, most certainly, also be done on the basis of phantasy.

In the first instance, this connection will tend to be with the mother or the mother-substitute. The neonate possesses an embryonic ego that is focused on its source of nourishment, which is usually the breast. That breast, or bottle, is pre-eminently in the baby's consciousness. The first relationships are with food. The baby experiences its first frustrations in that nourishment is not always available when the baby wants it. In phantasy the baby "splits" the breast into two aspects—the good one and the bad one. The baby loads all its bad feelings into the bad dimension and retains the good. This is the paranoid-schizoid position. The baby feels persecuted and withdraws itself into a position (schizoid, or disassociated) from which it can divide its feelings. The bad feelings will be murderous, and the baby wishes to attack the breast, but it also intuits that it is benign at one and the same time. All this is done on the basis of phantasy, supplemented by dreaming. In short, pain is to be avoided for the warm feelings of pleasure. The only way that the baby knows is to keep the good feelings in order to nourish the emerging sense of self. So the baby's thinking about the outside world (represented by the breast) is polarized. In time, the salience of phantasy will diminish as the baby gets behind the phantasy, so to speak, and encounters more and more of the actual, "objective" reality of mother. To put this another way: the baby sees that behind the explicate order of mother, which it has construed, there lies the implicate mother as she exists in reality. While phantasy is pre-eminent as a way of relating, the reality of the mother is not perceived in terms of what the mother feels as a separate entity and is in reality.

With subsequent experiences, and as the phantasy lessens, the baby comes to realize that the mother (breast) is both good and bad in reality. Once it has attained this mode of thinking, the baby can take up the depressive position. This position is the closest to understanding the nature of the reality the baby is encountering.

So, instead of keeping the good and bad feelings widely separated in order to defend from the primitive anxieties, the baby can now bring them together. Hence, the mother or mother-substitute is construed in the baby's inner world in terms of the total reality. Much later the infant can take up the tragic position (see chapter eleven), which is the realization that the causes of the mother being bad (and having elements of goodness) are to do with factors that mother cannot control. As can be seen, and as Melanie Klein made the subject of her writing, our adult world has its roots in infancy. In particular, phantasy is the key to understanding the neonate's world. In time, phantasy is tempered by reality testing and is seen as a necessary step in the process of being in touch with reality. In other words, phantasy is part and parcel of our process of construing reality. Sometimes one is led to think that human beings are acting out their phantasy of being adult the more they limit their imagination and the more they truncate the complexity and richness of their capacity to think.

This rendition is an unsophisticated version of psychoanalytic thinking. Nevertheless, I hope it is sufficient to show that thinking is part of our lives from our beginnings and is refracted from the inside world to the outside environment. As adults, our thinking about the real world is profoundly structured by our experiences of oscillating between the paranoid-schizoid (essentially based in phantasy) and depressive positions (based on the acceptance of the starkness of reality, which is depressing and is, at its most realistic, tragic).

The first thinking is about survival through the acquisition of nourishment (see chapter five). How we respond to that in the first instance is mirrored throughout the rest of our lives. Patterns experienced through relations with other people will evoke in us as adults the unconscious responses of the baby to its mother. When we encounter later reality that we do not want to entertain and so come to know, we split it into good and bad aspects by keeping them far apart. In time we learn from the object of reality that it is both good and bad, and so we attain the depressive and tragic positions.

Here, we can see that the Oedipal preoccupations of the baby in relationship with the mother or mother-substitute (with their unconscious features) are an integral part of how we think about all relations that fall into the domain of Sphinx, or are the subject of Sphinx. The attainment of RT+, which is a lifelong project, is always subverted by our adult wish not to have too much reality, and only if it gives us pleasurable, benign feelings. When we are caught up in this, we are in the thinking associated with –RT, which means that we are in the world of phantasy. The processes of thinking to discriminate between phantasy and reality, we attack in order to destroy the means of thinking.

I have tried to show the interrelation of oedipal preoccupations with Sphinx projects. What we perceive outside us is based on what we feel inside us. There is a continual modification of our phantasy world as we encounter the reality that is outside us. To be sure, this is a gross oversimplification, but it may go some way towards illuminating the processes of how we think. It is an attempt to flesh out aspects of the heuristic perspective I use, which hitherto have remained unwritten but have gradually been crystallizing in my consciousness.

A holistic perspective

I have been emphasizing the notion of context and the idea of the convergence of unique factors to activate thinking which is not reductionist. As will be seen throughout this book, I have increasingly been adopting a holistic approach to social science. I have the idea that everything is connected in a oneness, a wholeness, and my task is to find interconnectedness among environmental, contextual factors, which I sometimes am aware of through intuition. This means including all the evidence, which is daunting and perhaps impossible. For example, I have held for most of my adult life the view that unconscious factors play a central role in our lives and can be seen at work in organizations and groups. This is not a popular view to hold.

The Australian Institute of Socio-Analysis (AISA) has recently been advocating its version of socio-analysis in one of its brochures. They say: "Socio-analysis is the activity of exploration, consultancy, and action-research which combines and synthesizes methodologies and theories derived from psychoanalysis, group relations, social systems thinking, social dreaming, and organizational behaviour." To this, I can aspire to subscribe, knowing I will never get at the truth absolutely. The statement is an invitation both to omniscience and to impotence. On the one hand, there is the idea that all can be known and taken account of; on the other hand, each of us knows that this is impossible. We are left struggling, taking halting steps, stumbling, and, occasionally, achieving what we believe to be the truth. That way is to embrace the poignancy of the human condition, knowing that we shall never know the truth as an absolute.

CHAPTER TWO

The management
of oneself in role

The group relations training which continues to be developed and articulated through the Tavistock model is not an activity that is divorced from concerns about the larger society. Since these educational ventures began, there have been shifts in the larger society, and, for example, authority has become a "bad object" even though, on the surface, it looks as if we are living in stable, rational enterprises and institutions. In much the same way, the development of psychoanalysis as a discipline of thought and practice has meant that an analysis takes longer as analysands become more defended simply because there are more insights publicly available. My guess is that participants in group relations experiences, too, become defended. More positively, however, it can be said that having experienced, identified, and named particular social phenomena of an unconscious nature that can be rediscovered in each educational venture, hitherto unnamed phenomena begin to become apparent. Therefore I believe that there are two challenges before those who sponsor and take up consultant roles in such group relations ventures. The first task is to continue to identify unconscious social processes as manifested in group settings. The second task emerges from this and the history and traditions of the thinking and practice generated through this Tavistock model: to make explicit and to realize the political value of this work. This is the concept of the management of oneself in role.

In an earlier paper, the writer and a colleague attempted to put flesh on the bones of this notion. We wrote:

> The self-managing individual . . . is refusing to allow cultural assumptions to remain untested and he is disentangling the cobweb of myths and mysteries of our social institutions. He has to differentiate between what is conventionally agreed to be reality and what is reality for him. Thus, whereas it is widely accepted that the search for scientific objectivity requires the individual to suppress subjective judgement, we would turn this proposition on its head and postulate that objectivity is essentially the clarification of one's own subjectivity.
>
> But as he examines more closely what is inside and what is outside and tries to regulate the boundary between them, the individual is confronting those very cultural forms, hitherto taken for granted, that provide the defensive structures and thus confronting his own primitive inner needs that these structures satisfy. In giving up an external definition of "reality" and substituting his own, he is therefore giving up cements of certainty and security and substituting uncertainty and insecurity.
>
> Our argument is that the resultant disorder and chaos are the necessary risks and costs of undertaking change. Social change inescapably starts with self. [Lawrence & Miller, 1976, pp. 235–236]

Since we wrote that, I have puzzled a good deal as to how to make the content have real forms as part of living in industrialized societies.

In particular, I have been trying to come to grips with what meaning has to be placed on the phrase "the cobweb of myths and mysteries". What follows is a set of tentative working hypotheses about society and some thoughts on the possibilities of and constraints on the realization of the value of managing oneself in role.

Mass society

We have to acknowledge that the here-and-now of our lives is embedded in mass society. And the implications of this social fact must continually be identified and interpreted. There are, however, no really adequate theories, or even fully elaborated descriptions, that capture all the facets of mass society. Such major sociologists as Weber, Tonnies, Marx, de Tocqueville, and Freud in his *Civilization and its Discontents* (1930a) have all attempted to capture and elucidate the phenomena of industrializing societies, charting their causes and effects. But in the final analysis we are left with *apperçus*, at most working hypotheses, or sketches, of mass society that will change over time due to the very nature of such a society.

> One such set of working hypotheses can be found in the work of a literary critic: By the mass society we mean a relatively comfortable, half-welfare and half-garrison society in which the population grows passive, indifferent and atomized; in which traditional loyalties, ties, and associations become lax or dissolve entirely; in which coherent publics based on definite interests and opinions gradually fall apart; and in which man becomes a consumer, himself mass-produced like the products, diversions and values that he absorbs. [Howe, 1971]

This is not the whole picture. Some live in a world that is felt to be increasingly shapeless and is an increasingly fluid experience. To understand our experiences we are continually pressed to a psychic exploration of a set of intangible boundaries: certainty and uncertainty, chaos and order, the tolerable from the intolerable, destruction and creativity. Rational culture, so prized for centuries, is in the process of dissolution (McLuhan & Nevitt, 1972). So the concepts that have shaped our perceptions are found increasingly redundant because our perceptions of our experience are bursting the frames of our well-tried conceptualizations that once gave full meaning to life.

But the overwhelming experience is of social passivity. There is a wish, sometimes quite explicit and not so unconscious, that the State through its agencies will look after each individual. The governments of advanced industrial societies pride themselves on their ability to provide welfare services. Increasingly, however, it is expected that the State will always be able to find the resources to meet these demands. Such a primitive dependency arises when groups or institutions find it difficult to face the realities of the situation or feel that no solutions to their problems are possible. This is an outcome, or at least one effect, of what a colleague, Isabel Menzies Lyth, has called the "I want" philosophy of society, engendered by industrialized societies, which convert citizens into consumers—public into mass. As she puts it, the

> "I want" is little related to the realistic possibility of getting what one wants or to considerations of the sacrifices the "I" may require of others to get what he wants. This can be carried so far that people behave almost as though society's resources are unlimited. Political statements increasingly imply that all we need is more money: the resources it represents will somehow then magically become available. Money is treated almost as a thing in itself not as a symbol. This reflects a potentially psychotic and destructive social process, reflected in the rapidly diminishing real value of money. [Menzies Lyth, 1975]

There is a sense in which these unconscious processes of industrial societies are even more insidious. The "I want" is related to the feeling of envy that others may also want and get. And so institutions are developed in society to ensure that there is an equitable distribution of resources, thus further reinforcing dependency upon the State and its agencies.

The social passivity I am pointing to, then, is a strangely potent force. Equally, it is related to potentially psychotic and destructive forces. A socially passive mass spawns other crowdlike, unconscious social processes. The obverse of social passivity is exaggerated social aggressiveness, such as is demonstrated by urban guerrilla groups or some striking students, for instance. To shock the passive, the aggression has to be inflated. The socially passive react in a more defended fashion against the destruction of the aggressive activists, who, in turn, become more paranoid that they are not heard by the mass. So the violence has to be made even more monstrous.

Clearly, it is a social cartoon that I draw, but I want to hold firmly to the lineaments of destruction present in contemporary societies. Erich Fromm traces a connection between contemporary man's existential situation and destruction. The point is simple enough:

> If man cannot create anything or move anybody, if he cannot break out of the prison of his total narcissism and isolation, he can escape the unbearable sense of vital impotence and nothingness only by affirming himself in the act of destruction of the life that he is unable to create. Great effort, patience and care are not required; for destruction, all that is necessary is strong arms, or a knife or a gun. [Fromm, 1977]

Social passivity that is engendered, albeit unwittingly, by the State and its agencies and is also engendered in industrial and other enterprises means that individuals find it difficult to give meaning to their lives. They become isolated units, without a normal dependency on external objects, preoccupied with themselves and lacking in empathy; they may hold an inflated self-concept of themselves. Furthermore, what is unacceptable to the self-image is repressed and projected onto external objects, which are then devalued. It is but a short step to destroying external objects. These are narcissistic characteristics.

Other writers have pointed to this kind of disconnection from the realities of life using similar terms. Friedenberg, developing themes of R. D. Laing, suggests that we are experiencing a psychic closing-off on the part of individuals, a "psychological alienation which deprives people of the capacity to accept or even become aware of their own feelings" (Friedenberg, 1973).

This is familiar enough terrain. What is much more difficult to get a purchase on are the large-scale, unconscious social processes present in society. In the same essay Friedenberg makes the important point that in contemporary societies "the wielders of power have a vested interest in keeping the sovereign people alienated, it exacerbates their paranoia, but it diminishes their insight and self-confidence, and hence their political effectiveness" (Friedenberg, 1973).

The experience of political ineffectiveness is one of the major effects of the social and individual processes I have been identifying. Friedenberg's hypothesis is tenable. There is a fatal split between man and the institutions of society. Raymond Williams has argued that this split—what he calls "the crisis of the know-able community" (Williams, 1974), can be traced to the 20 months between 1847 and 1848 and found in the major novels written in that period by Dickens and others. The novelists of that period experienced extraordinary changes in English society. Agreed social and moral codes began to disintegrate with the advent of industrialization. For the purposes of this argument, the important point is Williams's hypothesis that this central process began to be apparent in society:

> An increasing scepticism, disbelief, in the possibility of under-standing society; a structurally similar certainty that rela-tionships, knowable relationships, so far from comprising a community or society, are the positive experience that has to be contrasted with the ordinarily negative experience of the society as a whole (or of the society as opposed to the local and immediate community). An important split takes place between knowable relationships and an unknown, un-knowable, overwhelming society. [Williams, 1974]

So we are in a position where it is believed that society is unknowable, is a "thing", is reification. This is one central myth of contemporary industrial cultures, and one that structures the per-ceived and felt relatedness of the individual to society. It is, then, understandable why the mass becomes socially passive and psy-chologically numb and amenable to the power of the State and, by extension, to the power of any institution and enterprise of society.

Although the novelists to whom Williams refers experienced this rupture of the felt relationship between the individual and society, others did not feel the change happening at the same pace. The dissociation was a more gradual process for the bulk of the population, and there was resistance. E. P. Thompson has argued that the working-class community of the early nineteenth century was the product of a "high degree of working class en-deavour" (Thompson, 1968). He has marshalled evidence to show that while the working class may have had their traditional roots of existence and essence wrested from a safe soil, they were able to articulate a political consciousness, to form a picture of the organization of society out of their own experience. There was a radical culture held by skilled workers, together with a sense that

Utopia could be realized. The early nineteenth century was, according to Thompson, the time of the

> most popular culture England has known. It contained the massive diversity of skills, of the workers in metal, wood, textiles and ceramics without whose inherited "mysteries" and superb ingenuity with primitive tools the inventions of the Industrial Revolution could scarcely have got further than the drawing board. From this culture of the craftsman and the self-taught there came scores of inventors, organizers, journalists and political theorists of impressive quality. [Thompson, 1968]

Again and again in the last century such men resisted attempts to be made into "tools" or "implements". Even "when they knew their cause was lost . . . they reached out again, in the Thirties and Forties, and sought to achieve new and only imagined forms of social control" (Thompson, 1968). But despite their heroic culture, with its dreams, visions, and utopian ideals, such men became what they feared the most: the proletariat; a dissociated aggregate of society; men and women converted from citizens to mass consumers. Now, a century later, we are in the midst of mass society, that "half-welfare and half-garrison society in which the population grows passive, indifferent and atomized" (Howe, 1971).

In this dissociation of the knowable from the unknowable, the social sciences have had their part to play. Indeed, the salient methodologies of the social sciences in a sense have legitimated the myth of the split between the individual and society. Practitioners of the social sciences have, for the most part, failed to use their imaginative capabilities. Subjectivity has been pushed out of scientific discourse. It may well be that this is because practitioners have been concerned about their own purity and have avoided situations and methodologies that might endanger their "professionalism". The danger for the social anthropologist has always been that he "goes native" and ceases to be a "professional". More generally, the stance of some social scientists has been to maintain an I–It, instrumental, pseudo-professional relationship with their world of "respondents".

A useful way of thinking about the social sciences and one that points to why social science practitioners may be failing to use their imagination has been advanced by John O'Neill, who suggests that sociology is best thought of as a "skin trade". In this context, sociology is not unlike the skin trades, such as haircutting or dentistry, which, like the professions of priest or medical doctor, are concerned with the sacredness and profanity that surrounds the human body. Because of the ambivalence felt about this, skin trade practitioners literally have to surround themselves with activities that distance them from their clients. Metaphorical skin trade practitioners, such as social scientists, are also caught in the same ambivalence. Hence the movement to objectify the subject of research, to convert the person into a collection of variables, for example. As O'Neill puts it:

> Much of the sociological apparatus functions, I suggest, to support a ritual of decontamination between the scientist and his subject. It is essential he view his subject only with professional eyes and that he resist the look in the eyes of the sick, the poor, and the aimless who turn his questions back on him. In this way the erotic symbiosis of talk is reduced to the interview schedule or attitude survey in which the client comes clean before the professional voyeur. [O'Neill, 1972]

My argument is that the social sciences ought to be a skin trade exploring the boundaries that are problematic—psychic, social, and political skins—because disorder is not to be kept at bay but entertained, understood, and worked with as a route to new forms of being that would include the political relatedness of the individual to society. Some research methodologies, however, because they protect the scientist from uncertainty, preclude this kind of knowing.

What Martin Buber has called the I–It relationship is often the organizing myth of the social sciences. The I–It relationship of the social scientist to his subject is often seen as being a proper scientific stance. But this is the inevitable outcome of the separation of the observer from the observed and rests on the presupposition that there exists outside any one individual person a "kingdom of order" in the sense that it is outside his/her will and desire. Hence, truth means the discovery of that pre-established order. The second presupposition is that a person's "cognitive apparatus does not materially affect the observation of this pre-established order" (Hampden-Turner, 1973). On these presuppositions are based social science methodologies such as behaviourism, functionalism, and operational research.

The question is whether the social sciences are to provide neatly ordered accounts of reality or whether the accounts are to reflect the complexity and the latent disorder. The behavioural sciences, for example, as Eugene Schwartz indicates, are a good instance of a particular formulation of the purpose of the social sciences:

> The thrust of the behavioural sciences is to stamp out disorder because the sciences cannot deal with it; to create activities that are conducive to control and hence to prediction; to make the complex simple because otherwise it cannot be comprehended. More serious is that science declared it a sine qua non that it must be objective by eliminating all subjective values and judgements, although, as has been shown earlier, subjective judgements were the bases of the axioms upon which science itself was built. Science, it is claimed, is thus neither good nor bad, but neutral. But if science is a-human in its neutrality by banishing all human qualities, is it not but a short step to become inhuman? [Schwartz, 1971]

All of these strictures can be applied to many social science practitioners. My major point is that such a conception of social science is not adequate for working with the complexity of reality. This is not an argument against measurement *per se*, as, clearly, certain features of reality can be quantified. The issue is whether or not the quantification is an avoidance of complexity. For example, the social scientist, in trying to understand what takes place in groups of people, attempts to reduce human group life to variables and their correlation. Not only is the choice of variables frequently faulty—chosen, often, because of their measurability—but also such an approach only interprets the outward facts of the situation. The basis of the behaviour of the participants—that is, what they hold in their minds about the situation and themselves in relation to that situation—is not taken into account.

The kind of difficulty this gets us into has been identified by a colleague, Peter Barham. In an earlier paper on group relations training (Barham & Lawrence, 1974), he referred to Poulantzas, the political scientist, who wrote of the difficulty: "in comprehending social classes and the State as objective structures and their relation as an objective system of regular connections, a structure and a system whose agents, 'men', are in the words of Marx 'bearers' of it—*Träger*" (Poulantzas, 1969). Poulantzas went on to speak of the impression thus given, that

> social classes of "groups" are in some way reducible to inter-personal relations, and the State is reducible to inter-personal relations of the diverse "groups" that constitute the State apparatus, and finally that the relations between social classes and the State itself as reducible to inter-personal relations of "individuals" composing social groups and "individuals" composing the State apparatus. [Poulantzas, 1969]

At this juncture I merely want to hold on to the view that this kind of impression is an inevitable outcome of the split between the knowable and unknowable community; the dissociation of objectivity from subjectivity; the division between modes of knowing. The healing of these splits, it is commonly believed, can only be brought about through "solving" interpersonal relations—the mechanics of relating. The subjective society carried inside the individual is disregarded. But I am beginning to believe that it is the society "in the mind", the internalized experiences, the introjected and projected experiences of that object outside us that we call "society", that need to be identified. My hunch is that if the necessary language could be created to explore these experiences of the fatal split between what is perceived to be knowable and the unknowable, we would in some way be able to make available for inspection the not so conscious social processes that I have been indicating, albeit in terms of a social cartoon.

It is to the lineaments of destruction, however, that I return. Mass society, I am suggesting, has more than its share of destructiveness. A major constraint on being able to identify and interpret this destructiveness rests in the very processes of an industrial society. Social passivity, psychological alienation, and narcissism are all interrelated. This produces social impotence, which produces passivity, and so on, as well as mindless destruction and violence. It would be too neat to see these in cause and effect terms. They happen, spasmodically erupting in confusing configurations.

What we can hypothesize, however, is that just as there is a fatal split between the knowable and unknowable of society and the how of knowing, so there is a fatal split between life and death. The presence of death is made absent, wished away in contemporary societies. In part this is understandable because the collective historical experience of people in the twentieth century has been of the arbitrariness of death and the realization that death can be manufactured like any other product. Wars, political purges, exterminations, and the rationality of the death machine of the concentration camp have caused a disjunction between the fact of life and the fact of death. The socially inherited, internalized rhythm of the sequence of life and death has been broken. Consequently, as Freud earlier identified in his "Thoughts for the Times on War and Death" (1915b), people become defended against the meaning of death as a process. The paradox is that the more people become defended against death and the inevitability of their own death, the more it becomes possible for death to be manufactured and split off from life. Destruction and violence, thus split off from the fact of death and in such a non-emotional climate, can be, at times, regnant.

But there are people who are identifying, exploring, and interpreting these frightening "public issues", to use C. Wright Mills's (1970) celebrated phrase. Almost predictably, it is left to some poets, and not the majority of social scientists, to make some purchase on these near-intractable processes I have briefly indicated. Alvarez in his recent study of suicide describes the work of what he has called the "extremist" poets—Robert Lowell, John Berryman, Ted Hughes, and Sylvia Plath—and suggests that they explore the experiences of the nihilism of contemporary, destructive societies. Since this cannot be controlled politically from the outside, he argues, the only way left is to try to control it artistically within the individual. This takes the individual, through the use of his feelings, to the friable boundary between the tolerable and the intolerable. And for Sylvia Plath this extremist impulse became "total and, literally, final" with her suicide as she explored "the nexus of anger, guilt, rejection, love and destructiveness" (Alvarez, 1974) of her life.

Here, I think, Alvarez identifies the major problem if the kind of exploration indicated is to be embarked upon. Because the mass—and ourselves as part of that mass—are reluctant to start the journey, those who do are made, at best, scapegoats and, at worst, victims. The public issues are neatly converted into "private troubles", again to use a telling phrase of C. Wright Mills's (1970). The individual who explores his own subjective experiences runs the risk of being converted into the "mad person", and then the remainder can hold the picture of being "civilized" and "contented". The impotence is locked away.

Nevertheless, my postulate is that the social sciences have much the same task as the extremist poets, which is, as Alvarez ends his book, to force

> its audience to recognize and accept imaginatively, in their nerve-ends, not the facts of life but the facts of death and violence: absurd, random, gratuitous, unjustified, and inescapably part of the society we have created. "There is only one liberty", wrote Camus in his Notebooks, "to come to terms with death. After which everything is possible." [Alvarez, 1974]

But I would want to turn around some of what Alvarez says. In particular, I want to suggest that getting in touch with the nihilism of society is, in fact, possible through political management from within the individual. Social change, which implies an inspection of social realities, starts from the individual considering his or her authority for being in a role in institutions of a society.

The management of oneself in role

My proposition is that this value has to be put into practice if we are to get in touch with, name, and interpret the kind of unconscious social processes in society to which I have been alluding. The realization of the value would be both a cause and an effect of this inspection process. This, it seems to me, is one way to create a shift in industrial societies in the direction of novel forms of living and existing in contemporary institutions. To put it tersely: the shift has to be "from having to being", to borrow from Fromm (1976). This means, I suspect, a reorientation of the individual's understanding of his or her political relatedness to the institutions of his society—a reorientation from having/not having power and authority as some kind of social possession towards taking authority for the nature of one's being as a system interrelating with other systems, be they other people, families, enterprises, institutions, or society.

I have been trying to indicate that we are imprisoned in our institutions and in societies. W. R. Bion in a recent interview talked about institutional imprisonment but pointed to some basis for hope:

> The trouble about all institutions—the Tavistock Institute and every one that we have—is that they are dead, but the people inside them aren't, and the people grow and something's going to happen. What usually happens is that the institutions (societies, nations, states and so forth) make laws. The original laws constitute a shell, and then new laws expand that shell. If it were a material prison, you could hope that the prison walls would be elastic in some sort of way. If organizations don't do that, they develop a hard shell, and then expansion can't occur because the organization has locked itself in. [Bion, 1976]

Institutions have locked themselves in, both politically and psychically; and so have, perhaps, the majority of the people who serve them. Consequently, the realization of the promise of the value of management of oneself in role, or some variation on it, or a more radical alternative, while it remains always a possibility, will always be constrained. There are the constraints woven into the fabric of mass society. These cannot be legislated away. No amount of rational planning will remove them or their causes but, paradoxically, will only reinforce them. So the starting point is the individual in his or her roles in relation to the systems in which he or she lives and works.

This has always been a concern of the group relations training of the Tavistock model. It has been, at times, an uncomfortable concern and has been reduced to interpersonal skill work, or consultants have been invoked as millenarian leaders. Fortunately, there have always been sufficient participants in a conference who have held doggedly to the primary task. There are some now who are convinced that the value of management of oneself in role has to be pursued. So, for example, one venture has been a working conference entitled "Authority and Social Innovation", which was

sponsored by the Tavistock Group Relations Training Programme
and *La Fondation Internationale de l'Innovation Sociale* based in Paris.
More important has been the continued development of what can
be called the "living methodology" intrinsic to the work of this
Tavistock model. The methodology is concerned to focus on whole
systems and their relatedness and not to be caught in the kind of
reductionism that characterizes so much of what passes for social
science. The methodology stands outside the scientific culture of
society in these senses and also because the method starts from
exploring what is experienced subjectively.

Evidence that the realization of this value is possible can be
found outside conferences. More generally, however, it can be
postulated that this value is one of the probable outcomes of con-
ceptualizing enterprises as socio-technical systems with open
boundaries.

The concept of socio-technical systems thinking is just over 20
years old and, since its first formulation in Trist and Bamforth's
(1951) "Some Social and Psychological Consequences of the Long-
wall Method of Coal-getting", has proved to be a particularly useful heuristic tool for many Tavistock research workers and others.
Essentially, the concept points to the interrelatedness of technical
and sociopsychological factors in production enterprises. Other
factors present are economic and political. The thrust of the socio-
technical concept has been to call into question the salience of
technology as determining social, political, and other relationships
within enterprises. As a result, organizational choice becomes possible, since it is possible to design forms of work organization that
optimize the best fit among social, psychological, technical, political, and economic factors.

One consequence of a socio-technical approach to organizational design has been the emergence of the concept of semi-autonomous work groups. The corollary of this idea is that every
individual who takes up a role in a work group, and by extension
in an enterprise, is called upon to manage himself in his role. This
is done in two ways: by managing himself in relation to his work
tasks and activities, and by managing his relationships with other
role-holders. And it is on the potentiality of and constraints on this
notion that I focus in this chapter.

To hold the view that individuals, enterprises, and indeed all institutions are systems with open boundaries is to begin a journey in organizational, political, social, and existential thinking that can cause a radical questioning of much of what is believed to be efficient organizational design. It can be postulated that if this journey were to be made, it could lead to a reformulation of the nature of the relationship between the individual, through his or her role, the work enterprise, and, by extension, society. Current ideas about bringing about compliance in enterprises would need to be overhauled so that the nature of the authority relationships within the enterprise, through its managerial representatives and employees, is redefined. My hypothesis is, however, that such a search for new meaning about that complex nexus can create such anxieties that people in enterprises very often revert to, or perseverate with, taken-for-granted modes of organizational design.

An example of the possibility of the value of self-management in role being realized was experienced by my former colleague, Eric Miller, and myself when we had the opportunity to act as consultants to the management of a factory that was being established on a green-field site. The task was to design jointly both the plant and the organization. The chosen base for the organization was the semi-autonomous work group—in particular, each task system responsible for the throughput was composed of workers who had authority to manage the transformation processes. A work group was defined as follows: "a set of associates who jointly accept responsibility for managing operating activities, process control, and correction to achieve agreed standards within a defined task boundary".

The importance of the introduction of the term "managing" in this context is not to be underestimated. In particular, it was being suggested that work groups were responsible for taking in imports across their task boundary, converting them into another state, and exporting them to the next system. This transformation process determined the primary task. Within work groups, workers were to be free to allocate roles for the execution of the primary task. Management, therefore, was a collective responsibility of the work group.

Such an idea cannot be carried out unless there is a change in the external environment composed of other systems. Two changes were to be important in this context: the conversion of quality control from a traditional control function to one of support, and a similar reorientation of production management. In this instance the quality control management (one of the services) saw themselves as providing the means for work groups to monitor their process controls at the boundaries of their task system and during the conversion process. Under this arrangement it became quite possible for each work group as a system to consider refusing at the import boundary materials or products that they did not think were up to standard. The regulation of the import and export boundaries of each work group as a task system thus becomes crucial, not only because it is through the management of boundaries that each system relates to another as an open system, but also because it affirms that the work group's authority derives from their collective primary task.

The political implications of management within a work group seem clear enough: it is a collective responsibility concerned with transacting across the boundaries of the system and coordinating the activities and relationships of one role-holder with another in relation to the primary task of the system. Thus each role-holder is not only concerned with the management of himself in his role but also with the management of the work group, which has to be held "in the mind". "In the mind", in this context, means that the individual in his role holds a *Gestalt* of the system as a whole with which he relates from his role, and that he can locate his work group as a system within the other systems of the enterprise. Consequently, decisions about the work and social life of the work group are located within that group, but have to be related to the realities of other work groups as systems with their primary tasks.

If the process of management is located within the semi-autonomous work group, what is the function of those who are officially designated "production managers"? Essentially, their role is to provide and regulate the conditions (materials, supplies, intelligence about the market, budget information, and technical expertise, for instance) for the work groups to manage themselves in their roles on the basis of the authority inherent in their primary tasks. On reflection, I believe that in addition they have an educational task, which is directed not merely at obvious information sharing but also at raising the political consciousness of themselves and their fellow workers. By this I mean exercising responsibility, authority, and leadership on behalf of the system as a whole—that is, acting as an ego to the system. Since all enterprises exist in turbulent economic environments, this function will become more important.

After three years the project ended because "the management" felt that they had gone far enough. There are two possible explanations for this, apart from the stated one. "The management" may well have found themselves bereft of a recognizable role. People change at different paces, and the lowest common denominator tends to hold sway. Even though "the management" had invested considerable enthusiasm and various kinds of energies for the success of the project, which all said publicly that they valued, anxieties had been expressed at various times by some managers that if this project continued, there would be no job for them. The other reason probably lies with the workers. On what journey was this project to take them? While they could and did express a high degree of satisfaction with conditions in the new factory, it may be that the demands were too high. Only those who see themselves as having the status of manager tend to manage a career on their life-chances. My hypothesis is, however, that the project and its new work experiences put into disarray the taken-for-granted assumptions made by most workers about the relatedness between themselves and management, both as a status and political aggregate and as a process.

But this is understandable. The consultants always saw the project as being an educational venture concerned with the politics of the involvement of the individual in his role in the enterprise. Without exception, all participants in the project, irrespective of their roles, had shared perceptions and constructions of the accepted organization of enterprises that were based on their discrete previous work experiences. They had all been inducted into one of the salient myths of organizations: management equals man-management.

Work in mass industrial societies is experienced as coercive. In part this is expected, because it is seen as providing the financial means to live in a consumer society. (The reality, as I have been

suggesting earlier in this chapter, is that citizens have been convened into consumers.) Consuming more social and other goods
has compensated for the frustration of ego needs and the ability to
exercise authority and autonomy in one's work role. (Having
more, wanting more, and envy of those who have more have replaced values about being.) When this has become intolerable,
when the sense of social persecution and social depression has
been allowed to be voiced, the result has been the "go-slow", and
other action. The repressed feelings erupt in violent actions. Usually, however, the over-consumption has been channelled into the
need to earn more, which has sanctioned those who have traditional political power within an enterprise to continue to make
work coercive and to continue to be able to define their role in
terms of managing other people. They, in turn, have their shared
myth that technology is value-free and neutral; that it determines
the plant and social organization, and therefore the political relationships in the enterprise. And for the most part they are
provided rationalizations by the motivation theory merchants
who hold the view that men have to be made into homunculi,
otherwise there will be chaos as people pursue their self-interests.
Figure 2.1 shows that it is a vicious cycle.

How can the cycle be converted into a virtuous one? An answer is beyond me at present. What I guess I know are some of the
issues to be faced. The vicious cycle derives some of its energy
from the basic assumption dependency (Bion, 1961) around which
organizations are mobilized. Individuals as role-holders and vice
versa take the dependency and social passivity present in the
larger society across the boundary of enterprises. Dependency of a
basic-assumption nature is pre-eminently available for study in
enterprises. In education (Lawrence & Hakim-Goldsbrough, 1973;
Lawrence & Robinson, 1974, 1975) and in industry (Lawrence et
al., 1975), one keeps rediscovering, as a consultant, the social process of dependency. Often it makes the consultant feel depressed.
This kind of experience I take, however, to be part of the role; he
is available for projections. The experience of basic-assumption
dependency has its outcomes: "the insidious costs of excessive
dependency [are] erosion of self-esteem, chronic feelings of helplessness and depression" (Menninger, 1972). These are present
very often in the consultant–client relationships, and the consult-

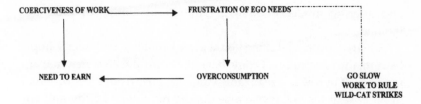

Figure 2.1

ant is available to receive these feelings from the client. These have to be contained and then made available through working hypotheses and interpretations, in order that the client should have an opportunity to reintroject them on his or her authority. And there is a sense in which this chapter has some of these qualities and an element of this task.

To acknowledge the helplessness, the social impotence, the loss of self-esteem, the social paranoia, the individual and social depression would be to enter the disarray, chaos, and uncertainty that the breaking of excessive individual dependency, or its collective counterpart, social passivity, would incur. Alvarez (1974) has pointed to the psychic territory: the exploration of "the nexus of anger, guilt, rejection, love and destructiveness". To this can be added that other complex nexus: the bond, link, relatedness, relationship, or whatever "it" is that joins or dissociates individuals through their roles to or from their groupings.

One constraint is that it is increasingly difficult for the individual to experience, let alone to name, these nexuses. Hypotheses to explain this difficulty have been offered. There is increasing narcissism; lack of questioning of taken-for-granted assumptions about authority; myths of political relatedness. Primarily, however, the constraint is anxiety against experiencing disarray. (In a mass society the freedom to experience anxiety is removed by the conventional belief that anxiety equals sickness and is to be wished away by means of tranquillizers.)

But anxiety, disarray, chaos, uncertainty are the seedbeds of creativity for renewed being. So I am postulating that we need to demystify assumptions about the social and political connectedness of individuals to society by putting them into doubt, by making them uncertain, interpreting unconscious social processes, and altering modes of knowing the social worlds of men and women.

Clearly, I am searching for ways of making real social hope. Despite the constraints, I come back to the proposition that managing oneself in role is a realizable value. It starts from the individual in his role in his enterprise questioning his responsibility and authority as a member of that enterprise. Hope cannot be placed in large-scale changes in society, in what passes for education in industrial societies, in consumer education, or in messianic movements. Social hope begins with men and women questioning cultural assumptions and taking authority for interpreting them, no matter where the search for truth leads. But that implies that they have made themselves sufficiently aware of the fact and process of death to make life worth the questioning.

CHAPTER THREE

Exploring the boundaries of the possible

This chapter attempts to elucidate some of the thinking involved in the kind of group relations training that was developed within the Tavistock Institute of Human Relations and is now conducted by its Group Relations Education Programme. For me, it is the most potent of methodologies because it enables one to distinguish between phantasy and reality. It also enables one, among other things, to distinguish between truth and the lie; to come to grips with projection and introjection, transference and countertransference, which are the basic "stuff" of human relations.

Since the beginnings in 1957, when the first conference was held in conjunction with Leicester University, as described by E. L. Trist and C. Sofer in *Exploration in Group Relations* (1959), there have been a number of institutional developments. Within the Tavistock Institute, a group of people, led by the late Dr A. K. Rice and principally supported by Mrs I. E. P. Menzies Lyth, together with Drs P. M. Turquet, R. H. Gosling, and E. J. Miller, pressed forward the particular version of group relations training with which this volume is concerned.

Between the first conference and those under the directorship of A. K. Rice, there occurred a critical division among those scientific workers of the Tavistock involved in group relations training. At the first conference the events were Study Groups and Application Groups. The former were designed to give participants experiences of the dynamics of small groups and the latter to explore how the learning could be applied in real-life situations. It was realized that while this design gave participants the opportunity to become intensely aware of the destructive and creative processes of the unconscious in Study Groups, there was a gap between such experiences and the world of work. Hence, H. Bridger introduced the Inter-Group Exercise at the second conference, which was held at Buxton in 1959 (Higgin & Bridger, 1965). Bridger's version of the Inter-Group Exercise provides participants with opportunities to form their own groups for the purpose of deciding on a programme of special interest sessions that would occupy the second half of the timetable for the conference. This event had a dual task: the study of group processes in relation to a particular project. A. K. Rice and his colleagues, however, believed that the educational objectives of conference would be better realized if events had a single task—that is, if the task of the event were framed in such a way that the existential nature of the event was pre-eminently available for study by all the participants. To have a dual task for an event would mean that the exploration of the "here-and-now" [*hic et nunc*] processes, which undoubtedly raise anxieties, could be defended against by participants. Thus the phenomenal stuff of unconscious group phenomena would be lost.

Since the time of Rice's directorship (from 1962 until his death in 1969) of this programme in the Tavistock, the conferences have had the title "Authority, Leadership, and Organization", or some variation on that. The focus of these conferences is on the exercise of responsibility and authority, and therefore of leadership and followership, in interpersonal and intergroup settings. This is a minimal statement because these concepts relate to others such as management and organization. Because the word "authority" occurs in the title, there is often the fantasy that they are authoritarian. Be that as it may, what needs to be stated at the outset is that the concern of these Tavistock conferences is about the political relatedness of the individual through his roles to his groups, institutions, and the larger society.

Other institutions have been founded to develop not only this version of group relations training but also related consultancy and action research activities. Because of the institutional seeding, it has been convenient to refer to this version of group relations training as the Tavistock model. It has, however, been taken on and developed by people who have founded institutions and is now, therefore, not just located in the Tavistock. In America there is the A. K. Rice Institute in Washington, DC, with a number of regional centres and affiliated institutions, such as GREX in San Francisco. In Canada, for a time, the Rosehill Institute of Human Relations also held working conferences. In Britain there are the Grubb Institute; the Scottish Institute of Human Relations; the Chelmsford Cathedral Centre for Research and Training; and, for a period, the Centre for the Study of Group and Institutional Relations based at Bristol University. Nowadays there are far more institutions offering conferences. In France, there is the International Forum for Social Innovation; in Germany, MundO; in Israel two institutions; and in Australia, the Australian Institute of Socio-Analysis. In Bulgaria there is the Bulgarian Institute of Human Relations. At the University of the West of England there is now a specialist course for the teaching of group relations. In addition, there have been a number of individuals who have introduced this version of group relations training into business and educational institutions, not all of whom I know.

The term "Tavistock model" refers to a heuristic framework for identifying and understanding what conscious and unconscious processes take place within and between groups of people. Its use, however, is both accurate and misleading. It is accurate in the sense that it has its beginnings in the Tavistock Institute and is still being developed there. It is misleading in two senses: first, the tradition is now located in a number of institutions, and so "Tavistock" becomes a common identifying tag; second, the tradition is a living one and is continually being reinterpreted by institutions in the light of changing circumstances in the environment; so the term "model" needs to be explored. The notion of a "model" can imply some "thing"—a reification—that is fixed and stable. Here the usage of the word "model" implies a tradition with identifiable, experiential, and intellectual roots that is being reinterpreted and reworked by representatives of different institutions. These differences are not to be obliterated but celebrated; one institution's thinking can inform other institutions. Predictably, technical leadership will move among the different institutions depending on how well their representatives are experiencing and interpreting across the boundary of their institutions. Somewhat ambivalently, therefore, I propose to refer to the version of group relations training that this book explores as the "Tavistock model". The reluctance, I hope, is understandable. Nevertheless, I believe that the heuristic concepts used by the institutions to which I have referred above are identifiable, and their shared usage ought to be acknowledged.

All these institutions are not founded merely for the task of providing group relations training. As in the Tavistock, the training has to be seen as complementary to other action research and consultancy projects. Hence, there is a good deal of interpenetration of ideas, values, and concepts from the research field to conferences and vice versa. Working conferences use such concepts as open-systems thinking about the organization of enterprises. The first text in this area was Rice's *Productivity and Social Organization* (1958). Other books have taken this idea about organizations, among others, further. There is *Systems of Organization* by Miller and Rice (1967) and Miller's *Task and Organization* (1976). Action research studies that have extended such thinking, relying on the heuristic concepts of the model, have been Richardson's *The Teacher, the School and the Task of Management* (1973); Miller and Gwynne's *A Life Apart* (1972); and an earlier text by Rice, *The Modern University* (1970).

This book also has to be situated in relation to other books and pamphlets that have set out this Tavistock model of group relations training. Of these, W. R. Bion's *Experiences in Groups* (1961) stands pre-eminent because it elaborates the working hypotheses and methodology on which this model is founded. To radically alter this method would be to establish a different model. Subsequently, in 1965, A. K. Rice published his *Learning for Leadership*, in which he meticulously described the working conferences in interpersonal and intergroup relations that had developed from Bion's ideas. Having set out the basic concepts and described the structure, culture, and activities of the conferences by using an open-systems analysis, Rice pulled together much of the key thinking about working conferences. There have been no major radical shifts since then. *Group Relations Reader I* (1975), edited by Arthur D. Colman and W. Harold Bexton, and *Group Relations Reader II* (1985), edited by Colman and Marvin H. Geller, have made available the best of the published material up to that date on the theory, method, and application of the Tavistock Model of group relations training. The important point, in respect of this book, is that because others have done the basic work of explicating the conceptual, methodological, and central values of the model as exemplified through working conferences, it is now possible to be free to be associative and to take thinking further. Nevertheless, I want to describe aspects of this training in order to provide a context for this book.

Aspects of working conferences

Working conferences for group relations training are usually residential and can last from a weekend to a fortnight. They are temporary education institutions and can be seen as open systems taking in members who have an interest in understanding issues of authority. The conference staff have two sub-roles: that of collective management and that of consultants. As management, they provide conditions for members to learn; in their consultant role, they interpret what is taking place from this role perspective. Essentially, they manage a process, which is to study group behaviour. This process is the transforming of feelings and ideas about authority into new ones. Hopefully, members will export themselves back into their institutions with fresh insights. The conference process is open-ended in the sense that the staff do not determine what members and they will learn. Experiences are provided through activities, and consultants attempt to interpret the experiences of these events as they occur. Hence, it does happen that some insight will emerge in a conference of which neither staff nor members were aware before.

Working conferences have a primary task. Among the most recent statements of task for these has been the following: "To provide members with opportunities to find sanction within themselves to experience and interpret the nature of authority and the interpersonal, intergroup, and institutional problems encountered in its exercise within the Conference Institution." The primary task is determined by the dominant import–transformation–export process, which is to study group behaviour. It is upon this task that the design of the conference and the role of staff are based. What members choose to do is on their authority.

"Living methodology"

The more I think about conferences, the more I am inclined to say that they are designed to provide opportunities for members to internalize and make for themselves a "living methodology" for inspecting the conscious and unconscious realities of groups and institutions and the political relatedness (authority, management, and organization) of individuals in roles within these configurations. "Living methodology" is a cumbersome term, but it carries the idea of the individual using his subjectivity and sensibility to explore realities, forming working hypotheses about the realities as he construes them, and testing the hypotheses with others as a way of arriving at some externalized, objective statement about the truth of the social situation as it is perceived from the role of member.

If we accept that what Kant called the *noumenon*—the thing-in-itself—is only known through phenomena and that we are only in a position to guess "that corresponding to these phenomena, which are something that we know about because they are us, is the thing itself, the noumenon" (Bion, 1974), notions about an education in a living methodology may become somewhat clearer. It is living in the sense that it is based on the individual testing his changing constructions and perceptions of his social world as an ongoing process. The method uses subjectivity but in the process takes into account the state of the person as an instrument. So it is not just a matter of perceiving but also of personally inquiring into how one arrived at a particular perception. One writer has captured something of what is involved:

> In a paradoxical way, then, objectivity requires the cultivation of specific subjective states, the disciplining of attention and selected habits of thought, the screening out of other sources of consciousness, control over emotions, and a commitment to private and public honesty, to care and precision, to technical statement and social cooperation. *Objectivity is a highly selective, highly developed subjective state.* [Novak, 1971, italics added]

What all this points to is that reality is not something exclusively "out there", that there is not a domain of order outside the individual that merely has to be discovered, but that the individual is a bearer of that reality. Reality is both inside and outside him or her. Furthermore, it is his or her construction of the phenomena of reality that is to be investigated. Ultimate reality, which can be referred to by such terms as "absolute truth, the god-head, the infinite, the thing in itself" (Bion, 1974), does not fall into the domain of knowledge. Ultimate reality can only be in a state of "becoming"; it cannot be known. And it is this idea of "becoming" that is to be held on to when thinking about modes of inquiring into social processes in groups and institutions. The "becoming" enables us not to fall into the traps of either solipsism or positivism but to engage with the creative tensions among what people believe to be realities and fantasies.

The role of the consultant

The pressing forward of this methodology is initially in the hands of the consultants. What follows is certainly not a prescription but my thoughts around this role. First, the relatedness between the consultant and a group is one focus of study. The consultant interprets from his role perspective. Whether that is perceived and experienced as having more power than that of the members is open to examination. The consultant interprets and formulates working hypotheses about the social processes, conscious and otherwise, that he or she understands to be present in the group. Transference phenomena are part of the data. But he or she is part of that configuration in the room even though he or she is not in the group and is not in the role of a member. If he or she becomes a member, his or her function which is sedulously to pursue the primary task, is lost. Yet the data from which the interpretation is derived are his experience of being pulled into membership on the one hand and extruded into limbo on the other.

Second, I sometimes explain to myself that the task of a consultant is a maieutic one in that it is to help members to realize their interpretations of the situation; in short, to exercise their authority to test realities (see chapter ten). Clearly, the role is not didactic in the conventional sense but is to puzzle out from a role perspective what social phenomena are present in the situation, to form hypotheses, and to further learning. It is fashionable in educational settings to talk about raising the level of consciousness. This educational context includes just that, but it also provides a model, through behaviour, of how one gets in touch with unconsciousness. This is part of the conditions that the consultant provides to enable members to undertake these tasks for themselves. Just as for the work group leader who is in touch with the primary task, there will be continual attempts to seduce the consultant into a membership role, preferably one that satisfies the primitive wishes of the members. But if this happens, transference and countertransference feelings will be removed from the situation, and the aim of understanding the nature of authority will disappear.

There is, third, a necessity that the consultant leads the group in a work fashion into problem areas for him/herself in his/her role in relation to the members with whom he/she is working. At the same time the consultant needs to understand the experience of containment, the ability to allow the members to "be" in their terms. The boundary between these two is always puzzling, just as are the limits of certainty and uncertainty, chaos and order, which are all personally defined.

Fourth, the consultant is working with his/her subjectivity and attempting to use him/herself as an instrument in the situation. The internal disentangling of what is being projected into the consultant and what is already there, having been introjected from his/her own past experiences, is a continual private task for the consultant. He needs to be able to work out, for example, how much uncertainty he/she owns and how much he/she is projecting onto the group when he/she leads into new areas of exploration by offering hypotheses. It is for this reason among others that those who have directed the Group Relations Training Education in the Tavistock have always undergone a personal psychoanalysis at least, and attempt to recruit staff for working conferences who will have psychoanalytic skills in their midst. To do otherwise is, to my mind, irresponsible.

Fifth, the consultant frames working hypotheses and interpretations on the basis of his/her experience in the role. These two terms are used interchangeably, though it would be better if only the former were used. A working hypothesis is the social science equivalent of an interpretation that I tend to see as being a more appropriate tool for explicating interpersonal relationships.

The working hypothesis is a sketch of the reality of a situation to be either elaborated or erased and replaced by another sketch. The working hypothesis is always an approximation—valid and reliable at a particular point in time of the relationship between members of a grouping in a conference and the consultant or consultants. Reality, as I have said earlier, is construed subjectively. In the course of his personal development, the individual has established a set of assumptions as to what constitutes reality and has organized his/her behaviour in relation to collective definitions of that reality. These assumptions and recipes for conduct give meaning to the individual's life. As important, they give some protection from fear and uncertainty, and so "even personal attempts to recognize and reconsider such deeply-rooted assumptions arouse anxiety and resistance" (Wilson, 1951). A working hypothesis, therefore, must always be directed at the space between the members and the consultant, not at a particular member. It is in the space between, so to speak, that the member's freedom to work or not with the hypothesis is preserved. The member then knows that what he/she decides is on his/her authority.

Dr Pierre Turquet, in his lectures, has a particularly useful passage on what he refers to as the "interpretation" (Schulman, personal communication).[1]

The interpretation

It creates usually a healthy pause where thinking and examining takes place. The interpretation has put people in touch with the here and now and releases certain phenomena that happen in the pause. Often members speak individually and closer to the task after an interpretation.

The interpretation has a certain content. So has the pause. It is important to observe closely the fact of the content of the interpretation. This gives usually clear information to the leader of what forces are in operation in the group and in the members. In the work group situation the content of the interpretation is clearly used for further efforts to tackle the task. The content of the pause that emerges after the interpretation should show this.

Turquet also pointed to the necessity for providing evidence for an interpretation—what he called the "because clause":

The "because clause" in the interpretation is very important because it is (a) "out of time" and emphasizes a long span of time of the group life; and (b) it gets at the repetition compulsions of the members of the group since it reveals the past and the motives operating which were, before the interpretation, out of touch with the here and now. The past, so to say, has to be differentiated from the here and now so those unrealistic historical motives can be given up. It is also the way and method whereby the interpreter is exposing his, or her own sense of reality and his understanding of what is going on at any moment. Thus he also, as it were, tests his own sense of reality. Often new ideas flow into the here and now after the "because clause" has been mentioned. The "because clause" in the interpretation differentiates the past motives from the present and thus, as it were, cuts off the repetition compulsion

---

[1]Here let me acknowledge my gratitude to Dr Gustav Schulman for letting me see his notes on Pierre Turquet's lectures to the Advanced Training Group held in the Tavistock Centre.

where the individual tries to repeat past history. When the leader takes this historical motive into the current reality he exposes it and can release the group to work more accurately on the actual task without the past interfering.

Ideally, members can internalize this mode of working and exercise their authority to interpret on the basis of their experience.

These experiences are possible through participation in a range of activities, each of which will have a primary task. Usually there are two events that are concerned with the study of experience in the "here-and-now" within different sizes of groups. There is the small (or study) group, which has 9 to 12 members with one consultant, and the large group, which is composed of the total membership, which may number between 35 and 40 upwards, with three or four consultants. Both these events are designed to enable authority and relationships to be studied, and they focus on intra-group relations.

It is around the small group that Wilfred Bion first developed the thinking that has now come to be associated with the Tavistock Model. Apart from his own writings (1961), and the account of his thought by Greenberg and others (1975), there are numerous other accounts, of which the most useful is that of Rioch (1970). Wilfred Bion not only emphasized the notion of groups being seen as wholes but also detected other dimensions: the unconscious processes.

His hypotheses about small groups have provided a set of heuristic notions for understanding what takes place in groups. Bion was able to see that in any one group there are simultaneously present two groups: the work group and the basic assumption group. The former functions like a mature ego does; its members operate by testing out realities through making hypotheses and exploring them. Such a group tries to discover and work on increased understanding of external realities in relation to the internal world of the group. Its members have the ability to stop and think, question the life of the group, make suggestions, allow free association, and make hypotheses. Such a group nurtures the skills of its members and recognizes their differences in a realistic fashion. It is a group that is not fixed to roles or to a structure or to past history or to an exclusive future orientation. Such a group can change according to the changing circumstances of the environment.

The work group has to be contrasted with the basic assumption group, which is the unconscious group—the group that operates on certain unspoken assumptions. Bion identified the basic assumption dependency group (baD), the basic assumption pairing group (baP), and the basic assumption fight/flight group (baF/F). None of these groups exists in a pure form, as does the work group, but Bion's descriptions provide us with benchmarks to understand the unconscious reality of groups. A baD group operates on the assumption that, or "as if", it is met to be dependent on one leader who is experienced as omnipotent and omniscient in contrast to other participants who feel the opposite. The leader is made into a kind of god. A baF group is one of action, and the role of the leader is to mobilize fight or flight in order to preserve the group. The mood is one of paranoia, and all such feelings have to be projected out of the group. The third kind of basic assumption group, baP, is one in which the mood is that of expectancy and hopefulness, and so two members will be paired, irrespective of gender, to bring forth a Saviour or Messiah. This can be a leader, an idea, or some version of utopia. Predictably, the messianic wish must never be fulfilled, otherwise the feeling of hope is lost.

Any group of up to 12 participants, Bion hypothesized, will oscillate among these various kinds of groups (Work, baD, baF and baP). A mature group will be able to mobilize and use these group cultures for the pursuance of work. Indeed, one set of basic assumptions keeps at bay the feelings associated with the other two. Whether the basic group is modifying the goals and activities of the work group negatively or not is always an open question.

This thinking around the small group has had the qualities of an architectonic paradigm for considering other group activities. The tendency very often is, however, to utilize Bion's thinking about small groups in relation to other group events, which is to press interpretations of their unique phenomena back into a small group mould of thinking.

One proposition can help us to do this: Bion's hypotheses are essentially about the myths on which groups of people operate. There is always in any group a conflict between the individual and the group. If we allow notions about individuals and groups being open systems, this conflict can become a positive way of testing realities in a changing environment. It is, however, not experienced as this very often. Rather, the individual is seen to be a closed system, and the group is felt to be a closed system. In such situations the fear of the individual is of being lost in the group. This can be described as the conflict between narcissism and socialism. In an attempt to solve this experienced problem, myths are created. The purpose of the myth seems to be to unite the aim of the individual with that of the group so as to bind them together in such a way that what is understood to be destructive conflict will be prevented. In small groups of up to 12 people the typical myths are the basic assumption myths. In larger groups different myths will be present. In general, the cultural language of myths is expressions of the forces that unite the group and contribute to the feeling of oneness between the individual and the group—a system-less world with no boundaries. In such a culture there will be resistance against naming the myth because the fear is that the unity of the group, with its attendant feelings of closeness and intimacy, will be destroyed. The fear is that if the myth is elucidated, it will take away the basic security of the group.

It is the shared myth, usually unspoken, that binds the group members together. This is, of course, an illusory togetherness that can be seen when the myth is interpreted. This creates a feeling of disillusionment, and the individuals never like it. The elucidation of the myth is difficult because it is usually unconscious and strongly clung to as common property. The elucidation causes a feeling of loss but frees the individual from illusory togetherness. This is the reason why an accurate interpretation of the myth can create a situation where members begin to speak individually. The basic assumption group tries to create myths and gather around these, in contrast to the work group, which tries to find unity around the task definition. The basic assumption group has a myth-producing atmosphere. There is the myth of Oedipus, myth of rumour, myth of sacrifice, myth of blissfulness and oneness, myth of marriage, myth of Robinson Crusoe, just to mention some of the usual ones. The Robinson Crusoe myth is about omnipotence where the members feel that they are in control and command of the whole environment and nature. Usually there is an atmosphere of exploitation and control where everything is done for the members' own benefit or the group's own benefit without thinking about the others. It is some sort of group selfishness where outside bodies, or even members in the group, can be treated like things or possessions. (To my mind this is the counterpart of narcissism in groups—group narcissism or group self-centred-ness. There is no sense of concern or ability to feel depression. Even apparently loving and good comments or deeds are done because of a selfish motive.)

Myths are created due to the basic assumption wishes for togetherness and easy life. They are kept away by accurate task definition, developing skills, reality testing, realistic notions of time boundary, realistic perception of external reality; in short, by vigorous and vigilant work group leadership. When these fail, myths are generated to focus on the internal life of the group, as a flight from the outside reality, which demands work and faces the individual with pain. The harder or the more frustrating the outside reality or the task, the greater is the need to turn exclusively into the internal life.

I think, also, that group life, irrespective of the size of the grouping, is organized around defences against the anxieties of uncertainty and chaos, which, in turn, produces myths. When an individual member joins a group for the first time, it triggers off in his memory models of his own past behaviour patterns and experiences in similar situations. There is a search for familiar models and familiar situations. There is, therefore, always a possibility that the here-and-now experience will be determined by past experience. The past represents something familiar, tangible, controllable, and secure. It provides a good opportunity to escape from the uncertainties of the moment. In basic assumption groups this happens especially.

I think that this is one of the essential elements of the mythologies of groups. An individual who is in touch with, or holds inside himself, a conception of primary task will be very much involved in the here-and-now, but will be trying to relate it realistically to the past and the future as he experiences it. He will start from the experience of the moment in its terms and work at its relatedness to the past and the future as opposed to construing the moment, in the here-and-now, in their terms.

The large group

Myths are pre-eminently available for study in the large study system or group. Until fairly recently the primary experience in a working conference has been felt to be that of the small, or study, group. This is, I think, because Bion's hypotheses best fit that situation. Increasingly, however, there has been a shift towards making the large group the primary experience by, for example, giving it first place on the programme each day. This is for two reasons: first, the large group and its immediate related activity, the median group, are recent, post-Bion discoveries. A. K. Rice and P. M. Turquet were the first to consult to a large group. Subsequently, Turquet developed what thinking there has been around this complex event. His two papers, "Leadership: The Individual and the Group" (1974) and "Threats to Identity in the Large Group" (1975), stand alone as the only sustained efforts to explore and explicate the phenomena of large groups.

The second reason why the large group experience is being made more salient is that it is an event that provides members with opportunities to study what I have called the crowd that lies behind the organization of every large-scale system or enterprise. I am becoming increasingly preoccupied with large group phenomena because it is possible to hear, with the "third ear", what is taking place in the wider society. The large group is a frame for catching what is unconsciously taking place in the society at large, even though that is not the stated preoccupation, nor is life in society the topic of discussion. It is here that we see the narcissism of individuals struggling with a phenomenon that is experienced as being akin to "society". It is here, for example, that we experience the two related myths that society is unknowable and that only the individual is knowable.

The institutional event

In this event there are two major groupings: staff and members. Members are free to form subgroups of their own choice. Management can either divide into a management subgroup and a consultant subgroup or stay as a staff group or management. Even if they stay as one group, they carry the two sub-roles.

As in the intergroup event, task, time, and territorial boundaries are specified. These, as in the former event, are for the convenience of staff; what members choose to do is on their authority. The focus is on the political relatedness of members and staff, and the task is to study what conscious and unconscious relationships are present or do not exist between them. It is in this context that the concept of "institution in the mind" comes into play. Both members and staff are relating politically to their perceptions of and visions for the institution within whose frame the action is taking place.

All these events have a single task, which is to study behaviour in the event as it happens in the here-and-now. A study group has the primary task of studying the relatedness in the group as it happens; the intergroup event has the task of studying relationships between groups as they occur. The group and intergroup behaviour is the focus of study. This has to be compared with events that have a dual task—for example, to form a group to make, say, a learning institution, and then to study the group processes by which decisions were made. This Tavistock Model concerns itself exclusively with single-task events, because group processes are then available for existential study without other factors that could be used as a defence against the anxieties of examining what processes take place at an unconscious level in group settings being present.

Review and application groups, orientation groups, and role analysis groups

I describe these four types of groups together because they essentially serve the same functions: to enable a member to consider his role within the conference as an institution and to consider what learning is appropriate to his back-home situation. All these events can be seen as providing spaces in the time of the programme for the member to consider his relatedness to the conference as an institution, as a paradigm of his relatedness in outside systems.

The Role Analysis Group was first thought out by Irving Borwick when he was at ITT. He saw that the application groups were limited when it came to working with managers in their roles. Essentially, the idea was to have managers situate themselves in the systems in which they were working and to work out the kinds of pressures they were experiencing. It has been found that it is a potent tool for enabling managers to understand the dynamics of their work life.

The conference is an open system taking in members who wish to consider issues of authority in relation to their work and other organizations. In crossing the boundaries of the conference, it is important that opportunities be provided for members to consider what is relevant in taking up the role of member, as opposed to merely attending a conference. Similarly, as members move towards the output boundary, they ought to have an opportunity to reflect on what is involved in taking up their outside role again. All these events can be seen as being between the inner experiential skin of the conference and the outer organizational one. They are designed to enable members to consider what authority they have in relation to various internal and external realities.

Conference plenaries

There are normally at least two conference plenaries. They are events in themselves. The opening plenary sets the task and administrative boundaries of the conference and points the membership towards the experiential events that are being made available.

The final plenary (or plenaries) is designed to provide opportunities for ending work relationships between members and staff without applying closure to the learning of the conference. It is important to understand that the "product" of a conference is a "process"—what has been called a "living methodology".

In this outline I have not attempted to describe in any detail what takes place in a conference and its events. Even if I had the ability, I would never capture their complexity of behaviour. A conference is there to be experienced, and whatever I might say about experience would be mine and would not be the same as another person's. Nevertheless, there are some aims and principles that would be shared by those organizing and staffing these conferences.

Aims and principles

I can do no better in this introduction than selectively recall from what is usually stated in the brochures describing a conference:

> A working conference is based on the belief that men and women can work more effectively, with greater satisfaction and, possibly, create an organization of their choice if they come to understand in a direct and personal way the dynamics of groups and inter-group processes within social systems. The overall interest of the Conference Institution is in the functioning of groups as wholes and not in the personality factors of individual members: the latter are for the private scrutiny of each member. The processes, both manifest and covert, of groups and social systems can best be understood when they are seen in actual operation. The Conference, therefore, offers an opportunity to examine what happens within, among and between groups, to work in the "here-and-now" of experience as it occurs.
>
> Such aspects of organizational life as task, authority, and role are examined in the Conference Institution. There are opportunities to become aware of discrepancies between the stated primary task of a group and the task it actually appears to be pursuing; to discover what differences there may be in perceptions of authority and management and what are the conscious and unconscious sanctions for exercising responsible leadership and followership. Such roles and others may not always be officially designated but can be invoked by groups for quite other purposes than the pursuance of the primary task. But these are all open to examination.
>
> In the work of the Institution the concept of boundary is important. Leadership (which may not always be invested in a desig-

nated leader) is conceived in terms of managing a boundary between what is inside and what is outside—for example, boundaries between group and organization, organization and environment. The Institution affords opportunities for examining the nature and meaning of such boundaries, including experience of the member–staff boundary in a variety of settings. Within this framework, members may also explore such related boundaries as those between the individual's inner and outer worlds, person and role, individual and group, leader and followers, group and institution, institution and environment. In this context authority is vested in and accepted by individuals and groups to manage transactions across these boundaries.

The Institution is open-ended in the sense that there is no attempt to prescribe what anyone will learn. This educational approach, therefore, with its focus on learning from the here-and-now of experience, implies that what each member learns is unique. It is on his or her own authority that each member accepts what is valid and rejects what is not. Through this process members may become better equipped to reconsider the exercise of their authority in institutions which exist in an uncertain environment.

The more I think about working conferences, which use the Tavistock model, the more I am convinced that they will lose their value if the focus shifts from authority and political relatedness. There is a continual pressure on staff in their consultant roles to explore only interpersonal relationships. The concern has to continue to be the exploration and explication of the real and fantasied relatedness of the individual in his roles to his groups, institutions, and society: that is his political responsibility and authority.

Because this is an uncomfortable concern, I suspect that a number of socially structured arrangements are established by people providing group relations training to defend themselves against the anxieties that such a concern arouses. These defences can resonate with the feelings held by participants who sometimes see themselves as consumers of experiences, which must be "good" and free of any psychic pain or anxiety. So all collude to avoid the challenges of the joint educational venture they could make.

The principal seduction I have already referred to is that group relations training is reduced to interpersonal skill work, as if the conscious and unconscious political processes and issues of contemporary institutions in societies could be smoothed away if people would meet people as people without any differences in sex, age, race, creed, political affiliations, or, indeed, authority and power.

There has grown, inevitably, an institutional way of avoiding insight within establishments for the provision of group relations education. This is the selection of staff primarily on the basis of nepotism. Once this happens, it is inevitable that the Lie is created and perpetuated. The lie is about why someone was selected to join the staff. The Lie is taken into the fabric of the staff culture. It can never be named, for the person who names it is unlikely to be invited back on the staff. What grows is a dependency on the Lie, which subverts the truth-seeking posture of the staff. The authority of the subject of the Lie can never be questioned, because that would raise questions as to the use of power and the evasion of authority on the part of the sponsor of the subject.

Because industrial societies engender social passivity in their citizens by creating and fulfilling the wish for dependency on the State, there are dangers that group relations training can resonate with the wish for basic assumption dependency. There can be collusion on the part of consultants to bring about this dependency and create "patients" of participants. This, in turn, unquestioningly defines the role of the consultant. Nothing is problematic. We can expect a mirroring of aspects of society in group situations, but if they are merely reinforced, they cannot be interpreted. So such a group situation becomes a socialization exercise and does not allow for any internalization of a methodology for questioning the *status quo* of the group setting, which, in turn, could provide a model of how the participants might start to question the status quo of their outside institutions. The other feature of the kind of group activity I am indicating is that social or public issues are neatly converted into individual or private troubles.

There is a good deal spoken about self-actualization in group relations training. The reason for the popularity of the notion of self-actualization is, I suspect, that its promise resonates with the narcissistic preoccupations with which so many people find themselves engaged. If self-actualization becomes an end in itself—a product—it is likely that the means employed to attain that end will bring about quite unintended outcomes. Such a self-centred search could be quite irresponsible in that it denies the freedom of others. Self-actualization can be understood as a process—a journey with no terminus. Victor Frankl starts from the idea of responsibility in relation to one's actual life situation and maintains that "man can only actualize himself to the extent to which he fulfils meaning. Then self-actualization occurs spontaneously; it is contravened when it is made an end in itself" (Frankl, 1964). In another context, Frankl has stated his perception of the issues: "By declaring that man is a responsible creature and must actualize the potential meaning of his life, I wish to stress that true meaning of life is to be found in the world rather than with man and his own psyche, as though it were a closed system" (Frankl, 1967).

The only gloss to be made to this formulation is to suggest that the individual be seen as an open system in various states of relatedness to other open systems in his social world. It is this notion of open systems interacting with open systems that needs to be held on to because it allows for the possibility of conflict as a social process. There is always a wish for some kind of homeostatic relationship—a perfect equilibrium between the individual and his society. This needs to be turned on its head, so to speak, and perhaps conflict—with both its destructive and constructive aspects—could be mobilized as a social process to forge new meanings as a basis for cooperation between the individual and his groupings.

To tie all this somewhat more together: my postulate is that group relations training is about exploring the responsibility and authority of the individual in relation to his social environments— the choices the individual has to face if he wants to feel in, of, with, for, or against his social groups and the institutions of his society. I think this comes down to the meaning he places on his relatedness to institutions. It is a matter of inspecting the taken-for-granted connection between the individual and society. Increasingly, it seems to me that the inspection of the subjective apperceptions of groups and institutions—distinguishing what is believed to be knowable from the unknowable, and the naming of the experience of the society "in the mind", as a way of externalizing or objectifying the meaning the individual puts upon himself, his social world, and its relationships—is the proper preoccupation of group relations training.

Exploring boundaries

As Kurt Back has demonstrated in his account of sensitivity training and the encounter movement, *Beyond Words*, such versions of group relations training have de-emphasized boundaries and as such have reflected in American society a trend that has been apparent in other industrial societies. In particular, this trend "has been to decrease the importance of certain social categories, such as race, social status, class background, and more recently even the biologically determined categories of sex and age" (Back, 1973). Furthermore, he rightly points out that such a trend, coupled with the high valuation placed on the individual and his relationships, is characteristic of millenarian movements in societies. Millenarian movements have wish-fulfilment as their underlying psychological mechanism and are created "to deal with unsatisfying reality" (Toch, 1966). That people in societies through their social institutions and other social arrangements experience unsatisfying realities has been documented at least from the beginnings of sociology as a discipline of thought. That, therefore, people have a wish to be reborn in another reality is understandable. Since industrial societies are characterized by impersonality in social relations, by the experience of alienation at work and even in the family, for example, it is quite comprehensible that there will be an unconscious, and often quite conscious, wish to create new social groupings that will be satisfying and transcend all other groupings. The point is that such millenarian movements have to offer "extreme hope for a quick solution of all problems" (Back, 1973).

By contrast, the Tavistock model has always recognized that boundaries are necessary but must always be open to inspection. Boundaries are necessary in order for human beings to relate not only to each other but also through their institutions. If there are no boundaries, relatedness and relationships are impossible because we become one—lost in each other, lost in institutions, lost in societies. At the same time it is readily recognized that boundaries can be used and experienced as impregnable barriers. Both the wish for no boundaries and the desire to remain totally imprisoned within a boundary are expressions of "rational madness" in that there is no desire to distinguish between fantasy and reality.

To cause fundamental questioning of boundaries and of their *rationale*, two events have been introduced: (1) The Praxis Event, which is outlined in chapter six, attempts to cause participants to question why they subscribe to boundaries and to examine why they are necessary. They are often fictions to avoid the reality. (2) Social Dreaming attempts to harness the unconscious and to show that the thinking of dreams informs our lives (Lawrence, 1998).

Both these events try to link with Bion's thinking, particularly as he developed it in his subsequent writings. Throughout his books and papers, his continual preoccupation with the group comes through. They are an ever-present challenge to our memory, and desire; to our human wish that everything reverts to the *status quo ante*. As long as group relations education continues and as long as it is not subverted by narcissistic claims on the part of the staff of conferences, the chances are that new, often surprising, insights will always be generated.

CHAPTER FOUR

Signals of transcendence

Self and Other

L arge groups are a feature of any programme offering group relations training. A large group is composed of all the participants in the conference, together with two or more consultants. The large group has the purpose, or primary task, of providing opportunities for the participants to understand the behaviour of the group as it happens in the here-and-now. It can be seen as an open system. The inputs are the contributions from the minds of the people who participate, which are transformed into insight on how to continue the work of exploring emergent realities in other contexts. This capacity to think, or entertain thoughts, by a participant can be understood to be the introjection of a mental disposition that exists because the group has the potential to engender an act of collective reverie. (I use the word "disposition" because I feel that terms like "apparatus", "mechanism" or "equipment" are too concrete and constraining to describe an inner process of mind.) Here, I am postulating that what is learned about the functioning of groups in states of cooperation, conflict, or anomie (non-understanding) is secondary to internalizing a methodology that I am describing in terms of a mental disposition. What people may learn is just how to experience groups in a conference, which they may find difficult to apply in other contexts outside of the conference.

The particular dimension of large group behaviour I am to explore is the relatedness and relationships between Self and Other. By "relatedness" I mean relationships in the mind; by "Other" I mean not only other people in the group, but also society, the world, the cosmos, and the divine. The large group, because it is made up of all its membership together with two or more consultants, is a unique opportunity to study a system—albeit a temporary one—with defined boundaries of task, time, and territory that differentiate it from the conference as a whole system and the environment, which we now conceptualize eco-systemically. All are present as Selves. I offer a set of associations around this theme.

The pursuit of the understanding of the Self and the Other I see as being conducted in parallel. To focus on one to the exclusion of the other is to be lost. Gouranga Chattopadhyay's translation, in a private communication, of two Sanskrit incantations from the *Ishopanishad* captures the dilemma:

> The person who tries to understand what is within a particular boundary, neglects what is outside and gets lost in darkness. The person who forgets the boundary and pursues what is beyond it gets lost in even greater darkness. The person who understands both what is within the boundary and what is outside conquers death within the boundary and gets in touch with the indestructible which is the infinite.

Large groups are metaphors of the larger, containing society, to be sure. Often it is possible to interpret what is taking place in the large group as being a mirroring of what is taking place in the larger society. This I want to push further by suggesting that there is an interdependence between the two, but that we must do justice to the part of society that we call the large group, which we happen to be experiencing in the here-and-now at a particular time. "The whole", as David Bohm puts it, "is not imposed but is in each part and each part is in the whole" (Wijers & Pijnappel,

1990, p. 31). To press this even further, I make the working hypothesis that in the large group the contained contains the container. The implicate order of the large group, if you will, contains the implicate order of society, and so on.

Meanings of participation

The methodology we use to understand the large group, or any other grouping, is participation. We partake of the experience that is the large group, and we take part in it actively. For this we have a heuristic perspective that derives from the pioneering work of Wilfred Bion (1961), who offered us a way of using psychoanalysis as a tool of cultural enquiry. To this has been added open-systems thinking. This is a minimal statement. One difficulty with this is that there can be such a focus on purpose, or primary task, that so much potential for entertaining thoughts can be truncated.

The methodology is borne, in the first instance, by the consultants. They are there to offer working hypotheses on the group's functioning from the perspective of their role as they participate. It is the group that is the focus, not the personality characteristics of the people present in the group. Ideally, the quality of the consultative interpretative voice will be such that participants, too, can find their voices to interpret for themselves, from their role perspectives, the experiences they are experiencing as these occur in the here-and-now [hic et nunc].

More and more, I see the work of consultancy as being derived from a hermeneutic–spiritual coming-to-know. Hermeneutic refers to the interpreting of scripture as text, but I extend this to all situations where language is being used to describe the experience of participating. The large group articulates and evolves a text as the participants give words to their experiences of being in it. There are texts within texts: the unconscious text embedded in the conscious material, the condensed material that is present. As a dream is a narrative—because that is the only way we can communicate the content of the dream to another person—so it is also full of incoherence and lacunae, which is how we may have dreamt the dream in the first place. The large group, too, has its incoherence, which may contain more of the truth than the spoken and received text to which both participants and consultants may be working. Therefore, the idea of hermeneutic is worth holding on to, particularly if we construe the term as being the activity of hearkening. Martin Heidegger (1953) writes: "Hearkening . . . has the kind of Being of the hearing which understands" (p. 207).

The idea of "Being-with" the large group in the different roles of participant, member, or consultant potentially makes us available for psychic, political, and spiritual relatednesses with whatever is defined as Other; other participants, other consultants, the group, other groups we would like to be in, we have known, the other of the containing society, the universe, the cosmos. Psychic and political relatednesses are well enough recognized. The term "spiritual" I want to employ in this context as being evacuated of all conventional religious meaning, and to use it in the sense of linking, being connected to whatever is the Other beyond ordinary sense data. Since conferences began, participants have become more aware of ecological issues, for example, which is a view of the world that is ultimately spiritual. "The connection between science and spirituality is through the ecological world view of science" (Wijers & Pijnappel, 1990, p. 67). To have talked about the spiritual, except in a conventional religious sense, twenty years ago in working conferences would have been to enquire into aspects that, then, were not part of the accepted domain of discourse.

Immanent and transcendent

When people participate in the large group and come to know the text, as I am calling it, in a hermeneutic–spiritual way, they lead in to bringing into being the unspoken—what is behind, below, beyond the text. This is parallel to the transcendent becoming immanent. Just as the analysand learns to know him- or herself through the lengthy process of remembering and self-discovery

while submerged "in the immanence of significance that transcends him" (Kristeva, 1987, p. 61), so does the participant in a
large group in some measure. The name given to that significance
is the unconscious. As Julia Kristeva goes on to say: "The analysand knows the unconscious, orders it, calculates with it, yet he
also loses himself in it, plays with it, takes pleasure from it, lives
it." In the world of the large group, it is not the individual unconscious but the unconscious of the group that Bion named as the
basic assumption group.

In particular, consultants offer working hypotheses from their
experiences of being-with the group in their roles to address the
significance and signification of the psychic, political, and spiritual
relatedness present in the context of the large group. They do this
in order to bring into consciousness the purposes, and the conscious and unconscious quality of relationships being evoked, as
participants voice their experiences of their participation, as they
engage with the primary task of the large group as an event.

Thinking 1 and Thinking 2

Another vertex can be taken on the links between the transcendent
and the immanent. It is the minds, both conscious and unconscious, of participants, whether members or consultants, that make
up the existentially animating spirit of large groups. Minds create
the text. Mind both produces thought and is available for thought.
David Armstrong (1991) has identified what he calls Thinking 1
and Thinking 2. In the former, thought or thoughts come out of the
process of thinking and owe their existence to a thinker. Such
thoughts are capable of exegesis, justification, and falsification.
Epistemologically, thinking is prior to thought. (See chapter one.)

In Thinking 2, thought and thoughts are epistemologically
prior to thinking. Bion (1984) expresses this idea thus: "Thoughts
exist without a thinker. . . . The thoughts which have no thinker
acquire or are acquired by a thinker" (p. 165). Such thoughts are
voiced as a result of the practice of attention and awareness. They
are, in my terms, an outcome of the hermeneutic–spiritual, psychic
posture of availability for the experience of experience, to borrow

Bion's phrase. Such thoughts just are, they are neither true nor false. They emerge from the not known, which is experienced as a frustration, a mystery.

Armstrong (1991) outlines the sequence from the not-known:

> When this not-known begins to take a shape that can be for-mulated, it is as if I were being introduced or "spoken to" myself, or as if we were being introduced or "spoken to" our-selves. This introduction or being spoken to oneself or our-selves is not to oneself or ourselves alone, but to oneself or ourselves in relatedness to something else: a person, a group, an organization, a society, a world or worlds. Which is to say, generically, that a thought in Thinking 2 is always located systemically. And this relates to the fact that the object of experience is always contextual and never "private." There is always an implicit presence of the other, internally and/or externally. [pp. 3–5]

The large group in a working conference is a public context, with boundaries of task, time, and territory. It is the meeting-place of Self and Other. That meeting can be explicated in Thinking 1 terms. The large group is then pregnant with "memory and de-sire", to borrow the phrase of Bion, so much so that it is difficult to hold on to what is the unique significance of the experience of the "part", in Bohm's terms, because it is suffused with memories of the meaning of other large groups at another time, in another place, in another country.

To exist in the large group without "memory and desire" is to be prepared to "keep the soul terribly surprised", as Emily Dickinson put it. It is in such conditions that Self and Other can be explored in Thinking 2 terms.

The imago of the cosmos

Working with the religious (nuns and priests) in large groups led me to understand that the relatedness they had with their God was manifested in their relationships not only with each other, but with the consultants as authority. This is well enough understood in terms of transference and countertransference.

What it has taken me much longer to grasp is that for the non-religious what is also potentially present in the mind is their relatedness to the cosmos, and what I find myself more and more preoccupied with is the presence or absence of an imago of the cosmos—so much so that I have the working hypothesis that it is the imago of the cosmos that structures relationships on the planet. To be sure, there will be variation because all humankind does not have a common picture in the mind of the cosmos. That imago may be a no-imago, the shadow, that is—chaos. This is consistent with Bion's idea that every thought has its origins in a no-thought.

To pin this down with examples: The organization of work enterprises has mirrored over time changing conceptions, and therefore imagos, of the cosmos. Crudely, nineteenth-century organization, with its hierarchy of owners, managers, and workers, mirrored current versions of heaven and hell and the notion that the elect would go to heaven, which is always located above.

Hell is no longer credible as we end the twentieth century, for we have lost the belief in damnation. For medieval Europeans, however, hell was real.

> Hell was likened to a slaughter-house, a hospital, a torture chamber, and all these variations of Catholic infernality come together in the predominant morphology of the drain through which the flesh, contaminated by the infected spirit, falls. All the sad relics, the world's rubbish, its dirty and lurid refuse flowed into this drain-like hell. In fact, in medieval iconography God is synonymous with perfect cleanliness, with light and dazzling splendour, whereas Lucifer is coupled with darkness, dirt and obscurity. [Camporesi, 1990, p. 15]

The images that survive for us of the industrial enterprise, the coal mines, the slums of London and Liverpool, evoke associations with the drain, with the underworld, the terrain beyond the Styx. In the twentieth century human beings took on the responsibility for damnation. Hell has been continually created for political purposes, as in the Nazi concentration camps, the Gulag, and the Killing Fields, to drain away the hated undesirables.

William Assheton, in a tract he published in 1703 (quoted in McDannell & Lang, 1988), was sure that heaven would not be a place of speculation where each admired the other's perfection, but a place where none were idle and would be incessantly employed "in mutual giving and receiving of commands from each other"—a place where, because it was God's kingdom, there would be "laws and statutes and governors and subjects, and those of different ranks, orders, and degrees"; but there would be no jealousy between the ruling and the ruled! (McDannell & Lang, 1988, p. 206).

In all this, Assheton, it can be hypothesized, was in part anticipating the emergent British class structure, which subsequently was to be realized and solidified through the Industrial Revolution and, particularly, through the hierarchical forms of industrial organization. Did he have prescience of future conflictual industrial relations as he outlined his ordered heaven?

But the imagos/no-imagos, of the cosmos and relationships on Earth do not remain constant. Hierarchical forms of organization were gradually supplanted by other models. Open-system organization (socio-technical systems) anticipated—perhaps it is better to say participated in—the revolution in science that has been taking place throughout the twentieth century. Open-systems anticipated both "(a) an ontological assumption of oneness, wholeness, interconnectedness of everything and (b) an epistemological choice to 'include all the evidence'" (Harman, 1992, p. 49). Such ideas are beginning to become integrated into organizational thinking as we draw on the images of holography, for instance. Open systems were always part of the early tradition of the Tavistock Institute workers when they tried to integrate both psychoanalytic thinking and open-systems thinking as they set about extending the domain of experience and knowledge of industrial and other enterprises. Here, however, one has to note that operationally open-systems thinking has tended in practice to degenerate into an instrumentality because the explicit openness of systemic thinking can be experienced as being limitless and, therefore, potentially chaotic. Today, in making a contextual analysis of a business in its market environment as part of an ecosystem, the range of factors to be taken into account can be bewildering.

The simple point I am making is that the imago, or no-imago, of the cosmos is construed from both projection and an introjection. We make our organizational forms to reflect our imago, or no-imago, of the cosmos and come to internalize it. We make life on Earth in the imago and no-imago of the cosmos.

The large group is no exception—it is, at once, the cosmos that is known, not-known, and the imago/no-imago of it. This is partly what I mean when I say that the contained contains the container.

Separation from the Other

Working conferences in the Bion–Tavistock tradition have for the most part been conducted in Indo-European languages. Julia Kristeva (1987) asks whether these languages "reflect a type of culture in which the individual suffers dramatically because of his separation from the cosmos and the other?" (p. 31).

I can answer this question in part. A few years ago I started in Dublin, Ireland, a series of conferences for religious, called "Authority for Faith", through the Religious Formation Ministry Programme. It was when I took the same design to India, where the majority of the membership was Hindu and not Catholic, that I realized that, though talking in English, the Indian members, whether Hindu or Catholic, had access to a different vocabulary to describe the transcendent, the spiritual, the numinous. The Other was construed differently. There was no wish for fusion between God and Man—rather, a striving to come to know the Other, the divine. There was, in the terms I am using, a different imago of the cosmos and, therefore, different kinds of relationships within the conference as participants engaged with the primary task of events. What I cannot find at present are the psychosocial roots of this difference.

The opposite of cosmos is chaos—where all is Other and in flux; where everything is separate, not connected, and random. One needs to be alienated in order not to be contaminated. Notwithstanding the elegance and beauty of chaos theory, chaos is construed, in folk understanding, to be the formless void of primordial matter, which by its nature is confused and disordered, uncertain and unpredictable. Managers of businesses readily talk of the turbulent environment of being in markets that are akin to casinos. Sophisticated managers try to work with models that allow them to bring order into chaos and order out of chaos as, for example, they initiate a change programme in their enterprise or rethink their marketing policies.

The imago of the cosmos as chaos is often present in the large group. One fear of the large group is that it could become a formless mob. Indeed, the large group has sometimes spilled into the mob as chairs are moved and the neat escargot-spiral shape is disrupted. Human beings have always known the power of the mob. We can regularly witness the mob on our television screens. Images of mobs become fused. There seems to be no difference between the behaviour of the mob in Toxteth in England, the one in Iraq screaming at the Western oppressors, the one in Rostock persecuting immigrants in their hostels, or those in Los Angeles or Seattle. To drive on a Sunday afternoon through parts of Jerusalem, where the extremist Israelis are waiting with stones to throw at cars with West Bank number plates, is to experience the fear of becoming a victim of the mob.

Arnold Zweig, writing in the early 1930s of the certain destruction of German Jewry at the time, describes the mob as only a novelist and a passionate participant could witness.

Individuals welded into a mass are moved hither and thither by the affects of the mass even as seaweed is swayed by the movements of the waves; the individual's stirrings and impulses being motivated by the hopes and the despairs which pulse through a soul which has become part of the mass-soul. Unceasingly this ferment goes on in our foundations; and what the psychoanalyst is able to disentangle, distinguish, and name in course of his analysis is, in the waking state, outside of the self-awareness of the average ego and the average group—even as the movements that go on in the depths of the sea are hidden from those who only watch the surface of the waters from the shore or from the deck of a ship. Before these depth-processes can be brought to light and become violently effective there is needed the impulsion of purposive ideas, repellent or attractive, as the case may be. Above all, there is requisite a cooperation of impulses before the group-soul can be unchained—the impulses of need, hunger, privation, or at least those of a mood without hope and closely akin to despair. [Zweig, 1937, p. 46]

The fear that the large group will take on mob-like characteristics is among the causes of survival behaviour in large groups. The Other is felt to be so annihilating that the Self takes unconscious defensive action. The Self mentally collaborates with the other Selves present in the large group to form basic assumption groups. Such basic assumption configurations are "the immensely powerful psychotic phenomena that appear in groups that are apparently behaving sanely, if a little strangely, groups that are working more or less effectively and whose members are clinically normal or neurotic" (Menzies Lyth, 1981, p. 663).

The basic assumption (ba) groups that Bion identified were Dependency (baD), Fight/Flight (baF/F) and Pairing (baP). To these Pierre Turquet (1974) added Oneness (baO), and I, with two colleagues, have added Me-ness (baM) (see chapter five). The paradox is that each of these ba groups is mob-like in that the individuals are absorbed into the temporarily psychotic mass. The distinction between reality-orientated behaviour of the work group and basic assumption behaviour disappears in the wish for survival. Consequently the ability to construct working hypotheses to test realities is expunged. The text being voiced is convincing and credible and delivered in Thinking 1 terms. Other thinking is swamped. The members co-create forms of rational madness, which, at the time, gives meaning to their existence.

The baO group is characterized by mental activity in which "members seek to join in a powerful union with an omnipotent force, unobtainably high, to surrender self for passive participation, and thereby feel existence, well-being and wholeness" (Turquet, 1974, p. 375). Turquet adds in the same paper that while in baO, "the group member is there to be lost in oceanic feelings of unity or, if the oneness is personified, to be part of a salvationist inclusion" (p. 360). In baO the Self fuses with the Other; the soul becomes part of the mass-soul.

By contrast, the baM group (see chapter five) is one where the Selves hold on to the version of self that can be called "Me-ness" and keeps all Others, however defined, at bay. The members behave as if the group were invisible and unknowable and, therefore, could not exist. Others are, in effect, made into non-persons. The horror is of fusion. It is a delimited or truncated self that is mobilized. The use of the pronoun "me" is to signify that it is not the "I" of the self that is being called upon but the object of the "I"—that is, the "me" of childhood, as in, "Me wants teddy". Consequently, other Selves cannot be related to, indeed no Other, because the preoccupation is with the survival of the "me". Cosmos has to be made into chaos and the world split into good and bad objects so that the "me" is always good. If you will, the cosmos-in-the-mind becomes phobic. Salvation lies, it is believed, in the solipsistic world of the "me". Here, one could say that solipsism and fusion are two faces of the same coin, that baM = ba non-O. To elaborate further: if ba groups are unconscious social systems of defence against the apparent difficulty of being in a W group that tests realities through hypotheses, baM's specialness is that it is a defence against both the W group and the ba groups as known. The paradox is that the organizing assumption is that only the individual can come to know anything because the group is not to be trusted, but the assumption causes the participants to collude unconsciously in co-creating and co-acting in the group I am calling baM.

To be sure, much of this can be described in terms of narcissism, but I believe that in large groups the behaviour is of the "I" of the Selves present in it being "driven into Me-ness" in order to survive what they feel to be the overwhelming Other that will cause the "I"/Self to be a non-person, a formless blob. To describe this another way: the culture of the group evokes the narcissistic elements and annuls other elements of the individual, which feeds into the group culture in an endless projection–introjection process to produce a climate of socially induced narcissism.

Survival and immortality

Pressing this further, behind the spoken text of a large group, which will have its story-lines of the basic assumption groups, the wish for survival is murderous. This is particularly evident in a culture of baM. The fantasy of murder of the Other is to protect against the fear that the Other will wipe out the individual Self. The hero is the survivor, triumphing over others, becoming ageless in phantasy as the younger generations are killed.

> The moment of *survival* is the moment of power. Horror at the
> sight of death turns into satisfaction that it is someone else
> who is dead. The dead man lies on the ground while the
> survivor stands. It is as though there had been a fight and the
> one had struck down the other. In survival each man is the
> enemy of every other, and all grief is insignificant measured
> against this elemental triumph. Whether the survivor is con-
> fronted by one dead man or many, the essence of the situation
> is that he feels unique. He sees himself as standing there alone
> and exults in it; and when we speak of the power which this
> moment gives him, we should never forget that it derives
> from his sense of uniqueness and nothing else. [Canetti, 1973,
> p. 265, italics in original]

Survival is part of the human desire for immortality—the wish to
draw the sting of death. It is not sufficient to exist for evermore but
to exist when others no longer exist. Ideally, the survivor determines the editing of the content of history, to deliver to posterity
an acceptable myth of how it really was.

This wish for survival makes for a large group that is suffused
with basic assumption cultures. It is totalitarian, ruthless, uncar-
ing. Its members cannot join together in the work of explicating
unfolding realities in the ways I have been trying to describe, join
together in activity that would make the transcendent immanent.
The ruthless group is a fearful group—fearful of experiencing the
Other, fearful of coming-to-know, fearful of Thinking 2, fearful of
the spiritual for it must dismiss even the possibility of the numinous. It is in such a group that the basest of feelings are rampant
and justified, because the wish is for survival and immortality.
Envy is the consuming passion, gratitude never acknowledged.
Melanie Klein knew of these:

> The key Kleinian insight is that greed, avaricious individual-
> ism, possessive individualism, and the like are not given; they
> are responses to fear (ultimately of our own aggression), a fear
> that stands in the way of caritas. It is this, I have argued all
> along, that makes Klein's view tragic. Our potential to love
> and to care for others is real; it is an expression of a desire
> whose power is exceeded only by its extreme susceptibility to
> fear. Here is humanity's tragic flaw, which we nonetheless
> frequently transcend in personal relations but rarely in the
> group. In these last four sentences lies the whole of Klein's

theory in so far as its relevance to social and political theory is concerned. [Alford, 1989, p. 179]

The large group always has choices. It can pursue *caritas*, truth, or it can follow evil. Time and time again, human beings are caught in the "tragic flaw"; it is the perennial global social dynamic. What is contained in the large group, in terms of basic assumption culture for survival, contains the container.

The large group, however, can contain much else. It always does, if only because of the presence of the condensed material that adheres to the text. The difficulty is to have access to this material, which is probably only available through the methodology that I am trying to describe.

Signals of the transcendent

Working in Ireland with a large group of nuns belonging to the order of the Presentation Sisters of the Blessed Virgin Mary, I was surprised by the announcement by one nun that "We must pray for the work of this group!" My anxieties rose. I had visions of a large group on its knees. I felt I was facing the Scylla of Flight or the Charybdis of Oneness, in addition to the basic assumption behaviour that my colleagues had been interpreting.

It took me some time to catch on that she was using prayer in her sense of working at the primary task, paying attention, coming-to-know the life of the large group with its implicate realities. Attention involves an act of concentration and a submission to what is there that is not of oneself alone. It implies a withholding of ownership, wishes, desires in order to experience reality as the Other. It is "hearkening". Prayer I now take to be an invitation to the act of reverie that makes possible a different mental disposition, which, as yet in the history of the group, is not available to participants in the group. What the nun's leadership resulted in was a thoroughgoing exploration of realities.

This experience reinforced in me the belief that basic assumption groups—with their preoccupation with survival, which, at times, becomes a political movement engaging everyone psychically—can be necessary phenomena. I would go as far as to say that they are transitional phenomena. There, to put it perhaps too strongly, has to be the experience of the temporary psychotic culture in order to find the Other. By this I mean that we never know what order is until we experience chaos; we never understand the meaning of sanity until we have touched madness; we do not know hate until we have loved with all our being. To be sure, some large groups only emerge from the basic assumption configurations but fleetingly.

But some do, and in so doing move from the trivial to the tragically profound plane, shift from Thinking 1 to being available for Thinking 2. To illustrate this: A few years ago, during a conference of the Institute of Group Analysis in Zagreb, with two other colleagues I took a large group. During one of the sessions, a priest, who is also a therapist, described his experiences with a patient who had AIDS. This young woman, as she was in the process of dying, wanted to have her childhood teddy bear and her Bible, but she could not have them because her parents had burned them. As I relate these simple facts, I cannot portray the intensity of feeling in the room, revealed through the stillness. The priest wept quietly as he recounted the experience, but one knew intuitively that he was crying for more than the girl.

Another member, a woman, described her feelings about the death of her mother and how she missed her. This was quietly volunteered as a statement of fact. A third woman went on quietly to describe her feelings about learning, just in the days before she came to Zagreb, that her mother had cancer.

I recall my own feelings at the time vividly. I knew that if any consultant made an intervention, we would "blow" whatever thoughts were in the room; I was intensely aware that these individuals, while talking from their unique experiences, were also making statements about humanity. The facts were biographically based, but the meaning was larger. There was not a hint of self-pity in the room.

No one offered interpretation; the experiences were allowed to rest. There was a sense of patience, but not of despair, in the room, and one felt that new thoughts were being thought of a Thinking 2 nature. There was an ambience of reverie and the presence of attentive hearkening. At the time, I felt that for me there was a danger that I would find a premature metaphor to order my disordered feelings. I felt metaphor would destroy the possibility of being with the incomprehensible.

The inadequacy of mental images became evident as a temporary sense of desolation came over me. Each person in the room seemed to be contemplating the mystery of being human—having a life, dying with or without hope, and the conundrum of living in the twentieth century. What has humankind become after millions of years of evolution?

I did have associations to Turquet's Oneness, but the oceanic feeling was not there, for the tenor of the group was of being committed to work. The group knew that we were in a mental space none of us had experienced before. At the time, I felt that there was an element of sacredness in the spirit of the place, the room in which we were working. On reflection, I felt myself to have been at some personal interstice in history, in the sense that one was posed with the perennial questions: How do things come to be what they are, and what future is there for us?

One interpretation of what happened in the 20 minutes I have briefly described seemed straightforward enough. It was about the "lost object."—a valid enough interpretation, invoking death, grief, and mourning. End of story. But is it?

It was about the tragedy of being human, to be sure. It was about alienation: the alienation of the girl from her parents because of AIDS—the alienation from her teddy bear, the classical transitional object of Winnicott, which implied that there could be no more transitions in life for her; and the alienation from her childhood Bible, from the record of the story of the Judaeo–Christian tradition to link humankind with death in a hopeful way. It was also, if I follow these associations, about all the alienation of Self from Other, the Other including a dissociation from the very idea of cosmos, of which the divine may be part of the whole.

The more I have reflected on the Zagreb experience, checking it with others subsequently, the more I have settled for having had the experience of "signals of transcendence", following Peter Berger (1971), who wrote:

> By signals of transcendence I mean phenomena that are to be found within the domain of our "natural" reality but that appear to point beyond that reality. In other words, I am not using transcendence here in a technical philosophical sense

but, literally, as the transcending of the normal, everyday world that I earlier identified with the notion of the "supernatural". [p. 70]

David Hay (1982) confirms aspects of the Zagreb experience and fleshes out Berger's insight when he identifies and analyses the evidence for transcendent experiences. In another context, he quotes one of the respondents, who has volunteered experiences for the data bank of the Alister Hardy Research Centre, which is devoted to understanding religious experience.

I was walking across a field, turning my head to admire the western sky and looking at a line of pine trees appearing as black velvet against a pink background, turning to duck-egg blue/green overhead, as the sun set. Then it happened. It was as if a switch marked "ego" was suddenly switched off. Consciousness expanded to include and be the previously observed. "I" was the sunset and there was no "I" experiencing "it". No more observer and observed. At the same time eternity was "born"—there was no past, no future, just an eternal now.... Then I returned completely to normal consciousness, finding myself still walking across the field, in time, with a memory. [Hay, 1990, p. 15]

The fact that the large group experience occurred in Zagreb is not lost on me now, as I see what is taking place in the former Yugoslavia. There, all is being defined in terms of Self and Other. Whoever is Other is a valueless object. Aggression, fear, and ruthlessness are partners against the human capacity for *caritas* and truth. The survival of Self is pre-eminent. The Other is to be annihilated, and if that means murder, so be it.

This illustrates the value of appreciating the relatedness between Self and Other. To be alienated from the Other and only caught up with Self is to see the Other as a valueless object. The wish is not to be related, to have no association. It is but a short step to *hubris*. The Other can be treated as something to be used. But for this to be effective, the Other has to be hated. In terms of people, the Other becomes a commodity—as in the slave trade between Africa, Britain, and America. The Nazis refined this notion of the Other as commodity. The hated Other was to be exploited in life, as slave labour and for genetic experimentation, and in death value was added to the corpse by economic use being made of hair and body fats.

The Other includes the physical environment in which we live. Increasingly, people recognize that we are alienated from our eco-systemic environment. Perhaps too late, human beings are trying to rectify their destruction of the biosphere, the diversity of spe-cies, and the earth's natural resources. These have always been regarded by human beings—certainly since industrialization, but already long before—as existing for their use, there to have value added to them. Crude oil is valueless until it is cracked to produce gasoline and chemicals. Whatever spiritual connection human be-ings felt and experienced was influenced by the image they held in the mind of the environment and their relatedness to it (contained in the imago/no-imago of the cosmos), which, in fact, as history proceeded from the times of the Enlightenment, became more characterized by dissociation.

I have been trying to say that the human species has the capac-ity, because of the mind, to be open to introjection and to project a mental disposition that allows us to be available for hitherto una-vailable dimensions of our experienced experiences. To put this another way: It is the mental disposition we bring to bear, and continue to bring into being, through our hearkening, in order to arrive at a hermeneutic–spiritual knowing, which allows us to bring into being what I have been sign-posting. There is, however, no prescription, except the self-discovery of reverie.

The Zagreb experience was not so much a turning-point in my thinking as a punctuation. What the experience did was to give me sanction to scrutinize and ruminate more on the significance of my own experiences in the Bion tradition of taking groups. It led to the kind of thoughts I have been trying to adumbrate in this chap-ter. It has made me try to come to know what may be present spiritually in groups, as well as being alive to the psychic and political phenomena; to attempt to be available for Thinking 2; to value reverie and attentive hearkening; to be available for any connections between the transcendent and the immanent; to be lost neither in the Self nor in the Other.

CHAPTER FIVE

The fifth basic assumption

with Alastair Bain & Laurence J. Gould

We write from our experiences in our roles as consultants to and directors of working conferences in group relations, in addition to our practices as social scientists, organizational consultants, psychoanalyst, and university teachers. We have been associated with group relations education for most of our adult lives, and each has tried to contribute to thinking on groups through participation and writing. In recent years our roles in conferences have been both as directors and as consultants; though we thoroughly enjoy the challenge of directorship, we find we are quite content to take up consultant roles to small groups, large groups, and so on because there is so much that is unknown about group behaviour. It also allows us to keep in touch as directly as we can with what is going on in groups of people who belong to later generations than ourselves. For us there is a symbiontic relationship between our practices and group relations education. What social phenomena of an unconscious nature we find in one context we test in the other and vice versa.

It is out of these experiences that we are now able to propose a fifth basic assumption group in addition to the work group and the three basic assumption groups that Bion adumbrated, to-gether with the one discovered by Pierre Turquet. This fifth basic assumption group we have named basic assumption Me-ness (baM).

The purpose of this chapter is to work out and explicate baM in groups, institutions, and societies following the Bionian tradition. BaM is linked to all other ba groups and to the W group. We can but reflect the particularized contexts in which we live and work. We are aware that within the field of psychoanalysis there is a burgeoning interest in the treatment of narcissistic disorders. However, we do not want to explain away baM in terms of indi-vidual narcissism as can be found in analysands and patients, because we are focusing on baM as a cultural phenomenon. More pertinent for us is the kind of social critique of post-industrial society made by Christopher Lasch in his *Culture of Narcissism* (1978), by Robert N. Bellah and his colleagues in their *Habits of the Heart* (1985), and by John Carey in *The Intellectuals and the Masses* (1992).

The work group
and the basic assumption groups of Bion

There are many renditions of Bion's formulation about groups, but none can replicate the richness of the original. Like his Brazilian and New York lectures, for example, *Experiences in Groups* (1961) requires close and repeated attention. Nevertheless, for the pur-poses of this exposition there is a need to give yet another account of his working hypotheses.

Bion's major hypothesis was that when any group of people meet to do something—that is, a task—there are in actuality two groups, or two configurations of mental activity, present at one and the same time. There is the sophisticated work group (referred to as the W group), but this group is "constantly perturbed by influences that come from other group mental phenomena" (Bion, 1961, p. 129), which are primarily what Bion called the basic as-sumption groups (referred to as the ba groups).

What is the experience of being in a W group? It is to be in a group in which all the participants are engaged with the primary task because they have taken full cognizance of its purpose. They cooperate because it is their will. They search for knowledge through using their experiences. They probe realities in a scientific way by hypothesis testing and are aware of the processes that will further learning and development. Essentially, the W group mobilizes sophisticated mental activity on the part of its members, which they demonstrate through their maturity. They manage the psychic boundary between their inner and outer worlds. They strive to manage themselves in their roles as members of the W group. Furthermore, the participants can hold in mind an idea of wholeness and interconnectedness with other systems, and they use their skills to understand the inner world of the group, as a system, in relation to the external reality of the environment. In a W group the participants can comprehend the psychic, political, and spiritual relatedness in which they are participating and are co-creating. The W group can be seen as an open system. The major inputs are people with minds who can transform experiences into insight and understanding.

Groups that act in this consistently rational manner are rare, however, and perhaps are merely an idealized construct. In actuality the behaviour of the people in the group is often on another dimension. This is ba behaviour. The genius of Bion was to recognize that people in groups behave at times collectively in a psychotic fashion, or, rather, the group mentality drives the process in a manner akin to temporary psychosis. Isabel Menzies Lyth makes the point with clarity that Bion saw that group phenomena were psychotic (Menzies Lyth, 1981, p. 663).

The term "psychotic" is being used in this context to mean a "diminution of effective contact with reality", to borrow Menzies Lyth's phrase. This is a group mentality with a culture that the individual, despite his or her sophisticated and mature skills, can be caused to regress to and to be temporarily caught up in primitive splitting and projective identification, depersonalization, and infantile regression.

Bion adumbrated three ba groups. The members of the group behave "as if" they were sharing the same tacit, unconscious assumption. Life in a baM group is oriented towards inner phantasy, not external reality. To identify a baM is to give meaning to the behaviour of the group and elucidate on what basis it is not operating as a W group. Bion's three ba groups are: ba dependency (baD); ba fight/flight (baF/F); and ba pairing (baP).

In the life of a group the participants will oscillate between the culture of the W group and among those of the ba groups. Each individual has a "valency" for a particular baM—"a capacity for instantaneous involuntary combination of one individual with another for sharing and acting on a basic assumption" (Bion, 1961, p. 153), be it dependency, fight/flight, or pairing.

What is the emotional experience of being in baD, in a culture of dependency? The aim of the members of the group, and the assumption on which they work, is that they have met in order to have a feeling of security and protection from one of their members. This leader is invested with qualities of omnipotence and omniscience. He or she is idealized and made into a kind of god. The feeling is that only the leader knows anything and only the leader can solve the reality problems of the group. Such a leader is a magical person who does not need information—he or she can divine it. In such a group the mentality and culture are such that the individual members become more and more de-skilled as information on realities becomes less and less available. There is an air of timelessness about the group, which results in the feeling that it will never end.

One phenomenon associated with this kind of group culture is that one person is made into the really stupid one, the "dummy", who has to be taught everything by the others, the collective "mummy". A similar process is to set up one member as being the object of care, which other members proceed to deliver. A variation on this is to create a "casualty"—someone who is made to feel inadequate, even to the point of temporary breakdown.

The experience of being in a basic assumption pairing (baP) culture is to be in a group enthused by the idea of supporting two members who will produce a new leader-figure who will assume full responsibility for the group's security. The wish, in unconscious phantasy, is that the pair will produce a Messiah, a Saviour, in the form either of a person or of an organizing idea around which they can cohere. The gender of the two people constituting the pair is immaterial. The ethos of the group is one of hopefulness and expectation. The crux, however, is not a future event but the feeling of hope in the immediate present. The group lives in the hope of a new creation: a Utopia—a utopian thought that will solve all their problems of existence. There will be no feelings of destructiveness, despair, or hatred. But nothing must be created in actuality; otherwise the hopefulness will vanish.

Bion's third basic assumption group is that of fight/flight (baF/F), which he sees as two sides of the same coin. What is the experience of being in such a culture? The unconscious assumption of the group is that they have met for action that is to preserve itself by fighting someone or something or by taking flight from these. The individual is less important than the preservation of the group. Understandably, this baM culture is profoundly anti-intellectual and will decry as introspective any behaviour that attempts to reach self-knowledge through self-study.

The leader in such a culture is of central importance because he or she is a leader for action, either into fight by attack or into flight. The ideal characteristic is that the leader be paranoid, without any hint of depressive qualities, and be able to name sources of persecution, even if they do not exist in reality. The leader is expected to identify danger and enemies unerringly and to feel hatred towards them. The group gives the leader the ability to turn it from fight to flight and back again—like the Grand Old Duke of York marching his men. The leader has derived power from the ability to play on the overwhelming panic that the members of the group feel.

The basic assumption oneness of Turquet

To these ba groups described by Bion, Turquet added a fourth: basic assumption oneness (baO). This is a mental activity in which "members seek to join in a powerful union with an omnipotent force, unobtainably high, to surrender self for passive participation, and thereby feel existence, well-being, and wholeness" (Turquet, 1974, p. 357). In the same paper he adds that in baO "the group member is there to be lost in oceanic feelings of unity or, if the oneness is personified, to be a part of a salvationist inclusion" (p. 360).

This wish for "salvationist inclusion" can be seen to operate institutionally when, for example, religious people give themselves over to charismatic movements. They wish to be at one with God, to have no boundary between the human and what may be the divine, and, for example, to speak in tongues. As the opposite of Oneness, we are proposing another basic assumption group that emphasizes separateness and hates the idea of "we". To state this over-neatly: baM equals ba not-O.

Basic assumption Me-ness: the context

BaM, we hypothesize, is becoming more salient in our industrialized cultures. Here, we are underlining that we understand baM to be a cultural phenomenon engendered by conscious and unconscious social anxieties and fears. In particular we are putting forward the idea that as living in contemporary, turbulent societies becomes more risky, so the individual is pressed more and more into his or her own inner reality in order to exclude and deny the perceived disturbing realities that are of the outer environment. The inner world becomes thus a comforting one offering succour. It is, perhaps, in this inner world that well-worn clichés can be held on to and rehearsed without fear of them being tested. "England is a green and pleasant land!" and "An Englishman's home is his castle!" can be believed in because the changing reality of the real environment and real experience of external reality are denied.

While there are always differences in national cultures, there are striking similarities, particularly between those that share industrial histories and aspirations. What they all share is an ambience of persecutory—loosely called stressful—feeling. In Britain, America, and Australia there have been economic recessions, which have hit the middle and lower classes. Unemployment has eroded the confidence of the managerial class, who had led themselves to believe that their job would always be secure. In Britain, the record of bankruptcies is unprecedented. So for people who tried to take responsibility for their own lives by taking a risk in setting up a small business, the result has been that they have lost their livelihoods and, in many cases, their homes.

In the United States of America, during recent years, the harsh impact of economic recession has fuelled the politics of hate. Interest rates plunged, bank failures soared, and the Federal Deposit Insurance Corporation was dangerously under-funded. Homelessness increased dramatically. In the face of all this, there was manic buying of shares, which drove the stock market upwards as individuals tried to secure a financially sound future for themselves.

In Europe we can only regard with misgivings what is happening in the former Eastern Bloc countries, which now share aspirations for the capitalist way of life. Russia itself is economically bankrupt and teeters on the verge of political collapse. Slovaks are now separated, in what the newspapers call a "velvet divorce", from Czechoslovakia. Within Slovakia there are 600,000 Hungarians who will want to assert their rights, and in Transylvania there is likely to be rivalry between Romanians and the Hungarian minority, oppressed and persecuted since the region was taken from Hungary and given to Romania.

Balkan politics, which so preoccupied statesmen and politicians before the Second World War, are being fought out again. Two-way ethnic cleansing in Kosovo has caused external powers to take part. War could start in Macedonia, where there are multiple rivalries; or in Sandzak, which is Serbian but inhabited by Muslims; or in Croatia.

The major social phenomenon that is appearing in these former Eastern Bloc countries, we hypothesize, is that there is a process of "tribalization" that is causing people to reaffirm their primary national identity. The process is complex because there is no neat coincidence between national identity and national territory. In Estonia, Latvia, and Lithuania, there are large populations of Russians left over from the days of the Soviet empire. In countries such as Poland and the Czech Republic there are Germans marooned as the result of historical processes and near-forgotten peace treaties. Predictably, Jews are beginning, once again, to suffer persecution as they are accused of undermining whatever country they are resident in. This is particularly so in Hungary, where one politician is using the same language and metaphors the Nazis had used.

As the monolithic political structures crumble in all these countries, we see individuals being pressed into forms of Me-ness that are becoming frenzied, as in the former Yugoslavia. The more general point we wish to make is that given the kinds of turbulence being experienced in all industrialized societies—and we have just given headlines—so the individual loses faith and trust in any structure, whether good or bad, that is greater than the individual. In short, as the environment becomes more persecuting in reality, one response is for individuals to cut themselves off from the effects and to withdraw into the inner world of the self. Another way of expressing this is to say that we are witnessing socially induced schizoid withdrawal. This is not to say that the individuals are schizoid in themselves, but that they are being made to behave so by their social and political conditions.

At the same time we want to hold on to what may be positive, and we can regard baM as a temporary cultural phenomenon, salient at this time in history. We can see the future as holding many challenges for the nature of the advanced industrial societies in which we live. These challenges are economic, political, social, ecological, and spiritual. They arise from cumulative changes in our environments, which interact together systemically. We are witnessing the creation of large unified economic markets, increasing international competitiveness, changing political, social, and cultural ideologies, shifting religious affiliations and beliefs, and continued revolutions in technology. As we have indicated, there is a reframing of relations between East and West and between the Northern and Southern hemispheres. Consequently we, in the West, cannot afford to harbour any ambitions, or even phantasies, of colonization—that is, mobilizing baD. We have to try to find ways of creating symbiontic relations that foster interdependence and collaboration—that is, eschewing all the baM configurations.

The repercussions of these changes can be interpreted as the beginnings of the ending of advanced industrial societies as they have been known in the past and the beginnings of societies that will have to be discovered. The turbulence of the eco-environment in which peoples of the world conduct their affairs paradoxically presents an opportunity to initiate transformations that use the best that has been learned from history and the best of thinking about desired futures.

At its most benign, we postulate that the experience of the culture of baM may be one that has to be gone through in order to achieve the kinds of societies that would be associated with a W culture. Just as the French Revolution mobilized baF/F to reach forward towards republicanism and democracy, just as Cromwell broke the baD assumption of the British on the divine right of kings, so may baM be a transitional cultural experience.

Basic assumption Me-ness

Our working hypothesis is that baM occurs when people—located in a space and time with a primary task, which is to meet to do something in a group—work on the tacit, unconscious assumption that the group is to be a non-group. Only the people present are there to be related to, because their shared construct in the mind of "group" is of an undifferentiated mass. They, therefore, act as if the group had no existence, because if it did exist, it would be the source of persecuting experiences. The idea of "group" is contaminating, taboo, impure, and, in sum, all that is negative. The people behave as if the group had no reality and could never have reality, because the only reality to be considered and taken account of is that of the individual. It is a culture of selfishness in which individuals appear to be only conscious of their own personal boundaries, which they believe have to be protected from any incursion by others. The nature of the transactions is instrumental, for there is no room for affect, which could be dangerous because one would not know where feelings might lead.

A major difference between baM and other ba groups is that in the former it is the group that is invisible and unknowable, whereas in the latter cultures it is the individual who is invisible and unknowable. In the cultures of baD, baF/F, baP, the individual becomes lost in the group. In baM cultures the overriding anxiety is that the individual will be lost in the group if it ever emerges. While ba groups in general are unconscious systems of defence against the anxiety of experiencing and testing realities in a W configuration, a baM culture is an unconscious system of defence against both the experiences of W and other ba groups. In a sense, baM may have come into existence because the others had previously been in existence. To state this as an exaggeration: it may be that baM is a result of the historical process of working conferences, which have now been running for nearly 40 years. People attend these conferences because they want to know about group functioning. They also believe that to experience ba behaviour is to be caught up in a process that they believe they cannot control. They wish to attain W behaviour as quickly and as effortlessly as possible—it is for this reason that they are present in the conference. There are powerful aspirations to know but also as potent reasons for not knowing—hence the emergence of baM, which is a resistance to both ba and W behaviour. The paradox is that while the architectonic belief is that only the individual can come to know anything, this belief causes the individuals to co-create and co-act in a baM group, and so they enter a ba group in spite of their efforts to avoid this experience.

In baM it is as if each individual were a self-contained group acting in its own right. A baM culture can never tolerate the collective activities of a W group because a baM culture has only individualistic preoccupations. A baM culture is more likely to pay attention to private troubles than ever it would to public issues—to use C. Wright Mills's classic distinction—because they have no relevance for the individuals.

Our elaboration of baM starts from Turquet's idea of the singleton. Turquet (1974) was writing in the early 1970s, and what he had to say was valid; for particular members it is still a way of understanding the transformation process they can go through as a result of membership experiences in a large group.

Turquet, in his analysis of the phenomenology of the individual's experiences of changing membership status in the large group, describes how the conference member comes into the large group as an I; more particularly, the "I" enters as a singleton wishing to make relations with others, even though not yet part of the group. While we fully accept Turquet's formulation, we are beginning to think that, nowadays, it is the "me" part of the "I" that is increasingly being mobilized. There is, we postulate, a stage preceding Turquet's analysis of the progression of the individual through the life of the group because the individual does not want to have relations.

Our working hypothesis, now, is that there is a new phenomenon in that particular individuals can get caught up in a mental activity that does not allow them to enter the "I"/singleton state and holds them in what we are to call the "me"/singleton state because they never want to experience membership of a group.

The pronoun "me" is the accusative and dative form of the pronoun of the first person. This fits the meaning we want to give to baM because the "I" becomes an object to itself—a "me", governed by the prepositions "to" or "for". Furthermore, if it were the "I" that was being mobilized, the "I" could empathize with the individual "I" of other members in the group, acknowledge that they too have feelings, perceptions, and understanding, and conceptualize that if a "we" were possible, the group could exist and achieve its primary task.

In using the idea of "Me-ness" we are harking back to the time when an infant becomes a unit able to distinguish between the inside and the outside. Winnicott, with his usual perceptiveness, writes:

> The idea of a limiting membrane appears, and from this follows the idea of an inside and an outside. Then there develops the theme of a ME and a not-ME. There are now ME contents that develop partly on instinctual experience. [Winnicott, 1980, p. 68]

Our view is that this stage of development is echoed when baM is mobilized in the group.

The evidence for this basic assumption group started to become firmly apparent about eight years ago. We give evidence from two sources: from the behaviour of members and staffs of working conferences and from what we have observed in societies. We offer "because clauses" (to use Pierre Turquet's phrase) to link the inner psychic states of individuals to the kinds of societies, institutions, and groups that people are co-creating in Australia, the United States, and the United Kingdom, which are the countries we know best.

Evidence from working conferences

It is a large group. During most of the sessions one woman participant always sits outside the arranged configuration of chairs. She
looks attentive as she sits, for the most part, bolt upright, often on
the edge of her chair. When asked by other members of the large
group why she has this seat, she replies that she wants to be separate. One assumes that she feels that she is not being trapped by
any structures. She states that in her view the consultants are imposing this structure. She attends the large group and all the other
events of the conference, but she never becomes a member. As the
days go by, one has a picture of a woman who will not join any
institution, as she wants to keep her version of freedom and her
individuality. She gives the impression of being the observer,
watching everything from behind a glass screen—detached, objective, unmoved, apparently content to be alienated. Withdrawal
and dissociation seem to be her way of life. It is difficult to guess
what her experiences may be because she never offers them, but
one assumes that she is processing them in some way.

In the same conference, another woman says that she had
never really existed as a child for her parents. She had been a non-
person for them. It was not a matter of rejection; she had never
been accepted in the first place. One could understand why there
was a necessity to hold on to a version of "me" in order just to
have survived as a person. This pressure to hold on to the "me"
part of oneself, in the sense that we are trying to give meaning to
the distinction between "I" and "Me", can be seen in other contexts, as we have tried to demonstrate above and will continue to
show in what follows.

In one session of a large group, one member said that she
dreamt of the film *Broken Mirrors*. She told the participants in the
group what the film was about. The story of the film is about a
sadistic murderer who captures women, ties them up, and takes
photographs of them while starving them to death. One of the
features of the film is that there is no interaction between the
photographer/murderer and the victim. The room in which the
film takes place is covered with photographs of previous victims
starving to death.

At one level, the volunteering of this film story of the relationship between murderer and victim represented the transference relationship that was felt to exist between the consultants and the members of the group. In phantasy, members experienced no interaction between consultants and the members of the group, and so the consultants were busy engaged in an activity that was akin to making a film of the mental life of the group as an object of study. At another level, we would suggest that the relationship between the murderer and the victim is a paradigm for the individual caught in baM. By this we mean that there is a sadistic photographing part of oneself which is busy taking snapshots of a suffering, starving part of oneself, and there is no interaction between the two. So the consultants come to be seen as sadistic by victimizing the members who are starving for insight.

In this conference it was noticeable that participants had great difficulty in talking about their feelings about themselves in any roles, about the context in which they were working, and about others. Feelings seemed to be being held in abeyance during the working sessions. This led on a number of occasions to people saying things like: "If I was to feel angry I would say 'X'." In baM, people do everything in their power to distance themselves from the feelings; they take a "photograph" and present that to the rest of the group and to the consultants as the "evidence" for what is going on within themselves. This is a logical consequence of baM, which can begin to be unlocked only when the members give their feelings of their experience. This would lead to an exploration of their relationships in the group and elicit their images of the group in the mind.

The activity of note-taking is unusual in working conferences. One member did so constantly during all the sessions. This same member had a dream, which he reported to the large group. His dream was that the director of the conference had a pimple on his forehead directly above his nose and that when the pimple was pressed, more and more pus came out of it. It is perhaps significant that the site of this pimple is the presumed position of the "third eye", and on reflection we wonder whether it represented an attack on participants' own capacity for insight, which was then projected onto the consultant who also had the role of director. The notes in this case, and the photographs in the other, replace insight. We can speculate that the model for this behaviour is that of the classical scientist regarding everything objectively, striving never to contaminate the findings with feelings, observations, or any activity that might skew the results.

Another member reported a dream in which she was having a baby, which was the child of a homosexual pair. In a baM culture "like links with like" (a phrase to which we shall return) and the only kind of birth that seems possible is a phantasized "birth" through homosexual pairing. It is also not a true homosexual pairing. We would hypothesize that the real relationship is "me with me" and that this is projected into a homosexual pairing. In a session towards the ending of this particular large group, males were linking with males and females with females, to the extent that one woman sat on another woman's lap. Mental heterosexuality, so to speak, and appropriate interaction and relating such that a "true baby" of insight could be born was taboo.

In an institutional event that has the primary task of studying the relationships between members in groups of their own choice and the management of the event who are the staff, we found that the membership formed three groups. In each of these groups we found that there was no internal differentiation of roles for task except that each had appointed a firm doorkeeper who kept all visitors to the group waiting outside the door of the group room. The groups were homogeneous in character. The three groups seemed to be turned inwards as though their task were to explore the interior life of the group, and not inter-group relations. The three groups in their concentration on their interior life represented an acting-out of baM at an organizational level. Another way in which baM was acted out was when one member formed a group of his own of himself.

The management of the institutional event found that the three groups had formed themselves consciously as sociometric chains. While it is an interesting way of forming groups, it avoids the pain of personal selection and rejection. It is apparently scientific and objective. The sole criterion is liking. Individuals ask others whom they like to join them, and so on. The nature of the group so formed was that they were "linked by liking".

The management, at one stage, had the working hypothesis that the model of learning being acted out was one of cohesion through adhesion, with like attracting like. This was seen as being akin to the pseudopodial process. This metaphor we take from zoology. A "pseudopod" refers, for example, to certain protozoa that form protrusions of any part of the protoplasm and so develop temporary processes for locomotion, for the purposes of grasping and attaching, or for the ingestion of food. This pseudopodial process is physical, as, for instance, in certain mosses, which develop a pedicel or footstalk in order to elongate. In baM culture it is a psychological way of relating.

Learning as a baM activity also seems to be a secretive process. What is learned by one person cannot be shared. The learning is for oneself alone. If any learning were to be shared, the phantasy appears to be that it will be stolen, taken away from one, and possibly be added to by another, with the result that the uniqueness of the individual learning is destroyed. Even worse, if one accepts thought or learning from another, one might have to express one's gratitude. Learning thus has to be acquired anonymously, preferably in as comfortable a fashion as possible, with the minimum of psychological disturbance. This means that differences have to be avoided because these might lead to conflict. It seems better to be in a state of anomie, just not understanding, than having to engage in either cooperative or conflictual relations.

This illustrates a major problem when the activities of baM are predominant in a group. There cannot be a joining with others to create something new, which is not simply an extension of or owned by oneself. This is why we suggest that the model of learning in such a culture is pseudopodial, because learning is not true reaching out and internalizing but a temporary and opportunistic "attaching" to something that is supposedly like oneself.

BaM represents an attack on the possibility of learning from relating to others. There is a difficulty just in "taking in", and all interpretations are experienced as persecutory due to the consultant's failure to acknowledge the "plumage" of the members—that is to say, their "marvellous Me-ness". This is because participants are behaving as if the group is not relevant and can never be used for their mutual advantage. In one sense baM can be regarded as an unconscious attack on any idea or person that could give dependability and be a resource for learning. This is because of the fear of basic assumption dependency. A baM group becomes a world of self-contained, autodidacts selecting what they want to know from whom they choose.

The group, of course, loses vitality, as it has an air of futility, because the taking up of a role for the purposes of the work of the group is seen as depriving others and, of course, oneself. Hence, the development of "creative apperception" (Winnicott, 1971, p. 65) within the individual, the group, and the enterprise is precluded, for the preoccupation is with the "me" in its selfish state. The "me" is starving and deprived, to be sure, but the unconscious assumption is that it will probably be fed only by its own self-reliant efforts.

When baM is the dominant basic assumption, there can be no exploration of authority. We have noticed (in our various roles as directors of conferences and as consultants to events) an increasing resistance within member groups to differentiate roles, and thereby authority, in order to work at the primary task. Notions that authority may be exercised differentially within a group and that this may help to press the task forward are often submerged in a rhetoric of pseudo-democratic egalitarianism, which can be viewed as one collective manifestation of baM.

The resistance to testing out boundaries and the limits of authority in a baM culture takes the form of withdrawal and passive aggression. Speaking one's thoughts takes place outside the stated events during breaks for coffee and meals. Within the events, the consultants may be induced into the illusion that the membership is present simply because their bodies are physically present. It would be more true to say that there is a "mental absence" within the group and that the members have taken up a spectator role—that is, one as the photographer. When members of a group are united in unconscious baM, they are acting to deprive the consultants of material to work on. There is no sense of a mutually interdependent, symbiont relationship. Consultants may be trapped into feeling that they have to fill the gap with more and more working hypotheses about flight (baF), which serve only to unite further the group in baM and passive aggression. The group "starves" the consultant, while the consultant tries to "feed" the group, which is not there to be fed (cf. *Broken Mirrors*). It all smacks of the parasitic relationship identified by Bion (1970, p. 95). One feels one is in a pseudo-group.

Consequently, in a baM culture members may believe that they are communicating when in fact they are not. One member reported to one consultant after her small group had ended that she had felt "quite emotional" during the small group and that this must have been obvious to the consultant. He was astonished, as she had appeared within the group to be the very opposite. This led him to think that in baM there is an unconscious belief that if something is going on in "me", others will know that it is happening without it having to be communicated.

Not surprisingly, when baM is dominant, there is little capacity for gratitude. There is no true interaction, so there can be no "baby" to symbolize learning, which if felt to have been gained has been born through a process similar to leaching—that is, similar to percolating. In a Me-ness culture there is no learning from history, from authority figures or role models in the past, from one's own experience or that of others. Psychic pain is minimized; one quotes from others but has forgotten the source; learning is instantaneous. Metaphorically it passes, as used to be said about some kinds of teaching, from the notebook of one to another without passing through the minds of either.

When discussing the feasibility of baM with Lawrence, Jonah Rosenfeld described his experiences in a German working conference in which he had taken part as a consultant. He said that he had never heard so many examples of cruelty recounted by members. One woman told of how as a child the meal consisted of boiled eggs. Each was set in an egg cup. When she opened hers she found an embryonic chicken which she was made to eat. A man told of how as a four-year-old he had been at the seaside with his parents. While they sat on the beach he had ventured into the water, got out of his depth and was drowning when a man came and rescued him. The man deposited him on the beach. The rescuer did not tell the parents and neither did the boy. He had never spoken about the incident until being in a group with Rosenfeld.

Rosenfeld's observation was about the cruelty of parents to their children that was sometimes witting, more often not. We speculated why he had been given this information. We thought it was because he was a Jew and an Israeli citizen, and that the German members were describing their experiences of cruelty to someone whose religious and cultural group had suffered because of the Nazi regime. But the more Rosenfeld reflected on the evidence the more he felt that he was being given evidence of how people's experiences had made them preoccupied with their individual survival and the necessity to hold on to the Me-ness of the "I". The "I" could be violated abominably but not the "me", the essential core, primitive identity of the self.

A supplementary working hypothesis for the incidence of baM is that this propensity for Me-ness is based on a split; the classical split between the imago of the good mother and the bad mother. The bad mother is split off into society—or, rather, projected into it—and badness is located in society or any of its intermediate institutions, such as work, the government, the economic market. External objects can then be blamed for the individual's unhappiness. Sadism comes into it because of this construction of a failed environment. A probable, logical sequence of thinking is: "You have owed me; you have failed me; you will therefore pay for it." By such thinking ruthlessness and selfishness become justified.

Any social figuration, such as the group or society, thus comes to represent the damaged and damaging object. The group is construed as an antagonistic object because it is deemed to be phobic. Consequently, the "me" who feels impotent and vulnerable, with real anxieties about obliteration, takes up a counter-dependent position to the group, which is succeeded by a denial of its very existence; only "me" has reality. This seems to be of the essence of baM.

Part of the experience of being in baM is of being present in a room with a set of other people who must never form a group because it is by unconscious definition a non-group; must never achieve a language that can make use of "we". It is to be in a scientific posture of observing an object. The object is always potentially threatening and damaging. It can never carry hope. It is disappointing and always frustrating. In such a situation there is no space for concern, for the mood is fatalistic—whatever happens, happens! All that one can do in such a situation is survive by keeping the goodness in and the dirty, messy, contaminating reality of the other out. There is no place for emotions, because the concern of the participants is that feelings be not-experienced and that they be not-expressed. Hence, life in a baM culture is ordered, calm, polite, and androgynous.

When baM is salient and activating the life of the group, the consultant to the group is made to feel that he or she has to work harder and harder giving working hypotheses and that each interpretation has to be better than the last one. The members seem to have retreated into apathy, and the consultant feels pressure to rescue, or save, the group from its arid, futile life. The consultant is made to feel, "If only I could make the right interpretation to unlock the stalemate". The consultant may continue to give working hypotheses that may seem "good enough" to him or her; in fact they may be pertinent, but they have no effect. In actuality the interpretations are likely to be about flight (baF), which is what the behaviour feels like because the flight is from the reality of the group as a group. Such interpretations may very possibly have a reverse negative effect in that the group solidifies increasingly into withdrawal and Me-ness. As a consultant, one is made to feel that one is not making contact with any members of the group; one is isolated, alienated. In a real sense, the consultant is either not present for the members in a culture of baM or felt to be a threat to individual survival—that is, the preservation of Me-ness. (Survival we can understand to be the meta-baM.) This consultant experience is a reflection of the fact that members are not psychically, politically, or spiritually present for each other.

We have been noting in recent years the dangers of a baM culture in working conferences. When we were not sure about our thinking, we could only describe our experiences in terms of dissociation, or of anomie, or of alienation, or of schizoid phenomena. Now we are more certain. We see that there is a tendency for some consultants and directors to act in such a way that they occupy space and become a central object of concern and admiration, needing to be nurtured constantly by other staff and by members of the conference. This, at its simplest, is the wish of some staff to be star performers; but we can now suggest that they are acting in a baM mode.

Bain has used the term "space invader" to refer to the kind of teaching situation where the teacher invades the space of the child, rather than allowing the child to learn and to work out for itself what it can do (Bain, Long, & Ross, 1992). This concept applies also to the inappropriate use of director or consultant's Me-ness in relationship to the primary task of conference events.

When this mental relationship of baM exists between group and consultant the chances are that pre-emptive interpretations (Lawrence, 1985) come to the fore. These are interpretations that cut off further exploration of reality because they are presented as a definitive statement, a final assessment or summary, an indubitable psychological fact and spoken sometimes quite punitively. Consequently, there is no space, because it is now invaded, for what can be called mutative interpretative work—that is, the offering of working hypotheses that themselves can be changed and will initiate transformations in the culture of the group. Another way of putting this is to say that pre-emptive interpretations are disguised "attacks on linking". What it also means is that there is no potential for group reverie, which is so critical for participants if they are to be able to make themselves available for thought and to develop thinking.

Bain reports that during a follow-up meeting to a Working Conference in Perth, Australia, a member said to him, "It's marvellous you're able to be here!" While Bain thought that there might be a wish of this ex-member to be dependent on him, it might be more that there was a need to flatter the director's marvellous "Me-ness"—"the plume he wears so well".

Here, it is worth drawing a parallel with psychoanalytic practice. Neville Symington, in an essay on Sándor Ferenczi, says that Ferenczi repeatedly emphasized the need for the analyst to be free of narcissism. If in the context of groups the consultant is caught up in his or her Me-ness, the group feeds into and off the baM culture. The group cannot be related to in an adaptive way. "We all know that in a love relationship there has to be a continual process of adaptation, because without it there can only be self-love or narcissism" (Symington, 1986, p. 195).

Participants can be "driven into Me-ness", as Jon Stokes of the Tavistock Clinic suggested during a discussion of the evidence for and against baM. This telling phrase captures not only our experiences of groups, but also increasingly our experience of living in contemporary societies, when we consult to industrial, educational, and church organizations. What Stokes's phrase signposts

are the cultures that we have co-created in our contemporary industrialized societies that cause people to behave as they do,
which, in turn, creates the culture that reinforces their behaviour.
In Bion's terms, the culture of the group is such that the individual's valency—that "spontaneous, unconscious function of the
gregarious quality in the personality" (Bion, 1961, p. 170)—is mobilized for baM.

Evidence from society

It begins to be evident that we are living in societies that increasingly reward Me-ness behaviour. The "yuppies" of the Thatcher
years are a case in point. Bain notes this rewarding of Me-ness
behaviour in relation to the career concerns of public servants in
Australia. For many in the public service, there has been a loss of a
sense of task and a consequent loss of organizational purpose and
structure, which leads to destructive greed and envy. The losses
experienced have eroded the idea of "I" as a system relating to
others; all that matters is how these changes have affected "me".
This fosters a culture of baM. There are, then, limited psychic,
political, or spiritual bases for developing social concern. Therefore, the main preoccupation of civil servants becomes that of
advancing their personal careers, and less attention is paid to public policies, which they might shape and for which they might take
responsibility and authority.

The more the individual is driven into Me-ness, the more selfish individuals become, for this is the only way that they can
survive in the social world. We note other instances of survival
behaviour in our societies. For example, there is an increase in the
bullying that takes place in offices, as described by Andrea Adams
in *Bullying at Work* (1992). The victim is driven to helplessness and
despair, impotence, and murderous feelings and has fantasies of
killing the bully, who may be a headmaster, a senior manager, a
head of department. The bully will have had a childhood of relationships with abusing authority figures and a history characterized by depression, anger, and violence. He or she recreates these
experiences when in a position of power because that of the bully

is the only imago of authority this person can elicit from his or her inner world. The bully's self-definition of Me-ness is such that he or she can have no conception of ruth for other persons who are objects to be manipulated.

For some time, Lawrence has been referring, half-jokingly, to the "Post-Thatcher Sadism Syndrome" (PTSS) in Britain. This arises from the Thatcher government and its successors' preoccupation with efficiency and value for money. While this preoccupation is supportable, what is not is the way in which the policies that ensue are implemented. For example, there is a reorganization in a hospital. People are invited to apply for the jobs that they may have been executing for a number of years without complaint from their senior management, their colleagues, or the patients. They are interviewed and rejected. One aspect of this is that one set of people (managers and consultants) determines criteria by which others in the system are selected or rejected. More precisely, as we understand the matter, use is made of doctrines of Quality Assurance and the Patient's Charter to implement policies with what is experienced as a vicious judgementalism.

We see another version of this Me-ness also in the ruthless, opportunistic behaviour of some business managers. The Guinness scandal would be a case in point. The most recent case in Britain is the "dirty tricks" campaign of British Airways in relation to Virgin Airways. British Airways' wish to succeed has caused them to think only of themselves and how they could win supremacy in their domain. Here we can speculate that there was an oscillation between ba fight and baM. One distinguishing feature of baM is that the enemy becomes an object, which has to be annihilated, not just conquered, by any means. There is, we think, a psychopathic element present in baM that is much stronger than in baF; a total absence of conscience. Ethics and morality are merely words. If British Airways had been successful one assumes that the management would have celebrated with no thought for the wrecking of a competitor who might provide a better service for the consumer.

The first inklings of baM came from the experience of working with religious (nuns and priests) on a series of action-research projects 20 years after Vatican II. During these projects Lawrence had the first glimpses of the phenomenon we now call baM. The key factor in all these action-research projects was that the majority of the known structures of the religious life had been removed as a result of Vatican II. At the time, Lawrence was preoccupied with the existential crisis that religious were in and wrote that they were experiencing the loss of a social world that had been ordered and regular and had a purpose. While this loss was a release for some because it brought freedom—as expressed in liberation theology, for instance—for a great many it was causing feelings of grief and mourning. We can argue against the quality of religious life before Vatican II and give evidence to show that it had many disadvantages in terms of the human development of religious because the emphasis was on baD. That is secondary to our main point, which is that, whatever its quality, the structures of religious life had provided a container into which uncertainty could be projected and certitude received back, or introjected. With the erosion of these structures, individuals were driven back into themselves, within their own personal boundaries, as the only sure anchor in a world of uncertainty. With hindsight it can be interpreted that religious were thrown into baM as a mode of survival.

As time has passed, one can see that this baM experience became for some a necessary, temporary basic assumption, for it has allowed many nuns and priests to come to redefine the religious life, as in, for example, their taking of the "option for the poor", enabling them to restructure their "apostolates" and change their lifestyle accordingly. So they have been able to reaffirm themselves in the new versions of the religious life, which are now more orientated to revelation through the processes of interpreting the Word in the light of the changing circumstances in the environment. There is, then, a sophisticated use of baM that can lead to a redefinition of work and new activities to further that work.

Some sophisticated uses of baM

Like all the other basic assumptions, baM can have its temporary uses for the ultimate furtherance of W. In the same way, for instance, that baO can be a transitional state that leads into transcendent experience, so baM can be of value for exploring realities. There is a necessity for all of us to withdraw deeply into ourselves, to plumb our own inner worlds in order that we can re-engage with the external environment. Sometimes this is called regression in the service of the ego. There is a necessity that periodically we assess the nature of our own feelings in order to disentangle what we may feel is being introjected into what we may be projecting and us. Although we have difficulty in ever identifying them with any certainty, we try to isolate what may be our countertransference feelings in order to find out what the transference feelings may be in whatever human context we are participating.

There is this work to find within ourselves what could be called "the moment", which is the capacity to arrive at a clarity of insight that cannot be avoided or gainsaid because it is as near truth as can be. That, of course, we are struggling with lies is not to be denied. BaM can be the temporary mental space we need to have in order to be out of the world to recuperate mentally and spiritually so that we can re-explore external realities without memory, desire, or the wish that they be other than they are.

There is a sense in which baM can be viewed as a dependency on oneself and one's own resources in order to have a basis of dependability to participate in and hearken to the realities of the environment. It can be a necessary withdrawal into the self to be able to make oneself available for thoughts and thinking and to be able to be attentive to external reality. BaM can become an introspective activity, which, for example, is difficult to achieve in a baF/F culture.

Bion makes reference to Freud's idea that particular specialized work groups make use of the activities of particular basic assumptions. Bion goes on to say that the Church or an Army has to hold on to basic assumption mentality and work group activity at one and the same time. Just as the Church is prone to interference from baD and baO activity, so is the Army from baF/F phenomena. Bion goes on to suggest that these ba groups are budded off by the main work group of which they form a part. The work group's purpose is "the translation of thoughts and feelings into behaviour which is adapted to reality" (Bion, 1961, p. 157). Here we are puzzling out the relationship between baM activity and work group activity, recognizing that "basic assumption mentality does not lend itself into action" (ibid., p. 157). Tentatively, we are suggesting that baM activity is part of the necessary experience an individual has to have as a self with a boundary in order to engage in terms of Work with whatever is the reality of the Other, be that other persons, the group as other, or the environment. We can see this operating in any group. One example is in a religious retreat, where baO and baM activities have to be budded off into specialized groups; otherwise the overarching W of a religious retreat would be destroyed. We see baM operating in a consultation to a business enterprise that is having to reorganize its resources for its future in an uncertain market environment. BaM activity, again, has to be budded off into subgroupings so that the human resources of the enterprise can be rediscovered in much the terms that have been used above. The W of the consultation, which is to engage with changing realities, is thus furthered.

Homo clausus *versus* Homines aperti; Homo individualis; *autonomous man*

BaM has social and intellectual roots, we are hypothesizing, which have come to justify this particular psychic position. Our concern is to find cultural explanations for baM rather than to reduce everything to narcissism. The intellectual roots lie in our immediate experiences of contemporary societies, as we have tried to indicate. There are, however, more profound reasons that are part of the emergent fabric of twentieth-century societies. Since Plato, through Descartes, Leibniz, Locke, Hume, Kant, Husserl, and Popper, there has been an endless circular argument about the individual and society, about the individual as the subject of knowledge and how that individual gains knowledge of the objects in the external environment. This solipsistic viewpoint carries the image of the individual being inside a closed container looking at the world of other individuals, each with minds, guessing at what is inside the others' sealed minds. Norbert Elias calls this conception *Homo clausus*. This conception of the isolated ego, of what he calls "we-less I's" (Elias, 1987, p. 266), he rejects, and for his own conceptual base he proposes *Homines aperti* (open people) who are linked together in various modalities and to varying degrees.

Open people recognize that their knowledge does not begin with them as individuals but, rather, that individuals learn from their historically determined environmental contexts through the ordinary processes of maturation and socialization. As Stephen Mennell (1992) points out, in *Die Gesellschaft der Individuen* Elias (1987) analyses the relationship between changes in the structure of human relations in societies with the concomitant changes in personality structure as part of a societal process. The image of *Homo clausus*, however, is a persistent one because it accords with self-experience and has existed since Renaissance times.

> The philosophers' *homo clausus* is just an externalization of this mode of self-experience: the sealed container in which we sense ourselves is sealed with the iron bands of the civilized self-controls forged in a long-term process. [Mennell, 1992, p. 193]

The sealed container has been an organizing theme of twentieth-century literature. Walt Whitman identified this as "the principle of individuality, the pride and centripetal isolation of a human being in himself—identity—personalism" (quoted in Tanner, 1971, p. 19). This has been the century of the celebration of personal self-actualization because it is believed that only the individual can work out his or her destiny in isolation. That isolation produces its own existential pain. Indeed, the theatre of the absurd explores one aspect of this anguish, which is the inability to communicate.

A gloss on this metaphor of the sealed container has been the twentieth-century intellectuals' dismissal of the masses. John Carey suggests

> that the principle around which modernist literature and culture fashioned themselves was the exclusion of the masses, the defeat of their power, the removal of their literacy, the denial of their humanity. What this intellectual effort failed to acknowledge was that the masses do not exist. The mass, that is to say, is a metaphor for the unknowable and invisible. We cannot see the mass. Crowds can be seen, but the mass is the crowd in its metaphysical aspect—the sum of all possible crowds—and that can take on conceptual form only as a metaphor. The metaphor of the mass serves the purpose of indi-

vidual self-assertion because it turns people into a conglomerate. It denies them the individuality which we ascribe to ourselves and to people we know. [Carey, 1992, p. 21]

The intellectual is in the sealed container and so can assert his or
her individuality because whatever is outside is a conglomerate.
This echoes the psychic and non-political and non-spiritual position of the participant in baM. The group of other people is an
undifferentiated mass in which people have no individuality and
are not worth knowing. There is an element of contempt present in
baM that is not so evident in other ba groups.

The paradox is, however, that while this has been the century
of *Homo clausus*, it has also been the century of communication.
Human relations in contemporary societies are importantly influenced by the plenitude of the mass media. This abundance of
information can generate anxiety because the television viewer of,
say, the Gulf War or events in the former Yugoslavia is left with a
feeling of impotence. At the same time, viewers have to make up
their minds about the rights and wrongs, the truth or falsehood, of
the information they receive, which is often complex and contradictory. Because we are living through the collapse of dogma and
received belief and, as Umberto Eco has identified, a multiplica-
tion of ideologies, the individual is pressed into becoming an
autonomous man—*Homo individualis* (Tecglen, 1992, p. 159).

While this has many positive advantages in that the individual
who can assimilate the information that is available can have an
unprecedented mental richness, questions arise as to what the nature of social life will be in the future. We feel that this trend points
to the emphasizing of the "I" and the "me", to the exclusion of the
"we" and the "us". There are, it appears, a number of factors that
increase the risk of baM phenomena in societies that, we have to
remind ourselves, are truly psychotic.

A related reason for the emergence of baM phenomena lies in
our beliefs as to how we gain insight and knowledge. Simply
stated, the engagement in baM, as we have hinted, may be a
throwback to a scientific methodology that we associate with
Newtonian science. The methodology of Tavistock Working Conferences celebrates different ways of coming to know what reality might be. The emphasis in conferences is on participation,

paying attention, and hearkening, which involves the participant as a whole person. This methodology, which sounds vague, near-mystical, obscure, and is downright subjective, may be a contributory factor in driving people into Me-ness, which is the posture of the non-participating, objective observer, regarding the group as a conglomerate, a mass.

Bion's hypotheses derive from a psychoanalytic knowing of groups. This has enabled us to see connections between basic assumption behaviour and the interpretation of what reality might be. Basic assumption behaviour is psychotic, albeit temporarily. The more permanent it becomes, however, the more are mature, healthy individuals capable of social contribution, because they have a capacity for rush, swamped in the basic assumption cultures of groups, organizations, or society. Donald Winnicott was alive to this over 40 years ago, when he showed how fragile democracy is as an achievement because it is always struggling against the psychotic, which may become the majority force in a society at any time (Winnicott, 1950). The more we can identify through experience and come to know basic assumption behaviour, the greater are our chances of interpreting the realities in which we live and transforming them so that human beings can become more mature through the quality of their contact with realities. Notwithstanding the sophisticated uses of baM, the major consequence of baM behaviour becoming salient and perseverative is that possible explorations of W and ba cultures are prevented and their potential experience rendered unattainable.

CHAPTER SIX

Beyond the frames

There exists a striking fourteenth-century Syrian miniature of the Archangel Gabriel. What disturbs the Western eye at first is that the bell of the horn that Gabriel blows bursts through the exquisitely limned frame that the artist has placed around the figure of Gabriel and the text below. Although the figure is flat and there is no sense of perspective, the visual effect of the horn bursting through the frame is to give the picture a third dimension—it jumps out of its frame. It is only on reflection that the observer realizes that Gabriel's horn cannot be contained within a mere frame, for he is the messenger of good news, having been visited by a vision (Daniel 8: 16–26).

In the context of this chapter, that is perhaps not quite so important as the simple idea that frames have both an inside and outside; they contain the space inside and leave undefined the space outside. Furthermore, frames are artefacts, which can be delineated at will. This is one leitmotif of this chapter.

Within the frame

Wilfred Bion was able to create hypotheses about the nature of human groups that took us beyond the frames. Compared with his predecessors, Freud and Trotter, Bion was able to make a quantum leap in understanding. In particular, he identified the basic assumption states that members of a group can take part in quite unconsciously while, at the same time, they are trying to pursue some work task. I believe this to be Bion's major, awesome contribution to our knowledge about groups.

Isabel Menzies Lyth has made the point well. In her review of Bion's contribution to thinking about groups, she notes that Bion insisted on "the use of the group *per se*, the dynamics of the group in the here and now, as the instrument of therapy and learning" (Menzies Lyth, 1981, p. 662). She goes on to write (p. 663):

> My second point concerns his elucidation of the psychotic element in groups. Previous reference to psychotic group behaviour had almost exclusively described gross phenomena, akin to diagnostically psychotic disorders. The subtlety of Bion's intuition was in pinpointing the less obvious but immensely powerful psychotic phenomena that appear in groups that are apparently behaving sanely, if a little strangely, groups that are working more or less effectively and whose members are clinically normal or neurotic. He describes the clusters of these psychotic phenomena as the three basic assumptions of dependency, fight–flight and pairing. They have in common massive splitting and projective identification, loss of individual distinctiveness or depersonalisation, diminution of effective contact with reality, lack of belief in progress and development through work and suffering. [Menzies Lyth, 1981, p. 662].

This is the second leitmotif of this chapter: how to explore psychotic phenomena in groups including any personal and social defences against such an exploration because of the anxieties invoked.

The focus of this chapter is on groups as an instrument of learning. At one level the chapter is about learning within the frames of groups as such, but it is also a record of going beyond these frames to fathom larger issues of institutions and societies. It also reflects my puzzlement about the unconscious or infinite world.

One of the outstanding outcomes of Bion's thinking about groups has been the growth of group relations training conferences. My purpose, however, is not to set out a detailed history, but to try to voice my preoccupation. What commonly is known as the Tavistock method, or model, arises from Bion's pioneering work. There have been other institutions that have risen and died, and yet others may now exist of which I do not know. The process that I am postulating influences the elaboration, through these institutions, of Bion's original insights about groups.

Through the growth of enterprises to provide group relations training there has been the phenomenon of institutionalization. From my role perspective as joint director of a Tavistock Institute programme of work, I find myself, at times, in the thick of this experience of institutionalization. Bion himself has identified this phenomenon:

> The institutionalizing of words, religions, psycho-analysis— all are special instances of institutionalizing memory so that it may "contain" the mystic revelation and its creative and destructive force. The function of the group is to produce a genius; the function of the Establishment is to take up and absorb the consequences so that the group is not destroyed. [Bion, 1970, p. 82]

There can be little doubt that Bion had the qualities of a mystic (cf. Grotstein, 1981, p. 33), if only because of his contribution to our thinking about groups. The paradox is that the disruptive ideas he first presented have resulted in an Establishment(s)—that is, the group relations training institutions to which I have already referred. I am in doubt as to whether "Establishment" is singular or plural; my postulate is that there is an Establishment "in the mind". Each institution (such as the Tavistock Institute, the A. K. Rice Institute, and the others) at times actually becomes the Establishment for the others. The Establishment "in the mind" is the ideal–typical institution purveying the very best of Bion's thinking and that of those who were immediately associated with him and who began the various institutions for group relations training. Here, I suggest, a number of individuals have been put into the role of representing the untarnished truth of Bion, Rice, and the others. Each conference sponsored by any one of these Establishments can be seen as the "group" in Bion's terms. The mystic, who could be a member either of the conference or of the conference staff, will have his or her disruptive ideas dealt with by the group, the members of which must preserve coherence even at the risk of new understanding. I can write more pertinently from my own experience. A few years ago I used the word "relatedness" in a conference staff group. Even though Turquet had introduced the concept earlier, I found myself regarded with puzzlement by my colleagues at the time. Now, "relatedness", as a term, is part of the language of any conference. At best, the Establishment(s) come, in time, to have a symbiotic relationship with the mystic. But the possibilities of commensal and parasitic relationships are always present.

The other aspect I want to pursue is the postulate that institutions for group relations training come, at times, individually to act as an Establishment for the others. Thus, at best, another institution can take on the role of mystic in the sense that the term is being used in this context.

This, however, is both complicated and enriched by issues of institutional transference and countertransference. Clearly, institutions themselves are not capable of transference, but their agents or employees are. Lomas, in his discussion of psychiatric clinics, makes the point that there is transference on the part of agents of clinical institutions towards their clients. He identifies

> a type of institutional countertransference, a transference of attitudes and feelings on the part of employees to the imagos that haunt the halls of the clinic itself. These attitudes and feelings, be they latent or manifest, inevitably cause such employees to become agents of the institution, executing the expressed mission of the organization, often without any regard for the clientele; and, worse, these attitudes and feelings cause such employees to carry out procedures that are in direct conflict with their own personal feelings. [Lomas, 1979, p. 548]

While a group relations training institution cannot readily be likened to a clinic, with its buildings and permanent personnel, it would be worth while to consider systematically the types of transference that occur between conference staffs and members, and between conference staffs and their Establishment(s) and the imagos of the Establishment in the mind. To avoid the disentangling of this and the testing of the reality or not of particular conference staffs being caught in the impersonalized procedures identified by Lomas, other institutions grow up with the latent task of providing a less painful experience than a Leicester Conference, as has been reported to me more than once.

All I can offer, at this point, is my experience that there are transference and countertransference feelings between agents of Establishments. So, if you will, the relationships and relatednesses of mystic, group, and Establishment and the dynamics of commensality, symbiosis, and parasitism come to be worked out at both interpersonal and institutional levels.

To put my concern in concrete terms: the felt pressure on the programme of the Tavistock is never to be innovative; it must be saddled with stability, certainty, and perseveration. But it must never disappear, as this would leave other comparable institutions with problems of rivalry for succession that would have to be fought out. So the idea of the Tavistock programme as a dead, hollow container or spittoon easily comes to mind, even though individuals as agents may feel differently within themselves. Essentially, I am also saying that the memory of group relations training conferences is so powerful because of institutionalization that new transformations, which might lead to a deeper ignorance and then a more profound understanding of groups, are constrained. As Establishments have grown to perpetuate the work of Bion, the world of groups with their psychotic phenomena is in danger of being defined for ever. The possibility of suggestion that might lead to tentative new insights can be squeezed out. Remember: "To define is to kill, / To suggest is to create" (Stéphane Mallarmé). The puzzle is how to generate symbiotic relationships between new ideas and the Establishment(s) and avoid the commensal and parasitic ones, to use Bion's formulation. This is another leitmotif.

Once in Ireland a motorist stopped his car to ask a pedestrian the way to Ballykinler. His informant said he could certainly tell him the way—"but", he added, "I wouldn't be starting from here!" I feel much the same about group relations. Working in conferences at times, I have a sense that with the institutionalization of Establishments a technology has developed. I purposely use the term "technology" to give the sense that, in the process of institutionalization, the perseverators of the Tavistock method/ model become technicians as opposed to being "makars", which is the old Scottish word for poets.

As, then, with any inheritance, there are puzzlements around what ought to be discarded in order to break through to some new understanding in the context of the times in which we live. What I am quite sure about, from my role perspective, is that to take psychoanalytic and Bionic thinking about groups out of this tradition would be to end it. And there can be a sense of an ending, as I experience it occasionally when working with some staffs of group relations training conferences who are preoccupied with pre-conscious material and not struggling to elucidate unconscious phenomena, or, alternatively, when I find myself part of a consultant staff that is in a pre-emptive frame of mind and is interpreting staff and member experiences in such a way that further exploration is truncated. It is in such contexts that mutative interpretations, which are those that engage with puzzling and lead to change, are destroyed.

What I am less sure about and continually want to question is the continued acceptance of the "frames" and "orders" that have been established and institutionalized to capture and explore the kind of group phenomena that Bion first illuminated. By "frames", I mean the "small study group", the "large study group", the "institutional event", and all the other events. In order to explore the phenomenal stuff of the existence of people in groups, we, in our roles of conference designers, draw outlines or contours around selected numbers and frame them. The figure 12 is traditionally a small group; 6, a very small group; 25 plus, a large group—or is it a median group? To be sure, there can be no identifiable group without such a contour or frame. But, at the very same time, it is known that such frames, outlines, or contours impose limits that have to be accepted by the people involved. Those limits become boundaries enabling the differentiation of what is inside the frame from what is outside. Nevertheless, they constrain the exploration of experiences and phenomena that cannot yet be imagined. The paradox is inevitable.

Another paradox arises when the "orders" associated with these frames and their selection are considered. I use the term "order" in the same way as does Max Weber. Some years after he had developed the concept of bureaucracy, which described the kinds of organization that man had evolved to execute tasks, he said in a debate:

> This passion for bureaucracy . . . is enough to drive one to despair. It is as if in politics . . . we were deliberately to become men who need "order" and nothing but order, who become nervous and cowardly if for one moment this order wavers, and helpless if they are torn away from their total incorporation in it. That the world should know no men but these: it is such an evolution that we are already caught up in, and the great question is therefore not how we can promote and hasten it, but what can we oppose to this machinery in order to keep a portion of mankind free from this parcelling-out of the soul. [quoted in Bennis, 1971, p. 144]

The theme of "order" has always been present in the work of the Tavistock conferences, with their emphasis on responsibility, leadership, authority, organization, and, now, the politics of relatedness. While the fantasy will persist that Tavistock conferences are "authoritarian", the commitment of staffs of such conferences is to exploring these dimensions of "order" in order to ensure that they are scrutinized and questioned. One way in which this is done is by holding to the psychoanalytic tradition of trying to make as explicit as the possible transference and countertransference feelings between the managerial and consultant staffs of a conference and the membership. The staff, in fantasy, will at times be seen as a privileged sub-group of the conference, at once destructive, persecuting, protective, benign. The collection of these transference feelings and the working through of them is one way that a staff can help the membership find its authority to take responsibility for making the conference a learning institution.

To be sure, there will be ambivalent feelings about authority. There will often occur, as a social process, a "rage for order" on the part of some members and staff that is reminiscent of Weber's insight, but there will also be a wish for absolute autonomy and freedom—even a hunger for disorder.

It is around this theme of order that the subjectivity of the individual is most closely engaged because order, while it may appear to be rational and logical, is often supported by unspoken and unconscious wishes for protection against the anxiety of finding authority to take initiative to feel and see beyond the orders.

The connection between the inner world of conferences and the external authority and power structures is easy to see. On the face of it, it looks as if internal and external management structures are matched. In fantasy and because of transference feelings the membership of a conference will tend to see them as exactly the same, even though the management of a conference may be directing its efforts to providing conditions for the membership to manage themselves in relation to their learning. Here I want to emphasize that I see conferences as being an opportunity for members and staff to re-affirm their capacities to inspect and question the social contexts in which they are existing. The hope is always that members will internalize from staff modes of inspecting the unconscious aspects of social arrangements and go on to forge their own perspective for questioning the social meaning of frames and orders.

A central heuristic tool for such questioning is provided through the concept of primary task. Every working conference on group relations is bounded in time, space, and activity. The boundaries (frames) of time and space are obvious. What is less obvious, on first inspection, is the boundary between work that is directed at understanding and non-work, which is to avoid insight. Here, there is a seeming paradox. The experience of Bion's basic assumption states (crudely and, by some, oversimplistically defined as non-work) within the boundaries of a conference and its activities comes to be the work of a conference. Work directed at coming close to what may be the truth of a situation can only be attained through the experience of the basic assumption states— the psychotic phenomena.

The ideal work of a conference is differentiated from other subjective experiences through the use of the concept of primary task. It is a heuristic device and not a prescriptive one, though it can be reduced to that by some practitioners. It is based on

> the proposition that every enterprise or part of it, has, at any given moment, one task which is primary. What we (E. J. Miller and A. K. Rice) also say, however, is that, if, through inadequate appraisal of internal resources and external forces, the leaders of an enterprise define the primary task in an inappropriate way, or the members—leaders and followers alike—do not agree on their definition, then the survival of the enterprise will be jeopardised. Moreover, if the organization is regarded primarily as an instrument for task performance, we can add that, without adequate task definition, disorganization must occur. [Miller & Rice, 1967, pp. 27–28]

In order to elucidate what is taking place, both consciously and unconsciously, among the people who make up the organization of an enterprise—and here groups of various sizes are to be included—the heuristic concept of primary task, has been further elaborated. On inspection, it is possible to differentiate between the normative primary task, the existential primary task and the phenomenal primary task. The first is the task that the people in an enterprise consciously and rationally know has to be performed if the enterprise is to survive as an institution. The existential primary task is the one that people believe they are executing. On occasion there will be agreement between the normative and existential task, but not at other times. The existential primary task is the individual's perception of the purpose of his or her activity. If the individual has internalized the normative primary task, the chances are that he or she will be able to take up a role in the system of activity. If the individual is concerned more with self-survival than with institutional survival, the existential primary task will be salient. These two definitions of the situation of an individual in role in a system of activity are conscious in the sense that they can be established through a question-and-answer process, for instance. What is less obvious is the phenomenal primary task. This is the unconscious task that is being pursued. It can be hypothesized that within any system of activity there will be this task sitting alongside the other two. At times all these will coincide to produce high-calibre work, but there may be tensions between the three. If the phenomenal primary task is salient in a system of activity, it is a mental world of the psychotic—that is, the basic assumption states of Bion. Although I am not certain about this, I would suggest that the existential primary task enables the neurotic quality of life in systems of activity to be identified. Certainly, the phenomenal primary task is the one of which people are not consciously aware (cf. Lawrence, 1977, p. 24). By holding these three versions of primary task in mind, it is possible to generate hypotheses as to the conscious and unconscious behaviour of people within the boundary, or frame, of a group or a larger enterprise with its fantasied and reality orders.

Working conferences have a primary task, but a conference designer can only state a primary task on behalf of the staff who constitute the collective management of the conference. For example, the primary task for the September 1978 working conference, entitled "Individual and Organization: The Politics of Relatedness", was stated as follows: "To study and interpret experiences of political relatedness within the conference Institution". Such a primary task definition differentiates the working conference as a temporary learning enterprise or institution from its environment. It also enables the people taking part in the conference—both staff (as collective management and consultants) and the members—to join the conference by taking and making roles in it in contradistinction to attending it. Without a primary task, there can be no conference.

Working conferences are based on the postulate that they are open systems interacting with their environment (cf. Rice, 1958 [1970 edition], p. 40; Rice, 1965, pp. 2–27). Essentially, a working conference provides opportunities for members and staff to transform themselves from a state of not knowing so much about groups into a state of further understanding groups at first hand through experience, as opposed to learning about groups from written sources, for example.

Within a conference boundary—itself a frame—there are such events as: the small study group, the large study group, the intergroup event, the institutional event, review groups, application groups, and conference plenaries. These have all been framed by conference designers in order to pursue the aim of experientially understanding group phenomena. Each of these events has a primary task that enables both members and staff to differentiate appropriate work from non-work. From the conference staff group—members of which have the two sub-roles of collective management and consultants—consultants are delegated authority to work with a section of the membership, say, in a small study group. It is unlikely that in the opening stages of a conference the members will have the political machinery to execute a similar kind of delegation, but in the course of a conference a shared sense of delegation by members of members is likely to increase, particularly within the inter-group and the institutional events. Indeed, the staff, both in their managerial and in their consultant roles, are working to enable the membership to find their authority.

To these have to be added other events, which do not appear on the programme of the conference. There is "the-event-of-the-staff-as-a-group" and, similarly, "the-event-of-the-membership-as-a-group-and-in-groups-of-their-own choice". I shall simply call these the staff group event and the membership group(s) event(s). About these, very little is known, because they are rarely open to direct study as they are regarded as being private. Nevertheless they are important because they influence other events in the conference.

To be sure, in the institutional event and in some versions of the inter-group event the staff is present as a group, and their behaviour is open to observation and interpretation as they make their roles both as management and consultants. In these events they are present as a staff group with work to do, but I am interested in the influence of the private events of the staff as a group and the membership as a group as they relate outside the stated, defined, framed events as sentient groups. Miller and Rice introduced the concept of "sentient group". They wrote:

> We have chosen sentient—"that feels or is capable of feeling; having the power or function of sensation or of perception by the senses", 1632 (*Shorter Oxford English Dictionary*)—as expressing most clearly what we mean without using the specialized vocabulary of psychoanalysis. We shall therefore talk of sentient system and sentient group to refer to that system or group that demands and receives loyalty from its members; and we shall talk of sentient boundary to refer to the boundary round a sentient group or sentient system. We shall also

use sentience to mean "the condition or quality of being sentient"(*Shorter Oxford English Dictionary*). [1967, p. xiii, italics in original]

Clearly, members can develop sentience only during the course of a conference, though it is quite clear that those who are acquainted beforehand might arrive at a conference with that potentiality. The chances are that a staff group will have more sentient qualities at the start of a conference than will the members. Within a staff group there may be tension between sentient sub-groupings and the staff as a work group. In my experience, this most commonly takes the form of a pair, which I assume, at worst, is a formation that is used by the pair and by the remainder of the staff, whose relations come to be influenced by the pair, as a defensive system against the anxieties of engaging with the psychotic qualities of the framed events. At the same time the pair comes to be used in exactly the same way as Bion identified when he described the basic assumption pairing culture—that is, a hope for creativity, but doomed to failure.

Sentient groups and groupings will develop and change within the period of a conference, both for staff and for members. From these groups and groupings individuals can be seen as taking up roles in the framed events and through their work experiences within them making sentient groups and groupings.

There is, then, within a conference and its framed events a substantial richness for learning, not all of which has been identified as yet. If we accept the inescapable paradox that to draw a contour, frame, or boundary precludes experiencing what is outside the frame, we can have an opportunity, if we give ourselves authority, to explore even more deeply within the frames of conference events. If the basic assumption states that Bion first identified are understood to be, in Conrad's words, "the heart of darkness" (Broadbent, 1979, pp. 193ff.), then there are opportunities within a working conference on group relations to be in touch vividly and vitally with unconscious processes.

One framed event, for example, that ever continues to stir me, whether as a member or a partaker of it, is the large group. This event grew out of the experiences that the members of staff were having in the 1960s in conference plenaries which occur at the beginning and towards the end of a working conference and are designed to offer a frame within which both members and staff can reflect on their experiences of joining, participating in, and leaving the conference.

Pierre Turquet, in his paper "Threats to Identity in the Large Group" (1975), points out that it was the inexplicability of the social forces in evidence in conference plenaries that brought about the specific study of large groups in their own right. A new frame was created.

From his experiences as a consultant to the large group, Turquet developed a rare phenomenological description of what takes place for the participating individual. His working hypothesis was that the individual member comes to a working conference, and therefore the large group, as a "singleton". Turquet introduced this term

> for this person entering into a new conference totally on his or her own, not yet part of a group but attempting both to find himself and to make relations with the other singletons who are in a similar state. As yet within the large group situation no relationships with other singletons have been established; nor do previous acquaintanceships seem to operate.
>
> One of the characteristics of a large group is that many of its members remain in the singleton state, unable, possibly unwilling, to join in and so go through the necessary change of state. This conversion process is part of the dislocation every conference member experiences as he takes himself into a world which transcends the usual parameters of his own individuality. [Turquet, 1975, p. 94]

Turquet develops his ideas about the conversion process available to the members of the large group. He or she can become an individual member (I.M.)—that is, convert from the singleton state as he or she struggles to make relationships with other singletons. Once the large group assumes some meaning for the individual and he or she tries to make a construct of it in the mind, the chances of converting to the "membership individual" (M.I.) are enhanced. To be sure, this conversion process is not without its risks, because the construct may only express the destructive feelings of the singleton and his fears of being annihilated by the large group and its members. So singletons can use the large group as a repository for negative feelings in order to maintain their own sense of a positive, individual boundary. There are, of course, other possibilities.

The struggle between the I.M. or M.I., or I.M. back to singleton states is experienced as flux. It is in these transitional states that the importance of the personal boundary, or external skin, is paramount. The dilemma can be stated as: "This is me; that is not me." With subtlety, Turquet goes on to describe the necessity for what he calls the "second skin"—the internal skin which

> is needed so that the singleton can separate himself out from his background, more specifically from the undifferentiated non-singleton matrix out of which he has developed and to which he might return again, if the I.M. status is not securely established, the various problematic processes having failed him and the defensive manoeuvres having broken down. [Turquet, 1975, p. 97]

This internal skin includes a history of past and present. Thus the here-and-now can be separated from the past by the individual that, for him or her, becomes "a background called the 'past'" (p. 97). Turquet goes on to say that this background boundary skin has another aspect: "While the presence of the past gives rise to a sense of continuity of growth out of all our yesterdays, the singleton's immediate experience is nevertheless one of discontinuity, of being different, of being other than he was yesterday" (1975, p. 97).

This sense of discontinuity and dislocation is very frightening but brings the singleton up against larger existential issues than just his or her private troubles. As Turquet says:

> Anxiety surges up with a developing content of annihilation, becoming fear of a void in which to be lost. Since internally nothing can be found, there is nothing there. The move to try and re-establish a "here and now" contact with the skin-of-my-neighbour can then be very quick. Macneice puts these aspects of the singleton's dilemma very aptly: "An historical sense is essential, which means that we must know how to be new. As contrasted with repetition—psittacism—on the one hand, and with escape from tradition—aphasia—on the other." He adds both graphically and dramatically: "We must sit in the seats of our ancestors, i.e., we must turn our ances-

tors out of them." As far as man in a group is concerned, whether it be large or small, that is easier said than done. [Turquet, 1975, pp. 98–99]

From Turquet's unrivalled exploration of the phenomenological experiences of large groups I want to draw out three points:

First, in a footnote, Turquet, using the *Shorter Oxford English Dictionary*, defines a "matrix" as "a place or medium in which something is bred, produced or developed and hence in the sense of a place of origin or growth" (1975, p. 96). As I understand it, at present there is a distinction to be made between a matrix and a framed event such as a large group. If you will, a matrix holds the potential creativity of a large group, and indeed the matrix qualities have yet to be explored experientially—or, rather, the tension between the matrix in the mind and the group in the mind.

Second, Turquet has set out some of the dimensions of dislocation available for members of a large group. The theme of dislocation is one that I want to hold on to. Later in the same paper Turquet introduces the neologism "dissaroy"—from the French *désarroi*—which is "a state of complete bewilderment or confusion". He writes:

"disarroy" becomes the overwhelming experience, including a picture that the world can never be the same again. The word "disarroy" is used here not only to describe the actual experience of change, with an inherent notion of disintegration and collapse, but also to indicate the presence of a wish to return to status quo ante, with further wishes not to know, never to return and would that he had never been there. [Turquet, 1975, p. 103]

The experience of dissaroy is thus essential for learning in that it is a fulcrum of experience from which the individual can tilt himself or herself in various directions for knowing and not knowing.

Third, I think that the large group is a framed event that gives us a glimpse of society as refracted through members and consultant staff at a particular point in time. There are public issues that are larger than the private struggles of the individuals as they engage with the experience of disarroy. To be sure, a large group can mobilize the topic of "society" as a defence against the problems of disarroy, but at other times there can be a real sense of

seeing how people are reacting to the larger group in the mind—
that is, society. At present, large groups seem to be characterized
by members, or more accurately singletons, having no potentiality
for experiencing any faith or belief in the dependability of any
grouping that is larger than a face-to-face one. Hence, large groups
become repositories for all that is negative and destructive in order that the individual as singleton can present himself or herself
in a pre-experience, pristine, narcissistic state. Disarroy is to be
avoided. This I can see mirrored in institutions outside conferences, particularly as the environment becomes more uncertain
and menacing.

Alongside these points, I want to set a personal experience that
occurred in a large group and caused me to think further in terms
of the leitmotifs of this chapter. Once, as a large-study-group-
taker, I felt that beyond the section of the membership I was
looking at I could see a "black hole". For me, the darkness of
bewilderment and chaos seemed unfathomable; the terror was
making me feel nauseous. I had visions of the whole membership
and the consultants being sucked into that hole, never to reappear.
In that moment two lines of a poem were born that became:

> Mind holes in blind space are ours of choice,
> questing neoteric echoes of our voice.
>
> [Lawrence, 1979b]

The pun on "mined" and "mind" is obvious, but "neoteric" was
used to give the sense of a "fresh" voice. Why "echoes"? I was
aware at that time that any voice echoes a past of other voices (cf.
Turquet, 1975, pp. 98–99, already quoted).

What was important, at the time, for me was the coming up
against the inaccessibility of experience *per se*. Words came to my
mind to fit the experience but, finally, took over and made an
experience. The astronomical metaphor became what I believed
was the reality of the time. Patterns of thought, perception, and
"understanding"—"memory" in Bion's terms—intervened to
frame the senses. And then it is an easy matter to associate mentally at a preconscious level. The experience comes to be named as
"blind space", "nothingness", of being in the "abyss", of seeing the
"void". But in naming what is believed to be the experience, the

possibility of knowing what the experience might be in itself is lost. To be sure, I could have expressed much of this in terms of Bion's transformations in O.

What I want to hold on to, at this juncture, is the overpowering wish for the ordering of experience—in terms of a metaphor, for example—within the frame of an event. I go so far as to say that there is a rage for order to defend against a sense of annihilation and a fear of disappearing into a black hole—into psychosis.

At the same time as I was becoming caught up in the astronomical metaphor, I started to have more elaborate fantasies as to what would happen (a) if the large group were to go en masse into the black hole or (b) if the participants in this large group were able to rise from their seats and spill all over the room as a crowd, even a mob, disordered and destructive.

Let me stay with the idea of "order". There is increasingly in conferences within framed events a rage for order in terms of memory. Bion once wrote somewhere about the hatred of learning from experience. Just because a working conference exists for the purpose of providing opportunities to study, at first hand, experiences in groups does not mean to say that the participants (both staff and members) will not be free from the hatred of learning. The hatred I see most clearly as being around discovering or tumbling into the psychotic experiences that Bion first identified.

Pressing this further: in my most disillusioned state I begin to have the suspicion that working conferences can be interpreted as well-rehearsed dramas with the title "*Oedipus Vivat!*" How far, at times, are both the staff and members orchestrating the fugue of work group versus basic assumption groups, albeit with variations?

To re-state what, in part, I have already said: have the frames (conferences and their events) with all their potentiality for dislocation, disorder, and disarroy that could lead to new learning come to be so potent that they have to be defended against mobilizing, for example, the rage for order? To be sure, the interpretation of resistance is a major pivot that can tip both the members and the staff into new learning.

But, at the same time, I want to hold on to much that is rich and positive in working conferences and try to build on what my predecessors in this kind of venture have discovered and illuminated, even though the capacity to speak with the dead is easily eroded. What is enormously exciting about working conferences and their framed event, such as I am puzzling around, is that, at their very best, they provide what Winnicott called a "cultural space". His ideas or formulations on the location of culture experiences make sense in relation to working conferences. His quotation from Rabindranath Tagore is apt: "On the seashore of endless worlds—children play." In puzzling around frames and orders, I see myself as exploring the seashores of endless worlds and wishing to play with the wonderment of a child, discovering for the first time.

Winnicott's main thesis is so succinctly stated that it deserves to be quoted rather than paraphrased. I quote the first three points:

1. The place where cultural experience is located is in the potential space between the individual and the environment (originally the object). The same can be said of playing. Cultural experience begins with creative living first manifested in play.

2. For every individual the use of this space is determined by *life experience* that takes place at the early stages of the individual's existence.

3. From the beginning the baby has maximally intense experiences *in the potential space between subjective object and the object objectively perceived*, between the me-extension and the not-me. This potential space is at the interplay between there being nothing but me and there being objects and phenomena outside omnipotent control. [1971, p. 100, italics in original]

I postulate that group relations working conferences offer individuals a unique potential space in which to be playful and creative between themselves and the environment of the conference. In turn, this experience can be transferred to other interfaces with environments. Working conferences can, of course, only provide a potential space that is analogous to Winnicott's cultural space. But, given that members have the opportunity, if they take the authority, to regress in the service of the ego—to experience, as adults, disarroy—within framed and contained time, space, and task boundaries of a conference and its events, the possibility of a novel cultural space being evoked and experienced is enhanced.

In the same paper, "The Location of Cultural Experience", Winnicott goes on to describe the third area, which is the one between "the inner or personal psychic reality and with the actual world in which the individual lives" (1971, pp. 102–103). Within the framed events of a conference, the possibility of rediscovering and remarking experiences in the third area is always possible (cf. Turquet's discussion reported above).

The search for the third area has preoccupied me for a number of years in the course of my professional practice as a consultant at the Tavistock Institute. By this I mean that I am trying to make opportunities for my client and myself to clear a third area for play and cultural experience. In relation to the subject of this chapter, I am aware how easy it is to have that area made into a desert full of memories and desires, rage for order, and a hatred of learning. How I have tried to struggle with a tradition, but avoiding psittacism and aphasia, in order to develop some something fresh, I shall now try to outline.

Outwith the frame

The leap beyond the existing framed events of working conferences to the interstices or gaps between them is what I now want to explicate. And here I am in difficulties in the role of a writer: on the one hand, I am under an obligation to communicate directly, but, on the other hand, I know that the thought processes that led me to explore beyond the frames into a fresh area for me were not strictly logical. My dilemma is well stated by McLuhan and Nevitt:

Beyond Exposition for Exploration
Civilized, rationally educated people expect and prefer to have problems described and analyzed sequentially. They try to *follow* your argument to a conclusion. They expect the conclusion to be your *point of view*, illustrative of your *values*. In contrast to the method of exposition is the method of exploration. This begins by the admission of ignorance and difficulties. Such statements will tend to be a tentative groping. The

blind man's cane picks up the *relation* of things in his environment by the quality of resonance. His tapping tells him what objects are adjacent to his stick. If his stick were *connected* to any of these objects, he would be helpless so far as orientation was concerned. This is always the plight of the logical method. It is useless for exploration. Its very strength makes it irrelevant. "Proof" of sanity is available only to those discharged from mental institutions. [McLuhan & Nevitt, 1972, p. 8; italics in original]

I hold to the idea of exploration of the interstices between the framed events about which I have been puzzling. What resonates in the spaces between them? So I cull a number of ideas from the text so far:

- frame, contour, space;
- order; psychotic, heart of darkness;
- "We penetrated deeper and deeper into the heart of darkness";
- "It was very quiet there . . ." (Joseph Conrad);
- memory, desire, the institutionalization of words;
- "I wouldn't be starting from here";
- makar;
- fugue;
- singleton, I., I.M., M.I., I. (Pierre Turquet);
- dislocation, disarroy;
- matrix = a place or medium in which something is born;
- "and live the space of a door that opens and shuts"(Samuel Beckett);
- the third area (Donald Winnicott).

To these I add other associations:

- Making it new
- In a land heavy with stones
- And each stone has a history (Robin Fulton);
- Interstice, gap, hiatus, lacuna;

- Ectopia, from the Greek εκτοπος = out of place, and in New Testament Greek, τοπος = desert; it can also mean a person's final resting place where destiny brings him;
- counterpoint, contrapuntal

And bear in mind:

> In any cultural field *it is not possible to be original except on a basis of tradition*. Conversely, no one in the line of cultural contributors repeats except as a deliberate quotation, and the unforgiveable sin in the cultural field is plagiarism. The interplay between originality and the acceptance of tradition as the basis for inventiveness seems to be just one more example, and a very exciting one, of the interplay between separateness and union. [Fulton, 1971, p. 99, italics in original]

But also think about:

> The visionary artist is the artist of the irrational, the obscure, the monstrous: his values lie not in order and discipline, but in inspiration, whether sublime or perverse. His subject matter is not the everyday world, but the ancient and dangerous archetypes which lie hidden in the deepest regions of the unconscious. If the danger to the psychological artist is barrenness, sterility, a vitality-destroying discipline, the danger to the visionary artist is incoherence, or even madness. To reside absolutely at one or the other pole means at the very least artistic death: either sanity bought at the price of sterility, or immediate experience of the unconscious at the price of psychosis. [Day, 1973, p. 468]

And:

> The spaces between the stones is where the survivors live.
>
> [Robin Fulton, 1971]

At Santiniketen, north of Calcutta in India, is the ashram of Rabindranath Tagore. There can be seen a sufficient number of his pictures to understand his development as an artist. His pictures are of an abstract nature. They arose directly out of his writing. As he corrected his poems by heavily scoring out words, lines, and whole passages, he found that the deletions made patterns. These he elaborated subsequently into paintings. What was ground be-

came figure. In much the same way the event I am about to describe arose out of the ground that was the figure of working
conferences.

Because of the kind of puzzlement that I have indicated in the
first part of this chapter, I had been brooding about an event that
would be contrapuntal to other recognized events in a working
conference. What I was quite sure about was that the event had to
be grounded in the tradition of group relations training associated
with the Tavistock Institute. At one and the same time the event
had to be within the task, time and territorial boundaries of a
conference and be ectopic. It had to be an event that provided
opportunities for both members and staff to take authority to be
out of their framed, ordered places in the conference life so that
they could look at the regular, framed events with fresh wonderment.

My anxieties were (and still continue to be) many: would I be
betraying the tradition from which I have derived so much?
Would I be in danger of creating an event with insufficient boundaries that would result in the anxieties of both staff and members
becoming so high that nothing could be learned? Was I in danger
of creating an event that would have untold effects on the work-
ing-through of transference and countertransference feelings that
are critical for the discovery by members of their authority to
interpret? Indeed, would the event be an elaborate system to defend against the staff's anxieties about transference feelings? How
far was I caught up in destructive feelings about conferences because of my growing disillusionment about the technicians?

The Praxis Event

The new event—the Praxis Event—was introduced at a working
conference at Gif-sur-Yvette in France in 1978. The title of the
conference was "Exercising Authority for Social Innovation", and
it was sponsored by the Group Relations Training Programme of
the Tavistock Institute of Human Relations and La Fondation
Internationale de l'Innovation Sociale, Paris. The conference programme included conference plenaries, a large study group, an

institutional event, and the equivalent of review and application groups, which were called innovation study groups. The primary task of the conference was:

> "To provide participants with opportunities to learn about and interpret their experiences of managing personal and social innovation within the organizational boundaries of the conference."

The French conference, because of its primary task, could allow for a new venture in group relations training. In particular, I wanted an event that would allow different opportunities for managing personal and social innovation than were available within the framed events. There had to be an opportunity for action and practice—that is, praxis.

With the authority of the staff as collective management, I, in the role of director, negotiated a primary task for the praxis event in a plenary session. The negotiation of a primary task was seen as being an essential element of the event, because it would not be given as in other events but be worked through in plenary sessions. The criterion that was made explicit was that the primary task of the praxis event had to be congruent with the primary task of the conference. What was set were the time and territorial boundaries of the event.

In the opening plenary of the event the point was made that once a primary task to which participants could give their authority had been negotiated, the director would give up his role for the period of the event, as would staff cease to be management and consultants. During the period the administrators would hold the conference management role. This is no different, in fact, from times in any conference when all the staff are deployed in consultant roles to events. Here the punctilious establishment of boundaries was to create the optimum conditions for containment and dependability in order that members and staff could be free to manage their explorations within the praxis event. Roles within the praxis event arose out of the primary task of the event.

I see little point in describing what took place during that first praxis event. I want to avoid premature institutionalization! My experience has been that each one is different. Now that it has been incorporated into other working conferences, I find, in terms of conference design, that it is better to have the praxis event before the institutional event, because what is learned from the former gives a new political dimension to the latter.

Rather, I want to give three associations. First, a participant in one praxis event subsequently wrote to me, enclosing a quotation from *The Selections from the Prison Notebooks* of Antonio Gramsci:

> The philosophy of praxis is consciousness full of contradictions, in which the philosopher himself, understood both individually and as an entire social group, not merely grasps the contradictions, but posits himself as an element of the contradiction and elevates this element to a principle of knowledge and therefore of action. [Gramsci, 1977]

What I take out of this is the notion that an individual is a social group in the sense that we each carry in our inner worlds a cluster of imagos of all our previous relationships and also a version of society in the mind. In addition, each person has the potentiality and possibly the experience of a range of roles. Some of these may be contradictory—for instance, a manager who is concerned about productivity, production, and profit is also a citizen who may have different views about the effect of some work practices on individuals. Such an individual may also be the parent of a young school-leaver who may not be able to get employment, and so on. The contradictions are apparent but are often not available for scrutiny in everyday life. This is because rarely can a way be found for doing so. So a praxis event can provide a space where societal puzzlements can be engaged with.

Second, it was within a praxis event that I discovered afresh what I shall call the Moment. I am aware that others have used this term and given it their meaning. For me, it is the discovery of an internal space where one has never explored—it may be between the first and second skins, which Turquet described, but I am not sure. The experience is of being in internal disarroy and then being able to put together feelings in a new way—for example, something of one's personal history and the present. It is a moment of internal making and is purely of feeling. It is the nearest I have come to what I understand to be an epiphany—that is, any moment of great or sudden revelation. My guess is that the praxis event provides a different kind of framed space and time for personal and social exploration than do other events. This is because it has a short history to date, is ectopic in the sense that roles are different from other events in a conference, provides a third area, and allows opportunities to experience a matrix rather than a group as such. Perhaps the strength of the praxis event rests in its contrapuntal quality—that is, being in the interstice of other events. Such conditions are conducive for self and social revelation.

Third, for a long time I have been disillusioned with the technical preoccupations of participants in conferences. At worst, this is a schizoid type of leadership that is very competent about the Tavistock method, group dynamics, and so on. Such leadership takes a long time to fathom because those in that role are very adept and skilled in interpretations. If this kind of leader is in the membership, he or she will be supported by others even though they become victims of the desperate processes that are engendered. Group psychosis is manipulated on such occasions. Such leadership is difficult to interpret because the leaders use interpretation in the service of the defence of their own egos. Hence, I am concerned to find complementary ways of understanding group phenomena to break some of the rituals I pointed to earlier in this chapter to get through to disarroy.

It is therefore through experiences in working conferences of the Tavistock, particularly the large study group and the praxis event, that I have been led to explore a different language to express what I feel groups are about. The praxis event, because it is new, results in one not being prey to memories and desires. In other events it is a conscious act to forget. Hence, privately, I find myself using words such as "soul" and "epiphany" to give meaning to experiences.

* * *

To conclude: I have tried to set out some of the thoughts that led to a new event within working conferences in the Tavistock (Bion) tradition. Despite my misgivings, I still feel committed to the kind of exploration of the unconscious and infinity that working conferences offer. Why? They are one of the few locations in time and space where individuals have a chance to reflect on the connections between private troubles and public issues—the nexus between the individual and society. For me, the experiences of working conferences with their framed events, and now having gone beyond the frame into the praxis event, have offered a glimpse of the "roots of creativity of the visionary artist" which Jung first described (cf. Day, 1973), to enter the heart of darkness.

I end with a seeming paradox: in framing the praxis event, by wresting potential experiences from the interstices between other framed events, I have drawn a contour, but, as is known, contours can signify arrest because they involve the acceptance of limits and restraint. But, in fact, as George Eliot observes in the Finale to *Middlemarch*: "Every limit is a beginning as well as an ending."

CHAPTER SEVEN

Emergent themes for group relations in chaotic times

I have given the name "immediate Transcendence" to that which has been experienced in the presence of a terrible negative element (The Third Reich), and can be consciously apprehended today and made our intellectual property. This immediate Transcendence and the whole depth dimension of life that forces itself upon us has, as its second face—without our necessarily having to invoke a personal God—godlike features. It is at once the existence, combination and actuality of exalting and purifying powers that carry us . . . and all humanity beyond ourselves, and is thus, properly speaking, transcendent and divine. No demonology of any kind is to be understood here. The Dark-Daemonic whose workings we have doubtless all felt only gives us the hem, as it were, and we ourselves have then to ring up the curtain on an all-embracing, all-permeating, omnipresent sphere of metaphysical forces lying immediately behind us and behind the phenomenal world.

A. Weber, 1947, p. 161

My task is to outline the thoughts I have for the development of the tradition of "taking" groups begun by Wilfred Bion as a way of understanding them and the contexts—institutional, societal and, I shall now add, cosmological—in which they are contained.

As, probably, for everyone interested in working conferences, it is the interplay between—or in the spaces between—consultancy and conference experiences that fascinates me because it is such a key source of thinking. And I cannot imagine a professional life without the experience of conferences.

Development—a working hypothesis

The first working hypothesis I offer is that

> development is a function of the capacity of members of an institution to extend the range of their interpretative voice through managing authoritatively the continual interpretation and making of their inherited tradition in relation to changing circumstances, both in the inner and in the external environments of their institution

(such as the A. K. Rice, the Tavistock, and all the others).

The obvious way of thinking about development is to think in terms of creating new institutions and going out to conquer, or colonize, the world in some measure. That seems to me to be putting the emphasis in the wrong direction. Rather, I am concerned to say that it is the development of the individuals within existing institutions that will fortify our interpretative voices in our environments.

I am putting the emphasis on institutional management rather than on the individual because I feel that if in the 1950s and 1960s our preoccupation was with dependency, autonomy, authority, and independence, which our institutions reflected in their structures, the possible challenge for a future is to create new forms of symbiont relationships not only between institutions but also among their members.

Bion's formulation of the nature of the possible relations between the creative mystic/genius and the Establishment gives us a
way of looking at and understanding how new ideas are dealt
with by the Establishment of an institution (Bion, 1970, pp. 62–82).

All I am saying is that within each Establishment (A. K. Rice,
etc.) there can be a possibility of working productively with the
mystic-genius–Establishment hypothesis, while taking into account the destructive aspects, in order that the relationship can be
symbiotic rather than commensal or parasitic. As Bion puts it:

> The institutionalizing of words, religious, psychoanalysis—all
> are special instances of institutionalizing memory so that it
> may "contain" the mystic revelation and its creative and de-
> structive force. The function of the group is to produce a
> genius; the function of the Establishment is to take up and
> absorb the consequence so that the group is not destroyed.
> [Bion, 1970, p. 82]

Clearly, the resources for development are members of the staff
that has been built up over the years. More particularly, I believe
that it is the institutional management's task to provide resources
for staff to develop themselves, including the bringing on of new
staff members, which should be the priority of the institutions
established to further this Bionic work.

The interpretative voice

We connect with participants in working conferences, and with
our everyday clients, through our interpretative voice and, sometimes more importantly, through our experience of lacking it. And
it is the nature and quality of that voice that interests me.

The metaphor that I use to convey my thoughts is that we
can understand groups of whatever size as being a spontaneous,
spoken text produced by the participants of their perceptions
and constructions of the realities of their contexts. The context is:
the individuals participating (within the context of their psychic
skins), the group, the conference, the society, the world, the uni-

verse, and the cosmos. Through participating in the group as a member, a text of what the truth of the reality is and could be is brought into being.

If you will, as we participate in our taker roles, we are using as a starting point the syntax of Bion on the Work Group and the Basic Assumptions, together with the added Basic Assumption of Oneness of Pierre Turquet, and BaMe-ness (Lawrence, Bain, & Gould, 1966—see chapter five). There is a good deal else besides: the syntax of psychoanalysis and of systems theory. In our "taker" roles our interpretative voice contributes to what cannot be put into speech, what is subliminal and is before the word.

* * *

My second working hypothesis is that

> the tone and quality of the interpretative voice will be related to four capacities on the part of the "taker":
>
> 1. the recognition that what is known is only compatible with the existence of knowers;
> 2. that there has to be a thinker to think thoughts;
> 3. that these two are related in the capacity to experience the various contexts and their inter-relatedness in terms of "container and contained";
> 4. the recognition that the spontaneous spoken text of the group is a selection from the "condensed material" that is potentially present in the context of the group.

To elaborate on these ideas:

> "The only things that can be known are those compatible with the existence of knowers."

This is Greenstein's Anthropic Principle, which is a remarkable device because, as he writes in his book *The Symbiotic Universe*:

> It eschews the normal methods of science as they have been practised for centuries, and instead elevates humanity's exist-

ence to the status of a principle of understanding. It operates in the realm of alternate realities, asking what the universe would have been like had some features of reality been different, and whether life would have been possible in such a circumstance. If the answer is no, we can be sure that features could not have been other than it is.

It involves a pretty trick of logic. Raise up your hand and look at it; you are observing yourself. But you are part of the universe—as you look, the very cosmos is observing itself. Now turn and glance at a tree. The very universe is still observing itself. Study the distances to the stars and the structure of atomic nuclei; still, one piece of the universe is observing another. Through our existence the cosmos has become self-reflective. But a cosmos devoid of life is unable to perform this remarkable trick.

One of the functions of these resonances is to ensure that their existence be known. [Greenstein, 1988, pp. 47–48]

While this notion, in some version, will always have been present for us, it does bring forth the thought that a group, of whatever size, is a mirroring of the cosmos in the mind. To extend this further: a working hypothesis could be developed showing the links between forms of organizations and the various interpretations of heaven propounded through the years. Hierarchies, for instance, may just be a secular rendition of Dante's *The Divine Comedy* or Swedenborg's spiritual universe.

The second idea—that there has to be a thinker to think thought—I take from Bion. In *Attention and Interpretation* he sets out his thoughts on a scientific approach to insight in psychoanalysis and groups. I am aware of the complexity of what he says; aware that thoughts thought can be a lie. I find myself continually perplexed by the capacity of conference staffs to create lies that they come to believe in order to preserve the staff group and its relationships.

The third idea is that neither of these is possible unless we possess the capacity to experience. More particularly, it is always the difficulty of experiencing our experiences, particularly those we have not experienced before. And here we should add, again to use Bion, to have the capacity not to know, to be able to suspend memory and desire, and, in short, to be available for Negative Capability.

The fourth idea is around condensed material. Presumably, like others, I am fascinated by what might not be being said in a group, and in awe at the amount of history and imagination—sometimes accessible, often not—that is in the group. It is the condensed material relevant for transferential discourse and exploration that one is trying to unlock. But also the participants in a group, including the taker, "are in the immanence of a significance that transcends them. This significance we give the name the unconscious" (Kristeva, 1987, p. 61).

I come back to the idea of the spoken text, which is a very small selection from the condensed material possessed by the unconscious but through experience can be known and thought on. The taker, for the most part, is the "container" for the thoughts of the participants. In this, of course, the taker "needs to have the capacity for reverie" in order that the participants can oscillate between the paranoid-schizoid position and the depressive one as they think thoughts on their experience.

(Parenthetically, I often wonder whether we should re-name the depressive position the "impressive" one, because it is the one that is reality-oriented on the part of the experiential thinker. The thinker becomes "impressed" in a variety of ways with realities that, while depressing because idealizations can no longer be held in the same way, is not repressing and can be liberating.)

Linking back to the proposed primary task of development: if the management of the institution (the Establishment, if you will) can carry, at times, the capacity for reverie, it could aid the mystic-genius/Establishment process and heighten the quality of experiencing, thinking, and finite knowing in relation to the infinite unconscious.

But this is not enough, for it is through the ability to entertain both the mystic/genius and the Establishment within each of us that the interpretative voice will be strengthened individually and collectively.

Aspects of the inherited tradition

As I have said, we have inherited a syntax for understanding group behaviour which was first formulated by Bion. More particularly, we have inherited and continue to make a methodology for understanding how one "takes" groups. There is a sense in which methodology is an understatement; for me, it is a way of life and thinking.

In thinking about development, I reflect on the history we have developed. Bion's ability to experience, to know (and, of course, not-to-know), and to think thoughts is well illustrated by Eric Trist in his chapter, "Working with Bion in the 1940s: The 'Group Decade'", in Malcolm Pines's *Bion and Group Psychotherapy*. Trist gives us an account of how Bion formulated the concepts of "group mentality" and of the basic assumptions. While he was struggling to formulate his hypotheses on the latent basic assumption and came up with the idea of the proto-mental level, Bion was aware that:

> he might be on the path of building a closed theoretical system and that he might even end up with a delusional product. Was he a bit mad to be giving serious attention to such ideas?

Trist continues,

> I replied that he had to have the courage of his logic, which had indeed led him to strange conjectures. The question of madness would arise only so far as he ceased to look for evidence to confirm or disconfirm them. [Trist, 1985, pp. 32–33]

Even though at times there is the risk that the basic assumption formulation can be treated as if it were a closed theoretical system, it was one of the gateways to a psychodynamic image of man based on psychoanalytic thinking and systems theory. The shift that Bion made was from using psychoanalysis in an ideographic way to a nomothetic one. And so we, today, can use psychoanalysis as a tool of cultural enquiry.

Trist also believes that after Bion's journeys into psychoanalysis and his study groups, there was a third path waiting for him, which is at the point of take-off in the last chapter of *Experiences in*

Groups (1961). We can only speculate what that journey would have been, but Bion does write of the badness of the group, and he does write of God and the Deity.

Aspects of the changing environment

When one re-reads the early writing of the workers at the Tavistock Institute, one is struck by how far ahead of the times they were. The formulation of socio-technical systems and of social systems as a defence against anxiety is a landmark in the history of psychodynamic thought.

It is an even more remarkable achievement when one considers the salient scientific culture of the times. The cultural context in which Bion and the early workers of the Tavistock had to operate was the post-war one of reconstruction and the beginnings of a firm belief in the efficacy of social engineering that had its flowering in the 1960s and 1970s.

The scientific context was one in which there was a belief in scientific methods based on logico-positivism. And it is clear that the kind of hermeneutic scientific method held today by us would have been decried, if not denied, at the time in the universities of the West, which are the key opinion-makers on such matters. (The hours each of us may have spent as students in learning social scientific methods based on a nineteenth-century version of the natural sciences, and fighting them if not intellectually at least intuitively, does not bear thinking about in late middle-age!)

From the tradition pioneered by Bion, we can make working hypotheses today on the nature of the psychic relatedness, taking into account both the conscious and the unconscious, among human beings in groups, institutions, and societies; and doing so using psychoanalysis as a tool of cultural enquiry, not in any therapeutic fashion.

In the late 1970s, simply by taking what was already contained in the Bion literature and the writings of A. K. Rice, coupled with experiences of working in conferences and in various institutional contexts, we were able to make more explicit the links between the forms of political organization that may be present in industrial institutions, for example, and the psychic constructions people had to make in their minds to endure in such organizations. This making explicit of the psychic and political dimensions of life in any kind of context is one that we can never lose. It is now part of our interpretative voice.

But the environment for receiving these ideas has changed enormously since the immediate post-war years. We now live, it is being more and more acknowledged, in an ecosystem—"turbulence" and "flux" are now part of the vocabulary of managers. The understanding of this may be reduced to understandable social, political, and ecological issues; but there is a lot more to be taken on board than just saving the whale.

There has been a revolution in the natural sciences. Starting from Einstein with his theory of relativity, our notions of space, time, and matter have taken us a long way from the Cartesian–Newtonian mechanistic view of the world, because that does not make sense any more. What is now emerging is a systemic view of the Earth in the context of a universe and a cosmos.

James Lovelock, the British scientist, has gone so far as to introduce the Greek goddess of the Earth, "Gaia", to explain this systemic connectedness, arguing that life goes on because the atmosphere and the seas and the Earth's crust and life on Earth all form part of a single living organism.

> The science of Gaia is new, exploring the planet-wide homeo-static process in which we share. But the concept is old, a rediscovery of what all earlier peoples have known. We are, in Lovelock's words, "part and partners in a very democratic entity". Formed of the fabric of Gaia, living amid the web of interdependent species and the traces of past lives, we cannot conquer nature without defeating ourselves. Recognition of this truth is fundamental to peace. [Barnaby, 1988, p. 10]

Whether or not one accepts the notion of the re-invention of the goddess Gaia, the fundamental hypothesis of being systematically connected cannot be denied. And Bion, metaphorically, intuits this.

What is stunning is the congruence between the methodologies of the new natural science and the methodology that we have inherited from Bion and from psychoanalysis in general. The new "scientists recognize that they are in the world of the imagination and recognize that Truth is always in a state of becoming". In some measure, the scientific culture has caught up with our kind of hermeneutic methodology. There is a new kind of sanction of what we represent.

So, as we try to interpret our environmental contexts, there is much more to be experienced of it and much more to be understood scientifically about how events and phenomena are systematically related.

* * *

My third working hypothesis is that

> we can continue to have development in our work if we can be extending the range or domain of our experiences of the contexts in which we live, including being aware of the accounts of experiences being formulated by contemporary natural scientists.

As the environment changes, the quality of our interpretative voice will be directly linked to our experiencing through feeling and perceiving, linked to knowing, not knowing, thinking thoughts, and testing for lies. I do not necessarily see these processes as being related in a linear fashion but, rather, as being systemically related.

Bion's formulation of the group as being a whole that is greater than the sum of its parts represents the systemic that has been taken much further by contemporary natural scientists in terms of the contexts in which we live. Bion was interested in the unconscious present in social configurations. That unconscious represents the transcendent, which is present, or immanent, in everyday life. So we can begin to make links between the systemic environment containing human beings who bring that environment into life, so to speak, in terms of knowing (the Anthropic Principle), both consciously or unconsciously. The moment we recognize these complex interconnections, we are taken beyond immediate phenomena and beyond ourselves. If you will, we are cognizant of the existence of metaphysical forces, which I prefer to refer to loosely as the "spiritual".

* * *

My fourth working hypothesis, then, is that

> future development will have to take account of the spiritual aspects of group life in addition to the psychic and political.

Here, I want to make quite clear that I am not talking about God and religion, which could be mobilized as a defence against the anxiety of dealing with a large totality than we have hitherto imagined that now is being developed by the contemporary natural sciences. But I am thinking that each generation has to re-make its imago of how people and all the things of the Earth are related in the context of the cosmos, and that this will be represented in some measure within the group, of whatever size. For example, we can infer the imago of God held by religious by disentangling their immediate here-and-now relations to authority.

While we may be more aware of ecological issues, however, we nevertheless experience ourselves as living in a world that does not make sense because it is perceived as chaotic. There is clearly not a truly symbiotic relationship between human beings and their environment. If anything, looking at the history of industrialization as it has unfolded, it is a parasitic one. Between human beings themselves there is little symbiosis—just taking into account the wars of this century and the terrorism that appears to be escalating.

At a more mundane level, in conferences we are often presented with a membership that brings into its context a mirroring of its experienced feelings of alienation, fragmentation, anxiety, and fear.

It is a puzzle to find even modest interpretations that can articulate and explicate a systemic view of the cosmos and the behaviour of men and women on the earth. There is a "badness of the group"—evil, if you will—that is present, which I now see as another aspect of transcendence. At the same time, I am aware of the dangers of being caught in omnipotent and omniscient interpretation.

I ask myself why the spiritual, or explorations of the transcendent, have rarely been part of the spoken text of conference life. At
worst, it has been denied; at best, it was heard by embarrassed
colleagues in silence.

To find some kind of an answer to this, I had to look at the
history of group study. The study of groups is a product of the
experience of the last major world war. It can be hypothesized that
it was the experience of social psychosis present in Europe in the
years before the last war and during it that gave the study of
group life an impetus. Before then, apart from Freud, McDougall,
and Trotter, the references are sparse.

Arnold Zweig, who was a friend of Freud, in his *Insulted and
Exiled*, published in 1937 starts his story—what he himself calls a
polemic . . . volleyed forth in a paroxysm of wrath—of the destruction of German Jewry with the events of 1933. In one passage he
describes what happens to people when they become part of a
mass:

> Groups are subject to a mental automatism which makes them
> think and act, not like grown-ups, but like children. . . .
> Groups react to truth as foolishly as children do. . . . The indi-
> vidual when incorporated into the group to which he belongs,
> loses precisely that amount of personal sovereignty which
> corresponds to what he accepts as a part of group-feeling. His
> understanding abdicates; his judgement becomes clouded; his
> need for intoxication, for the happiness of excitement for the
> delight of combining with other individuals by being fused
> with them into a mass, and of wherever possible, shuffling off
> on to a collective his individual responsibility for his existence
> and his actions—this need for abdication, this clamour for a
> leader who will mitigate fears of life and death, brings back
> the primal conditions of the horde into the clear light of the
> present. That is why the call to reason makes so little impres-
> sion on the masses, and why an appeal to their instincts is so
> decisive. [Zweig, 1937, pp. 43–44]

It was during the War that Bion had his important group experiences and immediately after that he formulated his hypothesis on
group behaviour. What marks off Bion—and the reason his hypotheses have stood the test of time—is that he started from the
psychosis that is present in groups. He had a capacity to see the

dark side of life—to connect the wish to be part of a mass, revelling in basic assumption land, with the abdication from being a mature work group member who proceeds to truth by testing hypotheses.

The fear of the psychosis of the mass must have been present in these war years. If we could understand more about that mass psychosis, we would be in a better position to address the puzzle of connecting the behaviour of human beings in the context of a cosmos that is a systemic whole.

To try to understand these years from 1933 onwards, in the closing stages of the war Alfred Weber wrote in his *Farewell to European History* (1947) offering new insights:

> An indefinable objective *something* broke loose that swept away values taken for granted and held to be unshakable, in a universal psychic wave. A collective super-personal force, chained and hidden till then, suddenly burst from captivity. Once it was out it was whipped up by every conceivable means and swamped, practically speaking *everything*.
>
> One can, of course, try to interpret it in terms of collective psychology or personal psychology, at will, by relating it to suggestivity and all its possible conditions, variations and assumptions. But we shall never grasp the real nature of a process like this.... It was the outbreak of forces certainly collective in origin, certainly stimulable by psychology and capable of being roused under certain conditions, but forces coming from greater depths than psychology ever plumbed. It was a sudden darkening of the mind that then set in, an occultation in which one felt the uncanny wing-beat of those powers whose effects one had read of in history books as the unaccountable appearance of psychic mass-epidemics, but which one had never appreciated as real, let alone actually possible within the body of one's own people. The wing-beat of the *dark daemonic* forces: there is no other term for their supra-personal and at once transcendent power....

Weber asks the question:

> Shall we, then, be so shallow-minded as to ignore the *deeper* level that is apparent here, the transcendental and the metaphysical level known to men of earlier times, of which but *one* aspect, one of its many sides has, under our very eyes, made

itself master of our lives for a spell? And if we come to grasp this level, even if only from this initial point to begin with, is that not the universal experience which will permit us to link up again, across a yawing chasm of nihilism, with bygone ages? [Weber, 1947, pp. 159–161]

Bion's recognition of the psychotic has placed us in a tradition of group thinking that is different from interaction analysis, T-groups, and so on. My hunch is that, very broadly speaking, there have been two developments on group psychology. One focuses on the person and personality, on growth and fulfilment, on creativity, and denies transference and, perhaps, the very unconscious. Here, I think of what I understand of humanistic psychology. The other strand to which we belong holds on to transferential issues but is aware of the destructiveness that can be present in groups of any size. This strand acknowledges tragedy and is prepared to live with Negative Capability and, following Bion's transformations into O, with mystery.

Oversimplifying, I want to find whether there are any connections, and alienations, between the Gaia-like qualities of the earth and the cosmos to the evil and good behaviour, conscious and unconscious, of human beings on the Earth, acknowledging the flux of both the creative and the destructive natural forces of the environment and human social process.

The terribly surprised soul

To further such a project, which cannot be defined in advance but has to be discovered in the "here-and-now" of the experience of being, I search for a way of experiencing, knowing, and thinking that will give cognizance to the possibility of the transcendent and the spiritual, both negative and positive.

* * *

Consequently, my fifth working hypothesis is that

a possible way of making such spiritual links is to re-invest meaning for the term "soul" or to re-make our imago of the soul for our times.

I am trying to use the term soul "as a transitional subject to get at the object", which is the truthful nature of the environment or the contexts in which we live. If you will, to rediscover the soul would be to begin to make transitions into creating richer and more elaborated texts in the sense I am using that word in this chapter.

A few years ago I published in French a short paper called "To Surprise the Soul" (chapter nine), which I took from a line of Emily Dickinson where she writes: "We must keep the soul terribly surprised." I took it that she meant that through the soul we can experience both the good and the bad of the contexts in which we live.

There is now a good-enough precedent for having the term in the English language to re-introduce the word "soul" into psychological discourse or, if you will, restore the psyche—that is, the soul—to analysis.

Poets are always allowed to use the word "soul", and, of course, religious have given it their own unique meaning in terms of the immortal soul, about which I have little concern because I do subscribe to Ernest Becker's (1973) idea that human beings are Gods with anuses who have to take responsibility for what they experience and create of what they inherited—an Earth aged over 4,500 million years. And here, I bear in mind William Alex's interpretation contained in his paper, "When Old Gods Die . . .":

> Deflated by loss of religious orientation and, concomitantly, enormously inflated through marvellous scientific, technological achievements, the ego of Western man now faces a new shock. It is the growing realization that science alone cannot do what 19th century man firmly believed it eventually would—the realization that it cannot control the potentially demonic forces inherent in the psyche of man. We are only too well aware, today, that no bomb ever exploded itself and no river or atmosphere ever contaminated itself. [Alex, 1971, p. 13]

As Bettelheim points out, Freud invited "us to follow him into the seeming chaos of the world of darkness of the unconscious and its irrationality". He, for instance,

> tried to correct and enlarge our ideas about our dreams and to instruct us about their meaning, hoping the familiarity with

the hidden aspects of our souls would permit us deeper, more complete understanding of ourselves. [Bettelheim, 1983, p. 69]

The point that Bettelheim makes, with the erudition of a native German speaker (pp. 45–61), is that the translations of ego, id, and superego are a misrepresentation of Freud's thought. He talked of the "I, the it, and the above-I", which are different aspects of the psyche all inter-related systemically with each other. This is more than talking about the mind and the intellect. As Bettelheim puts it:

> In the *Question of Lay Analysis* where he is conceptualizing the workings of the psyche, distinguishing the conscious from the unconscious, and distinguishing the functions of the it, the I and the above-I, he uses the term "soul" to describe what he regards as the overarching concept that takes in all the others. It seems natural to Freud to talk of man's soul. By evoking the image of the soul and its association, Freud is emphasizing our common humanity. [ibid., p. 71]

Freud, Bettelheim argues,

> spoke about the "structure of the soul" and the "organization of the soul" but these terms are usually rendered by translators as "mental apparatus" and "mental organization". Such translations are inadequate because they lose the exclusively spiritual meanings, which Freud had in mind when choosing his words. [ibid., p. 71]

The conflict in our soul between Eros and Thanatos can bring forth the worst and the very best in our thoughts and actions. Recognition of the worst possibilities—the destruction of all mankind—led Freud to his tragic view of life. But the best possibilities inherent in our soul sustained him even in deepest adversity.

In the end Thanatos wins, but the struggle in life to try to make Eros victorious is to live and enjoy the advantages of culture while recognizing that "An inescapable sadness is part of the life of any reflective person, but it is only part and by no means all" (p. 111).

Nowhere did Freud attempt to define the term "soul" and Bettelheim suspects that

> he chose the term because of its inexactitude, its emotional resonance. Its ambiguity speaks for the ambiguity of the psy-

che itself, which reflects many different, warring levels of consciousness simultaneously. . . . There is nothing supernatural
about his idea of the soul and it has nothing to do with immortality if anything endures after us, it is other people's
memories of us—and what we create. By soul or psyche,
Freud means that which is most valuable to man while he is
alive. [ibid., p. 74]

I have no wish to create any definition. I prefer it as a heuristic
concept to extend the range of experience and interpretation of
realities as they unfold in our minds. I can try to provide associations. For me, what is important in terms of the puzzle I have
given is that the soul, which includes but goes beyond the I, the it,
and the above-I, is the medium through which we are able to
reflect on our existence, not in a narcissistic way but reflecting a
state of rush.

Alan Bleakley, in his book *Earth's Embrace*, summarizes James
Hillman's exploration of the soul, contained in his *Archetypal Psychology: A Brief Account*, as follows:

soul is an unknown component that makes meaning possible.
Soul gives life and death meaning and purpose, the purpose of
life being the recovery of the perspective of soul. Soul "works"
through the metaphor of deepening, deepening events into
experiences: and has a special relationship then with the
mythical underworld and with death. Soul is communicated
in love; is at the heart of religious concern; and is the imaginative possibilities in our nature—the ability to experience
through reflective speculation, dream image and fantasy. The
language of soul is image. Soul is the middle ground between—body and spirit/mind. [Bleakley, 1989, p. 10]

If you will, going back to Freud, psychoanalysis is the giving of
meaning and speech to soul—making soul in our imaginative responses to the world.

Accepting what Weber wrote of the dark-daemonic, meaning
the transcendent and the divine, and holding on to what Bion
formulated about psychosis in groups, the finding of the soul may
help us to find an interpretative voice to address the puzzles of
living in contemporary societies in the context of a cosmos that is
in a state of becoming more and more known.

What I have been trying to say can be misinterpreted—at least from my perspective. And, of course, I can be totally wrong. I feel that, when speaking of this before, there is an attempt to split off what I might be saying about the possibility of recognizing transcendence in groups and institutions as being some introduction of religious ideas and therefore with no relevance for consultancy in industry.

Previously, I have been concerned to draw distinctions between what I call the "politics of salvation" and the "politics of revelation" (see chapter eight). Briefly put, my central working hypothesis was that consultancy, action, research, and, at times, the dynamics of conference staffs are driven by the wish to rescue, or save, other people from the life they have been experiencing by offering them some kind of redemptive message. This I contrast with the "politics of revelation", which is geared to fostering the responsible exercise of authority, both individually and collectively, so that people become generative of experiences, feelings, thoughts, and interpretation as part of the continuing process of knowing both the constructive and the destructive. Clearly, I am stripping the word "revelation" of any apocalyptic or prophetic connotations.

What I have said here is a continuation of that theme. In short, I have tried to offer a number of working hypotheses about development and its related processes for testing. The quality of development will be related to the nature of that testing by the work group characteristics of the members of the institutions for this kind of exploration of group life.

To conclude: I can summarize some of what I have been trying to get at through a quotation from Mircea Eliade:

> In the short story I'm writing (The Bridge), I am obsessed with getting across its secret meaning: the camouflage of mysteries in the events of immediate reality. Consequently, I want to bring out the ambivalence of every event, in the sense that an apparently banal happening can reveal a whole universe of transcendent meanings, and that an apparently extraordinary, fantastic event can be accepted by those who live it as something that goes without saying and at which they wouldn't even dream of being surprised. [Eliade, 1978, p. 205]

It is to a version of this "camouflage of mysteries in the events of immediate reality" to which we were introduced through the work of Bion. The "here-and-now" of group life is embedded in the historical and imaginative contexts of an unfolding cosmos. Can we lead ourselves on further to speak more elaborated texts of group experience in not only psychic and political terms but also in spiritual ones? If we do so, we might just be surprised by the occasional epiphany!

CHAPTER EIGHT

The politics of salvation
and revelation in the practice
of consultancy

The working hypothesis to be explored is:

There is the emergence of a paradigm shift from the politics of salvation to the politics of revelation in the practice of consultancy.

If you will, there is the beginning of change in the "mind set" that consultants bring to their work. In particular, I am concerned to explore the covert "scientific" thinking and related latent values that structure how consultants see the work relationships between their client–partners and themselves.

What are the processes of thinking that are leading to this change in perspective?

The twentieth-century heritage of thinking

Business, and consultancy, would be impossible without thinking and thought, for

> thought has a creative function ... to create what is there. In fact, almost everything we see around us in the world was created from thought, including all the cities, all the buildings, all the science, all the technology and almost everything we call nature. [Bohm & Edwards, 1991, p. 8]

To give a striking example: It was the capacity to work that caused Neolithic people at the end of the Stone Age in about 2,500 BC to start growing cereals and to begin to domesticate pigs, sheep, oxen, and goats. This remarkable leap in thinking transformed human beings of the time from being exclusively nomadic hunters, fishers, and gatherers of food to becoming settlers. From these beginnings agriculture as we know it developed. All of it has been achieved by thought.

The thinking and thought of our present century is characterized by a reliance on science and technology. This has been the century of staggering scientific and technological advances. The twentieth century began with one version of the natural sciences and is ending with another. Similarly, the thinking that has formed the social sciences has also been transformed, but to a lesser degree. This is because, for example, the methodology of psychoanalysis as it has developed since Freud, but particularly through the leadership of Jung, has always been striving for a celebration of the subjective and a recognition of the prime importance of the conscious and unconscious mind for the act of thinking.

The paradigm shift in the natural sciences in this century began with what can be labelled Newtonian–Cartesian ideas. They were founded, first, on an ontological assumption of separateness. The study of being and essences was conducted through the separability of observer from observed; of man from nature; of mind from matter; of science from religion; separateness of "fundamental particles from one another; separability of the parts of a system or organism to understand how it 'really' works; separateness of scientific disciplines" (Harman, 1992, p. 48).

The second assumption was epistemological (the theory of knowledge) and saw any scientific picture of reality as being based on empirical evidence derived from physical sense data. As Harman points out, from these two metaphysical assumptions have followed beliefs as to how knowledge of phenomena is gained.

The most important of these is objectivism—that is, the assumption that there is an objective world "out there", which can be studied by observation. Positivism assumes that the real world is what is measurable, and reductionism assumes that we come to understand phenomena by studying its elemental parts, such as "fundamental particles".

The ontological and epistemological assumption with which we began this century have their roots in the experiences of the greatest catastrophe to befall human beings in the known world. This was the Black Death, which began in Cathay in the 1330s and ended in London in the 1660s. It was an overpowering experience in that it carried off two thirds of the known population. Lasting as it did for over three centuries, it brought about a substantial shift in the way that people regarded their environment.

Both poor and rich were subject to the plague. The catastrophe caused people to become paranoid. They could no longer trust their environment, or, for that matter, the version of God that had informed their daily lives. They did not know the cause of the Black Death, and it took them a long time to discover ways of mitigating its consequences. Such a powerful destructive force ever present in people's lives had an effect on their thinking, which changed in two domains: that of spirituality and that of science. In actuality, the two were interdependent.

In the domain of the spiritual:

(a) The Divine was identified as being transcendent to the natural world. While this undoubtedly facilitates a deep and intimate Divine-human relationship it can also be seen as separating any idea of, what I shall call, god-ness from the natural world. If you will, the natural world becomes more profane and loses any quality that we might call "sacred".

(b) Within the Judeo–Christian tradition the focus in our

western spiritual tradition started to be on salvation dynamics to the almost exclusion of creation dynamics.

(c) There begins to be a constant presentation of Man as being transcendent to the Natural world.

(d) There grew a gradual belief in a transcendent future to which everyone should aspire and which is expected to usher in the millennial bliss. [McDonagh, 1982]

Each of these assumptions of transcendence has had far-reaching effects, if only unconsciously, in the minds of the peoples of the Western world—or, to update this, of the Northern Hemisphere. The first and second transcendence separate humans from the Earth–Cosmos creative dynamic, and the third and fourth from the natural world; and the fourth, in addition, shifts people's perspective from the "here-and-now" of existence to some future bliss, be it communism, fascism, democracy, or any form of millenarian belief.

All these transcendents together constitute a spiritual position. The word "spiritual" I use in the sense of "linking together". In particular, I am thinking of the linking "in the mind" of human beings to the Cosmos. In actuality, any previous linking together was ruptured. The Church of the times had the final say in what the nature of this linking was. But in a real sense the Church had failed and disappointed the people who had survived the Black Death.

The important consequence was that "in their minds" people became "dissociated" from the environment, which had now become persecuting. T. S. Eliot called this the "dissociation of sensibility" (Eliot, 1953, p. 117). More particularly, this transcendent–scientific perspective, which was forged as a result of the experience of the Black Death, produced resultant concepts, metaphors, and perceptions that give expression to "three pernicious dichotomies", as identified by Lawrence Cahoone (1988). (1) The split between subject and object—that is, mind and body, the inner and the outer world. (2) The split between the individual and his or her relationships (the solipsistic view point). (3) The split between human culture and the biophysical processes in which it is contained.

In the domain of science and the associated technology that it spawned, the ability to be an outsider to or split off from the environment meant, particularly through the invention of the telescope, that the world's phenomena were no longer seen as being part of a cosmic wholeness but, rather, parts of a complicated machine. This was the "new science" of the times.

From Galileo through Bacon, Descartes, and Newton there developed the version of scientific thinking that has just been described. The important point was that they were freed from the teachings of the Church and were able to explore reality as it seemed to be. This dissociation lasted until well into our present century. The result has been that human beings have come to see themselves as being in charge of their environment and that they can solve all problems.

This particular "mind set" of transcendent perspectives, which led to this version of science and of technology, is what lies behind the "Politics of Salvation".

Here, my working hypothesis is: the imago of the cosmos in the mind directly influences the nature of human beings' behaviour in and to their environment in which they make their experiences and co-create reality. This reality becomes a representation of the cosmos. Similarly, the cosmos in the mind is a mirror of the environment. They are mutually constructed through the psychic processes of projection and introjection.

The corollary is that if there is a change in the understanding of the nature of the cosmos, it will affect human beings' behaviour in the environment. This will include business behaviour.

For example, whereas at the beginning of the century people had a picture of Heaven and Hell as part of the cosmos, we end the century with no substantial belief in these. Piero Camporesi (1990) argues that the fear of hell has now virtually disappeared. For medieval people living through the Black Death, this was not the case. For most of us, as we near the end of the century, we have come to realize painfully that people make their heavens and hells on earth through their behaviour.

The politics of salvation

What do I mean by "politics"? I use the word in the sense of the "influence" of one person or party over another. By "salvation" I refer back to the salvation dynamics that were launched by the Black Death—in particular to the idea of a transcendent future.

The politics of salvation can be clearly seen in the missionary effort of the churches. The idea was to convert the heathen—that is, save them for Christ. And countries that developed empires were also caught in the same dynamic. To be sure, there were other reasons, but I am arguing that the principal rationale was to bring enlightenment to the savage.

The politics of salvation have been demonstrated through the "-isms" that have been a hallmark of our century: communism, fascism, capitalism, and, of course, democracy.

I took the idea of salvation originally from the "rescue phantasy" that can operate in therapeutic situations when the therapist loses sight of the task and becomes involved in trying to save the patient from whatever psychic ill they may be experiencing. In the dynamics of consultancy this is translated into "seeing the client system as being a system to be 'cured' and so offering solutions as a way of analysing unconscious material" (Dubbane & Lee, 1980; Lawrence, 1986, p. 62). There is in such situations an avoidance of the existential reasons for the consultants and client–partners to understand their present political, psychic, and spiritual condition.

In the practice of consultancy I think the politics of salvation can be seen in all the "packages" of interventions that are offered. One example, in particular, is the Quality of Working Life Movement. While this movement has laudable and the best of aims in a social justice sense, it is, nevertheless, based on the idea that the workers have to be saved from their conditions.

This century has seen the development of ideas on "social engineering". Essentially, I see the politics of salvation as giving solutions to people and not allowing them to define their life-situation for themselves and taking their own authority to alter it.

The emergent thinking
of the late twentieth century

What helped to cause the paradigm shift in the sciences in the twentieth century?—the discovery of quantum mechanics, to be sure. It was physicists exploring quantum mechanics who realized that they could not be like the classical scientists, standing behind a glass screen and observing, so to speak—scientists had to participate. Participation is the key word. It has two meanings now: "One is to 'partake of'. We partake of the whole within ourselves. The other is 'to take part in it actively'. Both are necessary" (Wijers & Pijnappel, 1990, p. 31).

This new understanding of "participation" has become being the essence of scientific enquiry, for it queries the idea of the scientist being behind a two-way mirror, watching what is going on, believing that the scientist is objective and divorced from the reality being observed.

The point here is that the scientist was no longer "dissociated" from the phenomena being studied. This method of experiencing through participation has been leading to new discoveries by scientists of all kinds resulting in a new version of creation dynamics, which turns on its head all previous notions of how the cosmos is organized and, therefore, the nature of the relatedness of human beings to their environment—that is, the ecosystem.

This change in orientation to methodology has far-reaching consequences. In particular, it has contributed to a new version of science. Now we have two new assumptions. They are:

(a) an ontological assumption of oneness, wholeness, interconnectedness of everything and (b) an epistemological choice to include all the evidence. [Harman, 1992, p. 49]

Under the rubric of "all the evidence", Harman includes:

- Those data admissible in the strict logical empiricism— namely measurements of physical parameters.

- Data depending on the connoisseurship of expert judges, such as those on which systematic (taxonomic) biology is based.

- Data which are essentially self-reports of subjective experience obtained in an environment that promotes high levels of trust and candour, subjected to sophisticated scepticism because of our known capability for self-deception, and checked in other ways wherever possible.

- The subjective self-reports obtained by "inner explorers" of various cultures. This includes the so-called "perennial wisdom" distilled from esoteric core experiences of the world's spiritual traditions. [Harman, 1992, p. 50]

James Lovelock has given meaning to the ontological assumption of wholeness. He found when studying the atmospheric chemistry of the earth that it could only be explained in terms of regulatory processes. Life on earth began, according to fossil records, 3,500 million years ago. Conventional theory is that species evolved in ecological niches. This, argues Lovelock, is far too simplistic, as life would have died out because of the natural processes of physics, chemistry, and biology, which would have destroyed the conditions that sustain life. Lovelock argues that life goes on because the atmosphere, the seas, and the earth's crust, together with all living things, all form part of a single living organism. He calls this living organism "Gaia", after the Greek goddess of the earth. Essentially, the idea of Gaia expresses the interconnectedness of everything that exists on earth. Here we can talk of "symbiosis". This is the mutual dependency between two organisms, such as a cow and the bacteria, which enable it to digest grass, which the cow could not do on its own.

There is another kind of symbiosis, however. This is the interdependence between the universe as whole, which is inanimate and not an organism, and the second partner, which "is alive, but is not any particular organism. It is not even an entire species. Rather the second organism is all organisms—life itself" (Greenstein, 1988, p. 189). Here, what is being pointed to is a gigantic symbiosis at work in the universe.

To understand this kind of symbiosis, we have to take account of the Anthropic Principle that Greenstein has propounded. This is: "The only things that can be known are those compatible with the existence of knowers." His hypothesis is that the cosmos brought forth life in order to exist. His argument is that for a single particle to exist, it must be observed. Subsequent steps in his argument are:

The first is to argue that what is true of a single particle is also true of a collection of particles: stones, planets—even the universe as whole. The implication is that the very cosmos does not exist unless observed. And the second step will be that only a conscious mind is capable of performing such an observation. [Greenstein, 1988, p. 223]

It is this kind of thinking that has made us realize at the end of the twentieth century that we live in an ecosystemic environment in which everything is linked to everything else. This holistic–ecological perspective is now fundamental. Systems theory, biology, and psychoanalysis are all holistic and so ecological. And it is this connection that is fundamental to spirituality.

My working hypothesis is that this paradigm shift causes a shift in the way in which we conceptualize consultancy.

To state this as succinctly as I can: the preoccupation of the politics of salvation is with change—that is, others holding power impose it from the outside on individuals or systems. The politics of revelation is preoccupied with the conditions and resources for the exercise of transformation that come from inside the person or system and are brought about through the people revealing what may be the truth of their situation to themselves and taking authority to act on their interpretation.

The politics of revelation

What follows I have to put in personal terms, because the thinking that goes into the politics of revelation can never be completed as by their nature they are always in an unfinished state.

My concern in consultancy and action-research is to create the conditions and resources for the politics of revelation to be realized on the part of the client–partner. This rests on the view that everyone who takes up a role in an organization has the capacity to manage him- or herself in that role. The idea of management of self in role was formulated by Miller and myself in the 1970s (Lawrence & Miller, 1976; chapter two), but it has never fully been realized generally. Ideas on Quality Circles intervened, for instance, which, if only unconsciously, were designed to give workers the impression that they were responsible for the management of their work. Essentially, Quality Circles never shifted the basic worker-management dynamic. It is an excellent example of the politics of salvation.

Now the idea of "empowerment" is to the fore. Miller describes his own work as directed at offering individuals methods for understanding the unconscious social processes they can be caught up in in order that they can gain greater influence over the environment in which they live and work. I am in complete agreement with his observations on the notion of empowerment. He writes:

> It is a term I avoid because of its ambiguity: between becoming more powerful and making more powerful. The notion of giving power is inherently patronizing—it implies dependency—and hence is of itself disempowering. Power cannot be given, only taken. That having been said, power and dependency are central issues for a consultant working with organizations. [Miller, 1993, p. xvi]

In the terms of this chapter giving power implies salvation—that is, rescuing others from their situation.

Consultancy and action-research I see as being conducted within a frame. This idea came in the late 1970s when with some Tavistock Institute colleagues I conducted an action-research study to launch democracy in a company, which I shall refer to as The Firm. The project hinged around the concept of System Future. Its primary task was to provide opportunities for the people in the Firm to explore what it was like to work there and consider what it could be in the future. As was written subsequently,

> Perhaps the most controversial aspect of System Future has been its initial organization. System Future was separate from the Firm. It started in our minds as being a symbolic space to which people could come on their authority to talk with us (the consultants) about their feelings, beliefs and wishes. We wanted to have the idea of people "seconding" themselves from the Firm to System Future for an interview or a discussion. . . . Space in this context also implies a time space, e.g., the duration of a discussion; a time out from life which would allow for reflection; a time in space to stand outside the skin of the Firm, so to speak. [Lawrence, 1980, pp. 72–73]

The encounters with the client–partner take place in what I now call, borrowing from Winnicott, the "third space" between the consultant and the client–partner. The key thought of Winnicott is:

> From the beginning the baby has maximally intense experiences *in the potential space between the subjective object and the object objectively* perceived, between me-extensions and non-me. The potential space is at the interplay between there being nothing but me and there being objects and phenomena outside of omnipotent control. [Winnicott, 1971, p. 100]

This potential space between mother and baby is a metaphor for the third space between the client–partner and the consultant. It is a cultural space in which meanings can be discovered. In the third space the "meanings" of the situation can be explored. Just what is meant by "planning" for example? What conceptualizations are there?

Winnicott, writing in his context, describes the "play" that takes place between mother and baby, which is the grounding for cultural experience. In the context of consultancy and action-research with adults in work roles I refer to the idea of "generativity", because the term "play" carries infantile associations.

What are the areas of generativity? The short answer is thinking and thought. Given that all business is reliant on thinking, not only for its day-to-day operations and the management of activities of conversion but also for anticipating the future by bringing new markets into being, the capacity to think is the major asset of the people in any enterprise.

Here it is useful to take the ideas of David Armstrong (1991) on thinking. He distinguishes between two kinds of thinking: Thinking 1 and Thinking 2. The former is characterized by thought or thoughts, which come out of the process of thinking and owe their existence to a thinker. Such thoughts are capable of exegesis, justification, and falsification. Epistemologically, thinking is prior to thought. In Thinking 2, thought and thoughts are epistemologically prior to thinking. Bion (1984) expresses the idea thus: "Thoughts exist without a thinker. . . . The thoughts which have no thinker acquire or are acquired by a thinker" (p. 165). Such thoughts are able to be voiced through the practice of attention and awareness. (See chapters one and four.)

All my consultancy work, in the last decade or so, has been pointing me towards trying to find ways of providing a third space between the client–partner and myself in role to be available for Thinking 2, because it is through this kind of thinking that innovation is more likely to happen.

Here, Bollas's idea of the "unthought known" is also useful. In consultancy we are preoccupied with the unconscious condensed material that is present in every encounter. We are vigilant to identify systems of defence against anxiety, following Menzies Lyth (1988), for example. It also is apparent to me that every encounter is pregnant with the thoughts about experiences in the client enterprise, which are known, at some level (the unconscious), but have not yet been thought and voiced. Bollas refers to genetically based knowledge that has not yet been thought of and constitutes "an inherited set of dispositions that constitute the true self" (Bollas, 1989, p. 10). In the context of an action-research project there are thoughts that are there in the enterprise, and are held by people about their experiences of work in the enterprise, which are unthought. The thoughts are in search of a thinker. The consultant becomes a temporary container for these thoughts to become available. It is this kind of thinking work that leads to insight. In my terms these are thoughts that come to be revealed—that is, they are a products of the politics of revelation. The essential point for me is about working with the client–partners in order to enable them to find their authority to interpret the psychic, political, and, possibly, spiritual realities in which they are working.

Even if there had been no paradigm shift in the natural and social sciences, the changes that are occurring in enterprises because of the use of Information Technology would cause consultancy to shift towards the politics of revelation.

Information Technology is transforming organizations. Everyone who has access to a personal computer can know equally about the information that is needed to manage. The old-style organization, where only senior managers had access to such information, is on the wane. There is an inevitable democratization process let loose in organizations because of IT.

Information Technology has been necessary because of the quantity of data that any enterprise needs to process into information for decision-making. Peter Senge makes a general point about organizations in the contemporary world:

> In an increasingly dynamic, interdependent word it is simply no longer possible for anyone to "figure it all out at the top". The old model, "the top thinks and the local acts," must now give way to integrating thinking and acting at all levels. [Senge, 1990]

The requirement increasingly is that people manage themselves in their roles at all points in the organization. The thinking that is required for people to do so is more likely to happen through the politics of revelation than those of salvation. Salvation is linked to the idea that there is someone who knows all, and the others have only part of the information.

In terms of leadership, we may have to rethink our conceptions of how leaders and followers are to be related in the future. Gilmore highlights one aspect of this in the context of changing forms of institutions:

> We may be approaching what Toffler calls "adhocracy". Our organizations are no longer the enduring institutions of old but assemblages of parts. The assemblage of a French designer, an American marketing organisation, and a Korean manager who join to produce a line of shirts may, within a year, shift some or all of its parts. Like movie-producers who assemble and disassemble the elements of a film, leaders and followers have to develop their skills at recruiting, joining, direction setting, organizing, and managing change among short-lived teams of people.
>
> We need to match hopes offering leaders who can articulate a genuine vision, infuse the organization with a sense of purpose, moderate conflicts, and defend the integrity of the enterprise with the realities of the instabilities of key relationships. [Gilmore, 1988, p. 247]

One consequence, in Senge's terms, is that the leadership task of tomorrow will be that of designers and not, in his terms, "crusaders"—that is, saviours. He sees the leader's task as being that of designing the learning process "whereby people throughout the organization can deal productively with the critical issues they face, and develop their learning mastery in the learning disciplines" (Senge, 1990, p. 345).

Following on these ideas, I want to introduce the concept of "symbiont management", which is a concept of organization that I am developing in a number of enterprises and take the opportunity to signpost in this chapter.

I take this concept from the ideas of Greenstein. If we have an imago in the mind that we are in a symbiotic universe, such an imago can structure the way we see actual relationships between ourselves and others and the environment in general and, what is our concern, relationships in the world of work. " Symbiont means an organism being in a state of mutuality with another" (Reid, 1962, p. 99).

One of the persistent myths of the late twentieth century is that individuals are autonomous—and this has spilled into the work enterprise. The idea of autonomy has been part of the aggressive posture that is often held in work enterprises. Aggression in work, particularly as associated with ruthless ambition, can ultimately destroy a work enterprise as, in turn, it destroys the aggressor.

We have tended to see businesses as being in competition with each other. However, I note the changes that are occurring. Managers of businesses are beginning to realize that they need to have what I am calling a symbiont relationship with their suppliers and, of course, with their customers. The motor industry, for example, which has always been characterized by aggressiveness towards both employees and suppliers, has moved to "lean production". What this means is that the authority for organizing work is in the hands of the people in the shop floor. What is also happening is that suppliers have long-term contracts, which contributes to high-quality components.

Conclusion

I have tried to outline ideas on the possible changes in consultancy practice from the politics of salvation to those of revelation. This is coming about through the changes in the methodologies employed, and the resultant conceptualizations of the natural sciences. At the same time, however, there are changes in enterprises themselves with the arrival of Information Technology, which changes authority relationships in the organization. What is also emerging is a greater emphasis on mutuality and support between role-holders rather than a reliance on competition, conflict, and aggression to execute particular primary tasks. This mutuality between role-holders questions ideas of individual autonomy, which has been a convenient myth of the twentieth century, for it has allowed people to justify their being dissociated from their environment of other people and whatever the cosmos may be.

CHAPTER NINE

To surprise the soul

We must keep the soul terribly surprised.

Emily Dickinson

Did the soul
Once see the universal mind,
And know the part, and know the whole?
  [*Sed mens* . . .
An cum mentem cerneret altam,
Pariter summam et singula norat?]

Boethius [c.480–524], *Consolations*, Vol. V, v. 20–21

Although it is an oversimplification, it can be postulated that until 1945 each individual had to struggle to make sense of a life, through achieving what he or she could to make it meaningful, while knowing, at the same time, that they must die. The agony and serenity of a life had, for the most part, a predictable but natural ending. Now that private interior drama, whereby the individual attains some heroic maturity, has to be set in the context of the public world drama of the fear of annihilation.

Man cannot deny that he has to live with the tragic fact that he has perfected the manufacture of death. Since Hiroshima in 1945, the extinction of humans as a species is a possibility. It can no longer remain an imagined, horrendous idea, as the Day of Judgement or Doomsday once could be. Man is also aware that even with limited technology, so to speak, he is capable of perennially resurrecting the Holocaust in different parts of the world. The technologies of death are in place for the annihilation of mankind. Man knows he can reverse the Genesis story.

While death is still a natural event and comprehensible as such because it is inevitable, it nevertheless can now be delivered as a consequence of political decisions and actions. And these choices may be exercised anonymously well beyond the control of individuals who feel that they are mature and have taken responsibility for their lives, irrespective of their political persuasions.

It is against this background that the questions that have always puzzled mankind take on a new poignancy, even urgency. As individuals, we find versions of our personal identity through periodically posing and pondering the question: Who am I? The other pivotal questions of a life link the individual more closely to humanity as a whole and, indeed, to the universe and whatever may lie beyond. These questions are: Whence am I? Why am I? Whither am I going? By posing and trying to find answers to these questions, the individual is caused to hear the echoes of history and the whispers of the spiritual, and to be anticipating the unknown of the future. But this can be so anxiety-inducing that the questions are rarely articulated, even privately, and so answers and further questions are avoided.

The answers to these questions for this generation, if made public, will depend on the state and awareness of the questioners. The working hypothesis being offered in this chapter is that in the West we could be on the edge of a new mode of awareness that could affect our collective interpretations of our existence. This edge is an anxious one, because it means scrutinizing the roots of our inherited modes of awareness and consciousness and trying to reach out to an emergent perception of reality that may proffer more questions than answers.

It will be against the spirit of this chapter if it as read as being a polemic. Too much harm comes from one set of people trying to convince another set that their point of view is right. This is intended to be an attempt to clarify some endings and beginnings in contemporary consciousness—wherever that might lead. By its nature and content, the chapter can be no more than a sketch of what the truth might be. If others are led to ruminate, it will have served its purpose.

It can be argued vigorously that our inherited modes of awareness have served Western humanity well because they have produced so much in the way of knowledge. The scientifically based technological achievements of this century are unsurpassed in history. At the same time, however, we have to live with the technology of death, and also make sense of a world in which drought and famine co-exist with space technology. Such paradoxes are so amazing that they are difficult to comprehend.

The capacity to be amazed and surprised may be a faculty that mankind in the West is in danger of losing. Despite the growth of psychology and the social sciences in general, man may already have lost the faculty of imaginative awareness and consciousness that takes him beyond his immediate, narcissistic preoccupations with survival in contemporary mass industrial society to link him with what may underlie existence. On the one hand, man knows he can manipulate what he classifies as the concrete realities of the natural world, but, on the other hand, he has an awareness of the existence of the supernatural. The latter is gossamer-thin and evanescent, so to speak, and may even be an outright intellectual construct without empirical substance. But it exists because it is experienced.

Once, Western man had a vocabulary to integrate these seeming paradoxes and mythically link himself and his life to what he intuited to be the universe. This faculty of imaginative awareness and consciousness was pre-eminently available when Western man could talk of the "soul" in everyday discourse. Now, that word is used almost exclusively by religious persons and, on occasion, by the poet.

The soul, it can be hypothesized, is that capacity of the mind to be self-aware and self-reflexive, and so it is the primary source of subjectivity. It is also the faculty of the individual to conceptualize responsibility and authority in relation to moral values, not just in the limited sense of good and evil, but in the larger sense of situating himself as a species in relation to a larger environment that can be destroyed or cherished by him. In this way he can begin to judge the limits between destruction and creativity; to be able to exercise will and rational freedom by discriminating among and judging his actions, which may be potentially creative and evil at one and the same time.

The near-demise of the soul has meant that man may have begun to lose the faculty or "instrument" to register surprise in a fundamental way. To keep the soul surprised is to be aware of and concerned about the predicament of mankind; to be alive to his destructiveness; to retain a shocked, uncompromising naiveté in relation to man's inhumanity to man.

The soul also bears the capability to experience wonder and awe in the face of creation, to ponder on what may lie behind the empirical facts, to be open to doubts, uncertainties, and mysteries by recognizing that the-thing-in-itself being contemplated will never be known absolutely. The soul nourishes truth as it becomes.

Such a series of suggestions as to the possible nature of what the soul could be would find no favour with some contemporary biologists, for instance. They would take the view that human beings are mere randomly organized chains of proteins and amino-acids whose purpose is to be machines for replicating genes. Because the soul cannot be identified materially, it cannot exist from this scientific perspective. But does this not mean that the complexity and preciousness of matter, however defined, is denied? Certainly from this perspective there can be no acknowledgement that matter might be connected holistically and even spiritually.

Such a view of human beings derives from a scientific perspective that structures patterns of apperception, awareness, and consciousness, which, in turn, determine the nature of truth.

A different perspective might reveal different versions of what the truth might be, or become. One of the exciting possibilities open to Western man as he enters the new millennium is that a different scientific perspective is being developed, which is a potential source of a new consciousness.

The question is: have we the courage to collapse our inherited, "traditional" scientific perspective, which is held by the majority in Western civilization, and engage with the new perspective, wherever it might lead us?

What can be called the "traditional" science has structured our twentieth-century consciousness. We inherited it originally from the Greeks, but Bacon, Descartes, and Newton formulated it. More accurately, our forebears made selections from their works. So, for example, the fact that much of Newton's experimental work was directed at alchemy has been ignored for the most part. In essence, however, the coupling of the philosophical principle that knowledge is only built up from self-evident propositions and their consequences, together with Newtonian laws of motion and causality, have resulted in enormous progress in the scientific venture and its technological applications. Such a view can have no place for what is "vague", which is deemed not worthy of attention, and hence what is termed holy or transcendental experience, which by definition is vague, has to be denied, irrespective of its vividness.

Such a view of the scientific endeavour is based now on a systematized pattern of perception (and therefore of awareness and consciousness) that starts from the assumption that reality is "out there"; is objective; and is independent of the observer. Reality, it is claimed, can be observed without changing it in any way. Traditional physics is based on ordinary sense perceptions and attempts to describe matter in terms of observable entities. These are composed of even more entities, which are situated in time and space and are related together in ways that can be determined by mathematical principles.

This system of science arrives at knowledge through the related processes of analysis, separation, differentiation, and splitting, intellectual processes that can only be applied to products of logical discernment. Nevertheless, this mode of generating knowledge led to the ultimate achievement: the splitting of the atom.

This construct of the scientific endeavour did not exist in a value-free cultural climate because it was paralleled and supported by classical Western spirituality. This made the Divine separate from and, therefore, transcendent to what became defined as the natural world. This allowed for and made possible a deep and intimate relationship between human beings and the Divine, but it also meant that the natural everyday world could not be a place where both the sacred and the profane could co-exist, interpenetrate, and illumine each other. The *numinous*—the totally other experience—had to be separated off and placed somewhere else other than in man's immediate environment.

By the same view, man had to be made transcendent to the natural world. Because the natural world was separated, and became alienated, from what can be felt to be the spiritual and the divine, man was justified in seeing and treating his natural environment as an object external to himself, which he had the right to use as he decided.

This right of manipulation became enshrined as a duty because all things on earth, by this definition, were construed as being in an unholy condition. Their usefulness could only be realized by man's capacity to transform them into something of value. The doctrine of "added-value" is at the heart of the contemporary industrial process.

As the consequent hubris of Western man waxed, so the "twilight of the gods" waned. Contemporary man has been near-successful in bringing about the demise of God.

Religious institutions may well have colluded with this as some of their protagonists have offered a theology that postulates that God is dead.

Religion, too, has at different points in history been distorted and used as a vehicle for millenarian fantasies that resonate with the unconscious anxieties of mankind who seeks ideologies and wish-fulfilment to quieten his fears. This phantasy that mankind will be delivered miraculously from his demonic destructiveness by the Saints of God, who will overthrow those seen as the oppressors and so inherit their true place of dominion over the earth, has echoed through history. So God, in a sense, was kept off-stage to be brought into the proscenium of the known world as a heroic saviour when life in it became unbearable.

To deal with his recurrent fears of being insignificant and of having a meaningless existence, and with his unresolved anxieties about death (which are often so powerful that their existence must be denied), men have had to create myths and ideologies to vivify the dream-world of mass man. Capitalism, communism, Marxism, Maoism, and all the other "-isms" have become the new religions. They attempt to provide rationales and answers as to how man can be connected with some hope to his immediate world.

But the world is forever situated in a universe which, by its mysterious existence, reminds man variously of death, chaos, mortality, nothingness, perfection, and also the experience of potential emptiness in the here-and-now of living.

The rise of the traditional science, as it is being called here, in Western civilization, together with its concomitant technologies, is associated with the near-demise of the supernatural and the near-liquidation of the theological enterprise. This scientific system of apperception has spread to other parts of the world and has become even more potent as it has been linked to the "-isms" of political ideologies. The death of other versions of "God-ness" (Hinduism and Buddhism, for example) is thus manufactured for new markets.

The concept of the soul-in-man, which appears to be common to all religions, thus has little to sustain it. Hence, only the rational, critical faculties of man can be mobilized to understand the world. There is little credence given to whatever might seem to be non-rational, or unconscious. It is therefore difficult for man to connect the outer world of science, economics, and politics with his inner world of dreams, of wonderment, of primitive anxiety, of the private acknowledgement that there might be something in the supernatural, the numinous, and that there might be a Divinity.

The paradox is that we may now be in a cultural state in which technology itself has become transcendent in the sense that it now has a quality of concreteness and potency that the spiritual once had for mankind. It is becoming apparent that the natural world of itself is losing its inherent power to limit the long-term consequences of man's application of technology. And man himself seems impotent to do so, even though he is not indifferent. There are ecological disasters aplenty to substantiate this proposition.

Technology, and the traditional sciences on which it is based, suffuses our lives. This is apparent from the language and metaphors that we use in the West. We do believe in "causes and effects". We talk of "engineering social change". We subscribe to "progress and achievement". We apply engineering terms to human beings with words like "stress". The metaphors we live by structure how we experience the world with its phenomena and events.

Western man—and increasingly the peoples of the East, as they continue to believe in this tradition, with its associated patterns of awareness, consciousness, and knowledge—seem to have the hope of salvation only through the power of politics. People have to invoke a sufficiently potent politic—such as a Star Wars policy, or SALT talks—that will vanquish their enemies. The preoccupation appears to be that there be a chosen nation that will survive any type of war. That nation, which will become an elite, will secure the future of the species. The resonance with millenarian fantasies is clear.

As mankind enters the first decade of the new millennium, however, some of us are now aware that despite the enormous triumphs of technology, which have suffused our language and consciousness while transforming our lives, technology is based on an inadequate system of perception and understanding of the nature of reality. Despite man knowing that this traditional path is likely to bring disaster, should what I am now to call the "politics of salvation" fail, he cannot turn back; indeed, he is compelled to go forward in his terms.

But one of the mysterious capabilities of mankind throughout history is that in the midst of his pre-occupations with the technologies of Thanatos, there still can be generated sufficient creative life force to sustain hope for humanity as a totality.

Out of the traditional sciences there has developed the new physics of quantum mechanics. A new story of creation and the nature of matter is being evolved in the secular scientific community, readily recognized as a story that is in a state of becoming. There is now through this development a possibility that mankind can discover a dynamic of creation that would render the politics of salvation redundant.

However, there is always a lag between the creation of a new story, or paradigm, and its acceptance by the larger community. Furthermore, science and technology have shaped the metaphors of our language, and so the gap will be that much harder to communicate across.

Given that the application of Newtonian physics to the Cartesian world view has brought humanity to the brink of annihilation in that humankind has proven it can reverse the Genesis story, can any new story of creation be heard in time to avert possible disaster? Can humans alter their patterns of perception, awareness, consciousness, and envisaging in time?

Why this new story? As physicists explored the nature of reality further, and further they found themselves having to abandon ordinary commonsense notions because they were being presented with a "raw" experience of what exists that could not be mediated by familiar concepts, and so they encountered paradox and uncertainty. The atomistic approach—and its related Cartesian- and Newtonian-based formulations—did not make sense any more.

The principal landmarks along this journey of scientific discovery have been Einstein's theory of relativity, Bohr's study of complementarity, the uncertainty principle of Heisenberg, quantum field theory, the Copenhagen interpretation of quantum mechanics, and Bell's theorem. Now there is the work of Bohm, who is developing these theories even further.

Quantum mechanics recognizes that reality cannot be pictured directly through the senses—however refined or sophisticated the scientific instruments to aid observation—but can only be imagined on the basis of second- and third-order data. The new physics is very much lodged in the domain of probability. The new physicists only claim to be able to correlate correctly experiences of reality. They describe the statistical behaviour of systems of matter and predict probabilities on the basis of existing, proven theories.

At the deep, sub-atomic level nothing exists in the way that we use that word ordinarily. Matter shows "tendencies to exist", and events show "tendencies to occur". At this level of exploration even the notion that there exist definable entities that exert forces on each other has vanished. They are related in other ways and in a holistic fashion that goes beyond our analytical, traditional understanding. Furthermore, for example, the idea that time has a linear, unidirectional flow has collapsed as it has been found that time can go backwards or forwards. Consequently, our received notions of causality are made inadequate.

The picture of reality that is emerging is of a holistically interconnected web that is not yet fathomed. It is not going anywhere. It just exists. It is. Perhaps, as Whitehead suggested, it is "pure thought".

This leap in apperception was made possible by the collapse of the myth, in the light of the evidence, that there is an objective world out there that is independent of us, the detached observers. As Heisenberg describes it somewhere, it is not nature itself but nature exposed to our method of questioning that we observe.

Scientists have stated that the new understanding of the issue is that it is the act of participation that is essential in the scientific posture, because in this way the universe is "brought into being" in some sense by the participation of those who participate.

The idea of participation in this sense brings us up against the symbols, language, and metaphors that we use to describe our awareness and consciousness of reality. The puzzle is to find expressions that will communicate the experience of the "suchness" of reality, which cannot be experienced directly in itself. This implies, as Planck put it, that the aim of science may be apprehended by poetic intuition but the intellect will never fully grasp it.

The experience of participation in this sense leads, as Bohm describes it, to a notion of unbroken wholeness which means that the classical ambition of analysis into parts, each separate and independent, may be impossible.

The mystics, who stood outside the predominantly accepted version of Western spirituality, echoed the experience of participation in the past.

The anonymous fourteenth-century author of *The Cloud of Unknowing* wrote:

> Therefore I will leave on one side everything I can think . . . it must be covered with a cloud of forgetting. And you are . . . to try to penetrate that darkness above you. Strike on that thick cloud of unknowing . . . and on no account think of giving up.

Anticipating Bohm, Meister Eckhart wrote:

> In the kingdom of heaven everything is in everything else. All is one.

The links between the mystic and the artistic and scientific pursuits have been clearly drawn by Einstein, who said:

> The most beautiful emotion we can experience is the mystical. It is the sower of all true art and science. He to whom this emotion is a stranger... is as good as dead. To know that what is impenetrable to us really exists, manifesting itself to us as the highest wisdom and the most radiant beauty, which our dull faculties can comprehend only in their most primitive forms—this knowledge, this feeling, is at the centre of all true religiousness. In this sense, and in this sense only, I belong to the ranks of devoutly religious men. [Einstein, quoted in Frank, 1947]

So the contemporary view of science takes us back to the place where thinking, sentient, awe-ing humankind has always been: facing the puzzle of creation with its mystery that can only be apprehended and comprehended if there is a subjective aliveness in the participator.

To be sure, we do not really understand this new story about the nature of reality. We can postulate that it is about cosmology though its lineaments are not known. Wholeness is there, certainly, but to develop a functional cosmology at present is an intellectually and emotionally daunting task. Indeed, it may be inconceivable at this time in history.

But some of us have to try to begin. A beginning might be made by being available for the experiences of participating in wholeness. But we can always avoid the experience, or not even experience it, by reverting to a predominantly analytic approach to reality.

It is the lacuna—the space, the gap, the interstice, call it what you will—between man and the cosmos that is the puzzle. To bridge that lacuna, in our minds, would be to re-interpret our patterns of understanding of our existence; to re-order our relationships with our physical, human, and potentially spiritual world.

This new story can all be explained away by invoking God, as the pious would do. But is that a good-enough response, for would it not be a betrayal of creation?

Certainly the churches, of whatever religion or denomination, could initiate an experiential enquiry into the implications of the links between the fact of death (with its contemporary political overtones), with the new awareness and consciousness that comes out of the new physics, and what we have learned to name as the supernatural, the spiritual, the numinous, the holy, the Divine.

This would be in the best of their tradition, as represented by the mystics of both East and West. Such an enquiry also could bring man to confront his imago, or non-image, of God. It is recognized that every succeeding generation must dissolve its imago of God and allow it to wither and elude his grasp; otherwise man becomes like his own idol. The image comes between him and what the image could represent and become. To take this kind of responsibility and authority to lead into re-interpreting the imago of God would be to re-interpret the Word in the light of man's potentiality to change his awareness of the cosmos and his place in it.

It is tempting to delegate this task exclusively to those who have an interest in religion. But irrespective of whether or not we believe in what can be called "God-ness", is it not important to try to re-interpret our contemporary patterns of existence?

We have seen where our traditional paradigms have taken us, and we can imagine where they might lead us as a species situated in a cosmos.

Some of us may have to join together just to experience an understanding of the nature of participation that leads into the emerging consciousness of the cosmos; but also find links to the contemporary realities of politics, economics, and ecology while trying, at the same time, to find answers for our generation to the oldest questions of a thinking mankind.

We may discover, or have to invent, a new version of the long-lost soul. But perhaps we dare not, for what we may apprehend just may be too surprising.

CHAPTER TEN

Psychic and political relatedness in organizations

T he nature of the connectedness between individuals and the organization of their employing enterprises is always a puzzle. The history of organizational theory is a reflection of attempts to understand and structure this key connectedness. One perspective that has rarely been used in organizational theory is that of psychoanalysis. In this chapter I am to outline a heuristic perspective that relies on psychoanalytic thinking for one of its elements and attempts to engage with the puzzle of the connectedness of individuals to their enterprises.

Psychoanalysis pre-eminently provides a method of investigation to understand "the unconscious meaning of the words, the actions and the products of the imagination . . . of a particular subject" (Laplanche & Pontalis, 1973, p. 367). All the cultural artefacts of man, which include the organization of their institutions—such as work enterprises—are products of his thinking and imagination. To be sure, people internalize organization as an experience, but they also put back, or project, into it their feelings. What organization means subjectively to the people involved is my chosen area of enquiry. I argue that the unconscious meanings are more important than the conscious, publicly accepted myths because the former both construct the myths and, at times, are also experienced as constraining. It is the recognition and the exploration of that space between those experiences that are felt to be constructive and those seen as constrictive that makes possible the growth of individuals as sentient, imaginative beings in institutions.

I can illustrate what I mean in part with an example. Geraldine Pederson-Krag, writing in 1951, questioned the then predominant view that work was not a precipitating factor in the development of psychic troubles. Her argument was that the hitherto taken-for-granted relationships between man and his work ought to be questioned because of the growth of the mechanization of labour and the factor of mass production. Her postulate was that mass production relies on the operations and motions of a great many individuals being integrated into pattern so that a particular product can be made. Consequently, it is this pattern of order that is actually productive, not the individual. She hypothesized that this pattern, with its related demands on the individual worker, imposes on the worker "a return of infantile living conditions" and, as a corollary, "a return of childhood emotional relationships" (Pederson-Krag, 1951, p. 436).

In workshops there may be very large machines, such as cranes and turret lathes, and there can be furnaces and rolling mills, and so on. The size and complexity of machines, particularly in heavy industry, tend to produce in people a sense of threat and personal inadequacy. The machine as an object is experienced subjectively. While a machine is only an expression of man's ability to use scientific knowledge, it can be experienced differently by the operator because of its perceived superhuman capacities. A worker is dwarfed by the power of the machines at his disposal. At the same time, he can have enormous strength literally at his fingertips, for example, when he uses a crane. Nevertheless, the worker feels that he cannot alter his environment in any significant way. He is part of an ordered pattern of production. As a result, a sense of unreality is engendered. This sense of unreality may be worsened by the noisy conditions, which make it difficult to check out reality through conversation with fellow workers.

As Pederson-Krag puts it, for workers in heavy industry:

> This is directly reminiscent of the individual in infancy before he could talk readily, when everyone was bigger and stronger, when chairs and tables were mountainous and had sharp injurious edges, when he could follow the dark universe with light if someone lifted him to press the switch, but when usually his greatest efforts were ineffectual to change anything. [Pederson-Krag, 1951, p. 438]

Because the worker in the pattern of mass production is cut off from outside realities, he is driven back into his internal fantasy world, the world of the daydream. This further infantilizes the worker because the daydreams can come to be generated to avoid the psychic pain of recognizing external reality.

The pattern of mass production relies on an authority structure whereby managers oversee supervisors, who, in turn, organize workers on the shop or factory floor. Everyone is subordinate to someone else. Such an authority pattern is directly reminiscent of childhood relationships with parents and teachers, and so it is the emotional relationships of childhood that are re-created and re-enacted in the work enterprise. Consequently, the individual worker is pressed to act at less than an adult level.

The pattern of mass production is an invention of man—a myth of organization. It is meant to be a constructive method for organizing people to make products, earn a livelihood, and generate profits. Nevertheless, it is constrictive in the ways that I have been describing. To be sure, workers in such situations have to find ways to avoid the pain of recognizing the constrictiveness of their experiences because they have little choice if they are to earn a livelihood in a consumer society.

This example illustrates, in part, how a psychoanalytic approach can yield particular insight into what takes place unconsciously in the minds of people in certain kinds of work enterprises.

From this and other studies a hypothesis can be made that the psychic relations and relationships of an enterprise create political relations and relationships, which, in turn, reinforce these psychic relations and relationships. The infantilization of the worker brings about particular non-adult views about authority in the enterprise (Lawrence, 1982).

This hypothesis can be pressed further, and we can postulate that there are constructs held in the mind to describe the connectedness between the individual and the enterprise. This can be called "relatedness". Individuals have a notion of how they are related to their enterprise as an abstraction. They have a picture in their minds. This relatedness structures their actual relations and relationships with others in the enterprise—for instance, between individuals and managers. On the basis of his experiences of relations and relationships their notions of their relatedness may alter. Essentially, relatedness enables individuals to make sense of actual relations and relationships.

The question I now want to address is: what concepts guide the practitioner in discovering what is in the minds of clients? My preoccupation is to find this out as a way of helping clients to disentangle what experiences of organizational life are felt to be constrictive or constructive. What goes on in my head and what provides me with sources for interpretation when I work as a consultant?

A heuristic framework

The basic postulate that guides a psychoanalytic approach to disentangle organizational life is that the individual can be understood to be living in a "double environment" at one and the same time. This double environment is both psychic and material. On the one hand, it is rooted in the life of the psyche and the body and in the unconscious. On the other hand, it is conscious and influenced by human relationships and culture (Guntrip, 1961, pp. 351–352).

The individual lives in two worlds simultaneously: the inner world of the mind and the outer world of relationships with others. The former can be said to be essentially the world of the past, the latter that of the present. The connection between these two worlds is often such a close one that it becomes confused and, on occasion, fused.

The inner world, of which the individual is not directly aware, is a private "society" of traces of residual images of relationships with other people experienced in the past. These have been people of influence for the individual by being the principal objects of his wishes, needs, loves, hates, and angers. These "objects"—or, rather, images of them and what they represent—come to be lodged subjectively in the mind of the individual and constitute his psychic structure.

The individual carries within himself all the experiences of his life. This is done in two ways: in memory and in the world of internal objects to which I have been alluding. The original ego that the individual possesses in infancy has the potential for growth. Through experiences with significant objects in his environment, particularly the mother, the complex structure of the ego is initiated. In brief, satisfying experiences of the ego with the mother will be internalized by the infant and stored in memory, but bad experience will be internalized mentally in an unconscious fashion as part of the world of internal objects. It is as if some experiences of relationships with objects outside us can be "digested" (Bion, 1962) because they are enjoyed. Other relationships will produce bad experiences, which cannot be absorbed into memory but are "retained as foreign objects which the psyche seeks to project" (Guntrip, 1968, p. 22). In fact, these bad objects of feeling are retained in our inner, unconscious world as dynamic processes in the sense that they are among the sources of energy for behaviour in subsequent relationships.

In this brief statement about object-relations theory derived from Melanie Klein, W. R. D. Fairbairn and H. Guntrip, I have been over-simplistic with the proposition that good experiences are remembered and bad ones retained only in the unconscious. Good experiences with objects in the environment may also come to be forgotten and repressed in the same way. Why they get repressed is unknown. Nevertheless, all these repressed good objects become "idealized" representations of relationships. When such objects surface from the unconscious in response to an actual transaction with another person, all these archaic characteristics are mobilized. Hence, when the individual falls in love, it is, in the first instance, not so much with an actual person as such, but with an idealized representation of a previously experienced object. The internalized object is used to project an image on to the live, loved object. Later, reality experience of the relationships with the new loved person cause the internal object to be modified. In these kinds of ways the individual can grow emotionally.

These transactions in relationships can be more accurately described as "introjection" and "projection". These unconscious processes are, however, among the earliest activities of the ego. According to Melanie Klein,

> introjection means that the outer world, its impact, the situations the infant lives through, and the objects he encounters, are not only experienced as external but are taken into the self and become part of his inner life. Inner life cannot be evaluated even in the adult without these additions to the personality that derives from continuous introjection. Projection, which goes on simultaneously, implies that there is a capacity in the child to attribute to other people around him feelings of various kinds, predominantly love and hate. [Klein, 1963, p. 5]

These two related processes become part of the individual's repertoire for making and unmaking relations for the remainder of his life. Introjection and projection are only possible if there is a boundary to be transacted across. The individual can be seen as a bounded entity with inner and outer worlds. The managing of these transactions is conducted by the ego. As individuals, we possess a mental process that makes it possible for us to distinguish between what is "I" and what is "not I". This process enables us to distinguish between what is in our minds and what we believe to be outside us and belonging to other people. The puzzling out of which feelings belong to us and which to other people is an essential feature of a relationship. This idea of the individual being a bounded entity can be extended, and the individual can be seen as a system taking in sensory data from the outside environment, processing them in some way, and then communicating with others. That this is done both in conscious and unconscious fashions is a basic postulate of psychoanalysis.

Wilfred Bion has described how individuals relate to their outer environment of other people in group settings, as described in earlier chapters. To Bion's three basic assumptions can now be added the ba Oneness of Pierre Turquet and basic assumption Meness (see chapter five).

An example of how people use culture techniques at both a conscious and unconscious level to solve their problem can be seen from A. K. Rice's investigation of an expanding machine shop in Glacier Metals. The line shop had to expand because there was an urgent demand for its products, but the process of expansion aroused acute feelings of anxiety in the workers (Rice, 1951, p. 143). Essentially, the workers cooperated with the expansion, but to cope with their feelings of being exploited and persecuted they created a negotiating committee for wage rates. This committee held all the feelings of fight/flight on behalf of all the workers. The negotiations about wages were bitter and prolonged until such time as the machine shop was fully operational in its expanded form and could engage in its sophisticated task of producing bearings for a competitive market. By then the negotiations had served their purpose, and a settlement was quickly reached.

Here we have an example of how people managed their feelings and gave meaning to their behaviour in a discrete work situation. On occasions, however, the culture of an enterprise may be dependent because the authority structure is such that the individuals relating to it can only take in—introject—data about being less than adult (cf. Pederson-Krag, above). This salient experience arouses primitive feelings of anger and hostility. These are "put out"—projected—by individuals onto various objects, such as middle management. The point is that it is the less-than-adult dimensions of the individual that are mobilized in the situation.

Here I am trying to indicate the political realities, which are born out of psychic realities (Lawrence, 1982). This is a two-way process (see chapter one for the relationship between Oedipus and Sphinx). There is a resonance between, for example, a Basic Assumption Dependency culture and the inner world of the individuals involved who can only co-act at a less-than-mature or sophisticated political level. The complexity of this resonance has been identified by Elliot Jaques (1955, pp. 478–498) and Isabel Menzies Lyth, who both use object-relations theory as developed by Melanie Klein. Essentially, Menzies in her studies of nursing hypothesized that its tasks involved the nurse in facing the stressful realities of death and other primitive fears. Consequently, in hospital there grows a social organization to enable nurses to develop methods for dealing with disturbing emotional experiences. This is a social system to defend against anxiety. One example would be of the methods of making decisions—so nurses tend to be given very precise instructions that have to be followed exactly. Another example would be of the nature of the relationship between patient and nurse, which tends to be "de-personalized" (Menzies Lyth, 1960, pp. 10–11).

The process whereby social systems of defence are created rests on projection. As Menzies Lyth puts it:

> Each individual brings into an organization his own personal anxiety that stems from difficulties or dangers peculiar to himself. . . . Anxieties dwell inside him on the basis of his experience from previous relationships. These psychic elements are for the most part unconscious and exist on deep and primitive levels of the mind where they take extreme and violent forms. [Menzies Lyth, 1965, p. 195]

To modify the inner world and to lessen the anxiety arising from it, individuals "project the internal situations into current real situations which then symbolize the internal situation" (p. 195). The external situation is then re-internalized by the individual. When this happens collectively, we can talk of a social system as a defence against anxiety. Such social defences, we find, are built into the "structure, culture and mode of functioning of organizations and acquire considerable stability and permanence" (p. 199).

A good example of such a social system as a defence against anxiety can be found in Berry's studies of the possible relationships in companies between policy formulation and accounting procedures. He found that the budgeting process acts to suppress uncertainty and anxieties about disorder for higher management. The development of this social mechanism results in subordinate managers making greater errors between budget and outcome. Berry's hypothesis is that:

> This outcome implies that the hierarchical position of the senior manager is protected or rather the anxiety senior managers have is managed by reinforcing their own feelings of success at the expenses of denying their subordinates any success whatever. The fear of failure was thus projected onto the subordinates. [Berry, 1979, p. 39]

As has been implied, enterprises are seen as social systems. The other element of the heuristic framework I use is that of the enterprise as an open system. Any enterprise takes in materials and other imports from its environment and manages the transformations into products, and so on, which are exported back into the environment (see Rice, 1970, pp. 31–47, 234–239; also Miller & Rice, 1967, pp. 251–269). Obviously, an enterprise imports people, machines, capital, values, and ideologies as well as information from the environment. These are all transformed in various ways and put back into the environment.

In puzzling out the relations between the social system and the technical system of an enterprise, I find myself increasingly attempting to identify the psychic and political dimensions to which I have been pointing. In this I would be holding on to an inter-systemic perspective, which sees the individual in relation to his work enterprise as an open, socio-technical system.

A maieutic method

I use the term "maieutic" to give the sense that in consultancy much of the work with client systems—be they individuals or groups—is to enable them to get in touch with their conscious and unconscious feelings and bring them to the surface. Consultancy is akin to midwifery in that it encourages the discovery of repressed, unconscious meanings and allows for these to be born into the world of the conscious. At the same time, consultancy is about the death of meaning in the sense that individuals and whole systems, for instance, can replace meanings that are more to do with defences against anxiety, with constructive alternatives.

I have to say that the method is continually being elaborated, and what follows is, of necessity, an interim statement on my part. This is because the continued work of consultancy allows the consultant to get in touch more and more with the defensive activities of his own ego in relation to bad objects. This then makes it possible for his clients to extend themselves.

Three preliminary points: in the first place, I share the view of Miller and Gwynne (1972, pp. 7–8) that consultants are research instruments because they are using their feelings. Consequently, consultants need to have undergone a personal psychoanalysis; there is no other way that I know of whereby they can learn to differentiate, as methodically as possible, between what they are introjecting from the client and what they themselves may be projecting. The world of feelings and meanings, if it is to be explored, requires that the initial explorer be as aware as possible of his own subjective, inner world and, more important, be committed to its continued exploration.

The second point is that the framework I have outlined is a heuristic one; a set of ideas for discovering what may be realities. Hence it is essential that the consultant be available to take in uncertainties, doubts, and disorder, bearing in mind L. C. Knights's dictum: "There is always the risk of anticipating and imposing when it is our business to discover" (Knights, 1959) and remembering that in the kind of consultancy I describe it is very often difficult to distinguish between patience and despair.

Thirdly, I see consultancy as a kind of exile. Because psychoanalytic thinking, particularly object-relations theory, is not widespread, this kind of consultancy is outside the predominant paradigms of knowledge. So there is an exile from the salient "disciplines" and schools of social science. But I believe that the act itself relies on being in exile; one is "in" the client enterprise but never "of" it, for instance.

Organizational development is an activity with a range of interpretations. It can have pragmatic goals—"improving efficiency"—idealistic ones, liberal ones, and so on (Miller, 1977, pp. 31–63). However defined, it is a political activity. At worst, it can be manipulative in that one set of people (managers or consultants acting as their representatives) impose their values—even liberal and humane ones—on another (Lawrence, 1979b, p. 15). At best, it is providing conditions for people to explore what meaning they put on their lives in a particular organization, so that they can take authority for understanding and managing the boundary between their inner worlds and the realities of their external environment. Hence, I do not accept a contract with a client unless it is clearly understood that I am acting in a potential relation to the whole enterprise as a system, not just to the management or any of the other employees or trade unions.

As I try to understand the psychic and political realities of the people in a particular enterprise—which I do through being available for interviews and discussions—I find myself trying to disentangle the various primary tasks that are being pursued by the people involved in the enterprise as a system. "Primary task" was a concept developed by Miller and Rice and owes something to the work of Bion (see above). Miller and Rice described it as follows:

> The primary task is essentially a heuristic concept that allows us to explore the ordering of the multiple activities (and of constituent systems of activities where these exist). It makes it possible to construct and compare different organizational models of an enterprise based on different definitions of its primary task; and to compare the organizations of different enterprises with the same or different primary tasks. The definition of primary task determines the dominant import-conversion-export system. [Miller & Rice, 1967, pp. 25–28]

Subsequently, I have tried to extend the range of this tool to include more explicitly the unconscious behaviour of people in an institution as a system. In this way I can, hopefully, get at what meaning life in a particular institution has for the participants. What Miller and Rice describe could be termed the stated primary task of an institution as a system. My experience is that people have a good idea of the stated primary task of their enterprise: to produce steel, for instance. I call this the *normative* primary task. Alongside this, other primary tasks will be pursued. People have minds and use the work system in different ways from what they know it ought to be for—that is, they manage themselves. So I have postulated two others: the *existential* and the *phenomenal* primary tasks (Lawrence, 1977, p. 23; Lawrence & Robinson, 1974, p. 10).

The existential primary task is the one that people say and believe they are carrying out—for example, to earn a livelihood. It is the meaning they place on their own behaviour in their systemic roles. The phenomenal primary task is the unconscious primary task that is being pursued by the people in the system. This is the basic assumption mental activity (of Bion, above), but it can also be an identification of any social system that is being used as defences against anxiety. For example, the activity of management develop-ment in enterprises can be understood to have the phenomenal primary task of acting as a buffer by absorbing the tensions be-tween the competitive individual aspirations of managers and the perceived, cooperative goals of the enterprise. If this task becomes salient, the chances are that the enterprise will be wasting talent. The anxiety of experiencing a disordered, rivalrous situation among managers can be kept at bay, however. The consultant or action researcher will hypothesize the phenomenal primary task, in the first instance, as being likely.

Related to this enquiry into primary tasks—and often I start from the null hypothesis that there is no primary task for the system—will be an inspection of the "institution in the mind" and "management in the mind". Both these terms were invented by my late colleague, Pierre Turquet, to describe elements of the re-latedness between the individual and the organization of the enterprise.

As I have indicated earlier, an institution (such as an industrial enterprise, a hospital, a school, or a family, for example) is no more than an idea—a construct—in the minds of the people associated with it. There will be different versions of the construct held by managers and workers, but essentially there will be some com-monality. Each person in his role will be related to his version of it. How plants and people are related, what is appropriate behaviour within plants and task boundaries, what are the differences inside and outside the boundary—these are brought together into a pic-ture held in the mind. At the same time, each person is related through his work tasks and related roles to other people. He takes part in a series of interactions that can be termed relationships. The same can be said for groups. Where there is a relationship, there is also relatedness in that each party in the interaction has a picture of itself, of the other, and also of the nature of the relationship between them. These pictures, or images, or ideas, or constructs affect the way in which each behaves. To some extent this must be a shared picture at a conscious or unconscious level, otherwise there is no basis on which they can interact.

Relatedness, however, can affect behaviour when there is no direct relationship. For example, in a large international organiza-

tion, the employees in one operating unit may have no direct relationship with either the Board of Directors or units in other
countries; but they have a picture in their minds of the Board and
the Corporation as a whole, and beliefs and fantasies about them;
and that experience of relatedness affects their actions and interactions.

The institution in the mind has psychic reality and so determines the political relations between those who are perceived to
have power and those who are subject to it. This would be management in the mind. On the basis of their own inner reality,
together with what is perceived to be the political reality, people
develop versions of management in the mind that are then mobilized in actual relationships that involve the exercise of authority
in relation to the primary tasks of the systems of work.

These notions are likely to be among the sources for a working
hypothesis to be offered to the client system. The working hypothesis is a sketch of the social situation. It is there to be elaborated on,
or erased and replaced by another, either by the client or the consultant. The transactions and the use of evidence around working
hypotheses allow both the client and the consultant to develop
and refine their ideas as to what might be the truth of the situation
in the client system (Lawrence, 1979b, pp. 6–7). The chances are
that there will be resistance to the working hypothesis because it
will probably be identifying unconscious social processes. "These
likely will have given meaning to life to the people involved and
afford some protection from fear and uncertainty even though
unrecognized" (Wilson, 1951, p. 22). The working hypothesis,
however, offers an opportunity to individuals to reconsider what
experiences are constrictive and constructive in order that they
may choose what social arrangements they want.

Here, it is worth distinguishing between two kinds of interpretations or working hypotheses. First, there are those that are
"pre-emptive" (see chapter six). By this is meant that their form
and content are such that the people in the client system can
change neither the hypothesis nor themselves. Secondly, such hypotheses have to be contrasted with those that are "mutative":
they open up possibilities for change.

To arrive at this point could be a long, painful journey for both
consultant and client as feelings and dearly held subjective experi-

ences are involved. In order to avoid the pain, it is always a temptation to take refuge in premature conceptualization.

To be in a position to employ the heuristic framework and develop working hypotheses, the consultant has to be available for the feelings and the meaning systems of the people in the client enterprise, ideally, by becoming a "container" for the feeling of the client system—a repository, a spittoon—and by being available for the good and bad feelings that are held about the institution and the parties with it. Some of his data will be drawn from the transference feelings—the feelings the people have about the consultant that are derived from their previous experiences of perceived influential figures in their lives. (See the discussion above of inner worlds, and the processes of introjection and projection.) But the consultant also has feelings about the client. These are countertransference feelings, which can include blind spots. If the consultant checks out these feelings with professional colleagues and utilizes the experiences of his own psychoanalysis, the chances are that both transference and countertransference feelings can be utilized fully to understand the psychic and political realities of the particular enterprise.

Political phenomena are cultural experiences, as are the social and technical arrangements of enterprises. The investigation of these experiences is the stuff of consultancy. Between the client system and the consultant(s) there is a "potential space". Ideally, this potential space is to be used by both to "play" in. I am not talking about games, but about play in the sense of creative living, of being able to have mental associations to explore the symbolism present in lived, cultural experiences so as to perceive the metaphorical skulls beneath the skin of living.

These ideas are derived from Winnicott, who was among the pioneer explorers of what takes place psychically between the mother and her baby. Part of his thesis is:

> From the beginning the baby has maximally intense experiences in the *potential space between the subjective object and the object objective perceived*, between me-extensions and the nonme. This potential space is at the interplay between there being nothing but me and there being objects and phenomena outside omnipotent control. [Winnicott, 1980, p. 118, italics in original]

What Winnicott is identifying is how the baby begins to differentiate between himself and the mother in order to make the reality of
her in her own right as an object outside himself. The space for this
to happen is what Winnicott described as "a vital area in the mental life of a developing person" (Winnicott, 1980, p. 199).

I am not suggesting that the potential space between client and
consultant is the same as that between the mother and the baby,
and that the consultant equals mother and the client is, thus, a
baby. Rather, I am suggesting that the potential space is between
persons with their subjective experiences of objects (other persons,
cultural phenomena, etc.), and the objects themselves have a reality that is likely to be different from how they are subjectively
perceived and construed by those called managers. The potential
space can be such that these essentially unconscious subjective
experiences can be "worked through" to obtain some objectified
stance. One trap for a consultant is to be caught up in "the rescue
fantasy"—that is, seeing the client system as being a system to be
"cured" and so offering solutions as a way of avoiding the difficulties of analysing unconscious material (Dubbane & Lee, 1980).

The psychic pain I have been referring to is often around the
issue of disillusionment. I suspect that often client systems invite
consultancy because they are either disappointed or disillusioned
with their own institutional system or want to be so. The ability to
be disillusioned is a mark of ego strength. It is the first step towards inspecting cultural realities and recognizing that it is
possible to make other realities.

The consultant can be seen as someone who is available to
receive feelings of disillusionment, disappointment, and despair; it
is not his task to project his own disillusionment onto the client
system but, rather, to make it possible for others to express their
inner fears and volitions. This implies that in the past the consultant has had experiences of disillusionment, disappointment, and
despair, coupled with the experiences of making hope.

My hypothesis is that the acceptance of the experience of disillusionment allows people to lead themselves into being depressed
about their social situation, and their psychic and political
relatedness and relations. If they can become socially depressed,
the chances are that they can get in touch with their own anger
about political arrangements in their institutions. To be in touch

with the feeling of anger allows people to disentangle their fantasies of persecution from real persecution. For example, management can be persecuting in reality. Once this has been achieved, the chances are that people can begin to remake their institutions and their organizations as they wish them to be because social hope is a possibility.

Essentially, the psychoanalytic approach to organizational life is designed to realize the value of the self-managing individual who refuses "to allow culture assumptions to remain untested" and so enquires into "the myths and mysteries of our social institutions" (Lawrence & Miller, 1976, p. 365; see also chapter two). The invitation to any client is to examine the meaning they give to their social institutions and their conscious and unconscious roles in it. Organizational development, like any innovation, invariably starts with self. To take this view, however, is to accept that the client may make political decisions that are at variance with what the consultant may believe. His task is to ensure that there is psychic space for the people in the client system to use their own authority to explore their psychic and political realities, wherever that quest may lead.

CHAPTER ELEVEN

Tragedy:
private trouble or public issue?

Acknowledging the past and the future

I am to assume the worst of scenarios in order to find resources for building some realizable hope for the future. That there is an urgent need for thinking of the future is evident if only because the techno-scientific processes that fuel the world economy are exploiting the environment to such an extent that the material foundation for human life may be destroyed (Hobsbawm, 1994, p. 584). The future is certainly fragile. The ability to breathe life into the future, or to render it dead, rests with human beings, possessed of minds and the ability to think. And the price of any failure to think will be darkness—the tragic end of humanity. That is the long, profound shadow that the future casts before, to echo Bion.

I am bleak because I recall that in the first 72 years of the twentieth century 120 million man-made deaths had been perpetrated. Pogroms, massacres, extermination camps, and wars brought about these deaths. The victims did not have any choice. They were herded to their deaths by the functionaries of extermination—employees, for the most part, of totalitarian regimes. The extermination was completed with logistical and technological sophistication. (I take these figures from Gil Elliot's 1972 book, *Twentieth Century Book of the Dead*.) What this conservatively estimated figure will rise to by the end of this century barely bears thinking about. We have to take account of the figures of the murdered from Africa, from Algeria, and now from Kosovo, from Chechnya, and so on.

Tragedy, then, has been a feature of the political landscape of the twentieth century. We find it too present in the social landscape as we learn how adults bring about the death of innocence in children through abuse. In a catalogue of human achievement by the end of the millennium, we have to take account of our ability to manufacture death. We may believe that we are one of the most powerful civilizations that ever existed, but we are experts in the fabrication of tragedy for others.

Consequently, the working hypothesis that I am to explore is:

A future cannot be brought into being until we experience and consciously call to mind the meaning and significance of tragedy, both as a private trouble and as a public issue at this point in history.

To anticipate my argument: tragedy (ranging from disappointment through loss to death) is construed by people as an intrusion in their lives, an impertinence of fate. Tragedy, we have come to believe, is not supposed to happen and is to be wished away. Life should be trouble-free. Because we believe that man is superior to everything else that exists on earth and is, therefore, god-like, we have no means of integrating tragedy into our lives. Tragedy we "split off" onto characters in films and television drama, and into the weak and the "under-classes". If tragedy, however, is seen as being an experience that is part of the texture of life, it can be integrated into the shaping of a life. And until we understand tragedy as a private trouble, we cannot comprehend tragedy as a public issue. To put this another way: I am beginning to think that the more we deny the existence of tragedy in our private and public lives, the more likely we are to bring it into being because somewhere, someone is having the kind of psychotic thinking that generates tragedy.

Psychoanalysis cannot be "applied", nor can organizations be made to match the circumstances of the psychoanalytic situation. Psychoanalysis has to be "made" in the social context. I find it a useful distinction to hold in mind that my focus is on the Sphinx thinking present in the organization (see chapter one), as evinced by people managing themselves in their roles. The other perspective—Oedipus—which is to do with the ego and the psyche of the person in the role, I leave to the therapist or psychoanalyst. What I do is to try to disentangle the shared psychotic anxieties my clients may be defending from, for instance. I try to make sense of the situation by trying to deconstruct the taken-for-granted conscious order of the situation by unravelling the unconscious phenomena (Bollas, 1989, p. 23). Then I would be engaged in an elaborative process—that is, trying to make new meaning with the client for the situation, be it in terms of, say, marketing, or future planning, or organizational structure, or whatever subject is under discussion.

Much of consultancy work focuses on trying to elicit the "unthought known" (Bollas, 1987). My experience of late has been that one unthought known is the cognizance of tragedy, which cannot be addressed publicly. In private conversation people admit to tragedy, saying that their myths of the future are distressed. They have little sense of the millennium being a time of major transformation in the world as it once was for futurologists. People are frightened of tribalism in its various manifestations, they have a sense of cultural disintegration, and they are impotent in the face of drug culture and the incidence of crime. Normality, as it once was construed and known 20 years ago, has transmuted. People can chart the changes that are occurring: technological, globalization, information technology, the dominance of market forces and the volatility of the global economy, for example. However, they cannot give any real meaning to their impact and cannot predict the consequences of the convergent systems that are now forming. All hope that they will be benign. Against this background individuals try to make a life, but tragedy visits them, even in the workplace. I think of companies that are failing because the management's thinking is out of touch with the reality of the market-place. Consequently, they cannot be creative, and they persevere with old strategies that are no longer of use in a changing market. I think of health systems whose management thinking is based on a totalitarian state of mind. As they pursue the "bottom line", trying to make a profit or to break even, they become more rigid in their thinking; as they strive after certainty, the staff have a lurking fear of redundancy as they become older. I think of a religious order, which by the year 2019 will have no nuns if no postulants come forward. Role holders in each of these enterprises are facing endings, or deaths of various kinds, but for the most part they deny the fact, although they know it, if unconsciously.

My thinking on tragedy began from reading Neville Syming-ton's description of a female patient who was extremely angry. She had passed through the paranoid-schizoid position and had attained the depressive one. But then she moved on to a third position, which Symington calls the "tragic position". He describes the patient, who came to realize that her present psychic position was not the fault of her mother, or her father, or herself. Other factors of fate had intervened, in that when she was a child, her father had had to work abroad because of the economic situation in his own country. It was this that caused the difficulties being suffered by her family and herself. When she realized this, it brought her into touch with the human condition. Symington concludes that both the paranoid-schizoid and the depressive positions are a defence against this "deeper abyss of non-meaning", which is represented by the tragic position (Symington, 1986, pp. 275–276).

The person who is in the schizoid position feels futility and hopelessness, and so life has no meaning. The depressive position carries feelings of guilt, but it is the one from which the individual is in touch with realities as being an admixture of both the good and the bad. It is the psychic position that enables the individual to begin to care for others—to exercise ruth—in his or her environment. We tend to see the depressive position as being the one from which it is possible to lead a creative life. Symington surprises us with the hypothesis that this and the paranoid-schizoid position, in the Kleinian framework, are defences against—or ways of avoiding—the impact of the tragic position. In Symington's description we read of the patient who makes the link between tragedy as a private trouble—all her personal, psychic pain—with tragedy as a public issue—the economic situation of her childhood. It is the recognition that puts her in touch with *la condition humaine*.

The connecting up of tragedy as a public issue and tragedy as a private trouble—though this may be a gloss—is made by Christopher Bollas in another way. He finds that as part of the elaborative process of psychoanalysis it is useful to think of the idea of destiny, distinguishing it from the analysand's sense of fate. Bollas describes some individuals who come into analysis as having "psychotic ideas and pains [and who] can be described as a fated person" (Bollas, 1989, p. 32). They have, if you will, private troubles. They are certainly operating with what Winnicott called the false self and are living compliantly without "creative apperception" (Winnicott, 1971, p. 65). They only recognize the world and its details as there to be fitted in with or reacted to. Compliance, in this sense, carries a feeling of futility. Such a person is in a psychic trap in that he "will project into his internal objects split-off parts of his true self, thus giving internal objects a certain further power to fate his life" (Bollas, 1989, p. 33).

The evolution of the true self is possible if a sense of destiny can be rescued. Shackling experiences of the past can be loosened by the mobilization of the destiny drive, which allows the true self to be sought. This is possible because "a sense of destiny would refer to the parts of the self which have not been split-off and remain 'inside' the subject giving him a sense of being on the right track" (Bollas, 1989, p. 33). The working through, so to speak, of the consequences of articulating the burden of the chains of fate to recover a sense of destiny, in my view, starts from an acknowledgement of the experience of a "tragic sense of life", and, of course, a discovery of the feelings, which may be no-feelings, of the tragic position. Otherwise the individual is locked in either the paranoid-schizoid or depressive positions, condemned to oscillate between the two.

The fated person remains embedded in an inner world where the configuration of self and object representations causes individuals to repeat the same scenarios. Such a person has a limited sense of a future because the external world is mapped and construed by the inner one:

> The sense of fate is a feeling of despair to influence the course of one's life.
>
> A sense of destiny, however, is a different state, when the person feels he is moving in a personality progression that gives him a sense of steering his course. . . . People who have a sense of destiny also invest psychically in the future. This involves a certain necessary ruthlessness and creative destructiveness, of the past and the present, in order to seek conditions necessary for futures. [Bollas, 1989. p. 41]

The themes of fate, destiny, and the future are addressed in an original way by James Hillman. He understands some analysands to be living in what he calls the "picaresque mode". This metaphor comes from the "picaresque novel" in which the protagonist lurches in a discontinuous fashion from happening to happening, event to event, but never experiences his experiences. The principal character, the "picaro", is a bit of a rogue, or knave, likeable but feckless. He does not develop, improve, or indeed deteriorate. Hillman hypothesizes that case histories have different fictional styles and says of the picaresque patient that the narrative recounted in the analysis "ends abruptly without achievement for there is no goal so the denouement can neither be the resolution of comedy nor the fatal flaw of tragedy" (Hillman, 1991, p. 80).

Hillman argues for the analyst and analysand to have an awareness of a larger range of narrative possibilities, which includes the tragic and the comic. This is not to choose one mode over the other, but to have them equally available for exploration. "For even", writes Hillman, "while one part of me knows the soul goes to death in tragedy, another is living a picaresque fantasy, and the third engaged in the heroic comedy of improvement" (p. 81).

These psychic progressions, as described by Symington, Bollas, and Hillman, are made possible in psychoanalysis through the use of transference and countertransference in that the analysand uses the analyst as an object into which to project parts of him or herself in order to recuperate them later as the analysand elaborates his personal narrative in search of his true self. Through the work of what Strachey called "mutative interpretation", the analysand is able to construct within himself a reconstituted self, so to speak, who is capable of taking responsibility and authority to engage in creative living by managing him or herself in various roles. The centrality of experiencing, thinking, and linking become critical for this exploration.

But the vast majority of individuals are not in therapy or psychoanalysis. Nevertheless, what we can learn from psychoanalysis can illumine and inform some of our experiences in our roles of, say, teacher, manager, or consultant. These roles attract feelings of transference and invoke countertransference. To be sure, we do not use these feelings in the same disciplined way as the psychoanalyst strives to attain. But by being objects of transference, we can be available for complementary role holders to articulate their sense of fate and destiny, to voice their feelings of futility and hopelessness; of those experiences associated with the depressive position and of their unthought but known tragic sense of life that they may feel in their work. I certainly encounter people who in their roles are struggling to move from the picaresque mode to ones in which both tragedy and the comic are present. Certainly, I feel that heads of enterprises often have an opportunity to disentangle the enchaining of fate delivered by the global, electronic environment from their own and their enterprises' destiny.

My hypothesis is that increasingly fate is very present in the global environment. The salient experience of life in the closing years of the millennium is of it being discontinuous, a series of near-chaotic events for which people can find no shape. The well-known armatures to a life, which were installed by capitalism and industrialization, have melted in the post-modern heat of electronic events. In such circumstances, people become pressed into the picaresque mode, which is essentially to be manic. It is their only remaining defence against the depressive position and an acknowledgement of *la condition humaine*, which comes from a recognition of the tragic position. In the psychic state of a picaro the individual's preoccupation is with survival. While there is an element of the comic present in their lives, they have no access to any available myths to account for the tragedy that they are not experiencing.

The death of tragedy
and the loss of a "tragic sense of life"

What myths we have to account for tragedy come from drama. Tragedy we are familiar with through the plays of Shakespeare and the ancient Greeks. The irony of tragedy is the reversal of intention. The hero intends happiness and well-being but brings about misfortune. King Lear wanted peace in his old age by dividing the kingdom between his daughters, but he only brought about a divided family and his own estrangement. This was because of *hubris*—that is, pride. The audience sees this as a tragic error, or flaw. The fall of the protagonist, while a humbling experience for Lear, is accompanied by the recognition of the consequences of his misdeeds. Lear, thus, comes to develop a fuller understanding of his behaviour and values. As Lear says of himself at the end of Act IV, he is a "very foolish fond old man. / Fourscore and upward, not an hour more or less; /And to deal plainly, I fear I am not in my perfect mind".

It is this self-understanding that balances the negative features of tragedy. This is what makes tragedy compelling. To oversimplify: whereas comedy encourages laughter as we look detachedly at society and the foibles of people, tragedy involves us intimately. Comedy brings understanding to the audience through the role of objective observer, but tragedy illumines our lives through our being involved participants. Tragedy requires a balance between what is possible and what is impossible. It is, therefore, an externalization of the struggle between fate and destiny that we can introject as an audience. Implicit in tragedy "lies the belief—optimistic, if you will—in the perfectability of man", which Arthur Miller points to in *Tragedy and the Common Man*. The optimism of the perfectability of man shines through tragedy to illumine the possibilities of a life that could be brought into being, to be set against that which we have realized.

All great memorable art has its roots in tragedy. David Cairns, author of *Berlioz*, talks about the inner landscape of Beethoven's Ninth Symphony, and he quotes Maynard Solomons:

> Beethoven's Ninth Symphony has been perceived by later generations as an unsurpassable mode of affirmative culture,

a culture which, by its beauty and realism, some believe anaesthetises the anguish and terror of modern life, thereby standing in the way of a realistic perception of society.... The fatal and destructive error behind such attitudes is this: if we lose our awareness of the transcendental realms of play, beauty and brotherhood which are portrayed in the great affirmative works of our culture, if we lose the dream of the Ninth Symphony, there may remain no counterpoise against the engulfing terrors of our civilization, nothing to set against Auschwitz and Vietnam as a paradigm of humanity's potentialities. Schiller had urged that the artist "multiply ... symbols of perfection till appearance triumphs over reality and art over nature". The symbol is of perfection—the Ninth Symphony and the late quartets, the trumpet call of Fidelio ...—these keep alive mankind's hope and sustain its faith in the possibilities of human renewal and survival. [David Cairns, private communication]

As it is, tragedy in English literature flourished only very briefly, for 25–50 years or so at the turn of the sixteenth and seventeenth centuries. The twentieth century saw the death of tragedy. Not even Ibsen or Yeats could match the likes of *Romeo and Juliet* or *Coriolanus*. George Steiner gives us one reason for the death of tragedy: the political inhumanity of our times, which has brutalized language, with the result that words no longer carry their full meaning.

And because they [words] assail us in such vast, strident numbers, we no longer give them careful hearing, each day we sup our fill of horrors—in the newspaper, on the television screen, on the radio—and thus we grow insensible to fresh outrage. This numbness has a crucial bearing on the possibility of tragic style. [Steiner, 1961, p. 315]

While I am not disagreeing with Steiner, my hypothesis is that we lost the ability to think and write tragedies and therefore continue to explore their significance, not just because of the devaluation of the word but also for reasons to do with the way that we think and feel.

It is no coincidence that the apogee of tragedy was in the seventeenth century, and that its demise began then. It was in that century that human beings came to believe in the mechanistic philosophies, which have shaped our civilization until very recently. The universe was conceptualized as a machine, and the idea firmly took root that God was transcendent to Man and Man to the Universe. The world of nature existed for Man to exploit. To this was added that Man could engineer a millenarian future whereby he could control his future, other people, and all the natural resources of the world. This was the time when a new idiom for human beings to relate to their environment was formulated. Material progress became Mankind's new deity, and Faustian Man the new ideal. What this has brought about has been the destruction of nature, which in time will affect society as we know it, and ourselves as inhabitants.

The political inhumanity of human beings goes with the Faustian myth that everything exists on earth for human beings to make use of as they will. (This is now enshrined in the doctrine of "added value".) Faustian man fuels his actions by his fantasies of omnipotence. He believes in his own delusion that he has triumphed over death because he denies it. This century is the one in which people have come to defend themselves against death. Geoffrey Gorer, in a now classic paper of 1955 pointed to the fact that death was a taboo subject in capitalist–industrial countries. Because of the decline in religious beliefs, there are no acceptable explanations of death. We are left alone with the myth that we can live without myth. While I am not arguing for the revival of the kind of religion that offers salvation in an afterlife, I am arguing for the acceptance of death as part of the process of living and, thus, making a connection, or making links, between life and death for our times.

It is the making of links between life and death that spurs human beings to achieve and transcend themselves by finding a sense of destiny, because it is the discovery of death that heralds the discovery of the hunger of immortality. At the same time, the discovery of death is also a realization of the tragic sense of life. The struggle with the tragic sense of life and the acceptance of death's finality—that is, no-life as we know it—allows human beings to consider immortality. This I am taking to mean as the leading of a significant, useful life, at best a creative one, based on non-compliance. If you will, leading a life that is not totally focused around narcissistic concerns but is struggling with the

complexities of what Bion called "social-ism" (Bion, 1992, p. 122).
Immortality causes us to think of why and how we exist, and in
Bollas's terms, to see the interconnection between fate and destiny,
which places before us the choices between good and evil, between creative living, based on the experience of the depressive
and tragic positions, or paranoid-schizoid, compliant living. Otherwise we are condemned to the picaresque mode of living; the
unthinking, unexamined life; living on what Arthur Koestler
called, somewhere, the trivial plane and not the tragic.

Making a future

Thinking of the finality of death spurs thoughts on the shortness of
life. The evanescence of life has troubled mankind through the
centuries. As Unamuno put it:

> From the poets of all ages and from the depths of their souls
> this tremendous vision of the flowing away of life like water
> has wrung bitter cries—from Pindar's "dream of a shadow" to
> Calderón's "life is a dream" and Shakespeare's "we are such
> stuff as dreams are made on," this last a yet more tragic sen-
> tence than Calderón's, for whereas the Castilian only declares
> that our life is a dream, but not that we ourselves are the
> dreamers of it, the Englishman makes ourselves a dream, a
> dream that dreams. [Unamuno, 1921, p. 39]

Even if we are a "dream that dreams", we know it will end in its
present form. Whether or not there is another form of dreaming
when we are dead is unknown, but it has to be discovered. The
idea that we are a dream that dreams is a metaphorical truth—
certainly a poetic truth. This apparently outrageous hypothesis I
base on David Bohm's contention that we live in an unbroken field
of the wholeness of thinking and that we live in an unfolding
universe. It unfolds by making transitions through thinking from
the *implicate* order to the *explicate* one. As events unfold, the explicate order becomes more apparent—it becomes—from the matrix
of the implicate order of being. These orders belong to an unbroken whole because they are connected in a primordial, cosmological sense.

The transformation of the implicate into the explicate is possible because of thinking, moving between being and becoming. Everything that exists does so because of human beings' capacity to think. Landscape, industrial culture, information technology would have no substance but for the capacity for thought. It is human beings in their context who bring forth the tension between fate and destiny that allows them to see that there is a tragic position.

The transformation of the implicate to the explicate is also made possible through dreaming and day-dreaming, which are the first forms of thinking that we experience, because our unconscious mind—the space of no time, and no space—is able to speak with our consciousness. Freud illustrated this process in part when he described creative writers making use of day-dreaming:

> The creative writer does the same as the child at play. He creates a world of phantasy which he takes very seriously— that is, which he invests with large amounts of emotion— while separating it sharply from reality. Language has preserved this relationship between children's play and poetic creation. It gives [in German] the name of "*Spiel*" ["play"] to those forms of imaginative writing which require to be linked to tangible objects and which are capable of representation. It speaks of "*Lustspiel*" or "*Trauerspiel*" ("comedy" or "tragedy": literally "pleasure play" or "mourning play"). [Freud, 1908e [1907], p. 144]

I am not suggesting here that to lead a creative life we become writers, but I am hypothesizing that part of the thinking into being and becoming—dreaming into being and becoming—a future, an explicate order, involves pleasure play and mourning play: that is, comedy and tragedy. My hypothesis has been that we cannot make a future until we recover a sense of tragedy, the tragic sense of life, both as private troubles and as public issues. Until we recognize that an essential part of *la condition humaine* is that we human beings bring much of tragedy into being through our mindless destructive urges, we are condemned to be picaros, subject to the whims of fate, unable to recover a sense of destiny.

In *Antigone*, Creon, very late in the action of the play, comes to the realization of his folly. His wife and son are dead, and he takes responsibility for their deaths with the lines:

Lead me away, I have been rash and foolish,
I have killed my son and my wife,
I look for comfort, my comfort lies here dead.
Whatever my hands have touched has come to nothing,
Fate has brought all my pride to a thought of dust.

Old models of articulating tragedy and comedy may be redundant—quaint, even—in a post-modern world when our cultural artefacts bombard and attack our capacity for thinking and linking. Nevertheless, we have to rediscover the words to engage in pleasure play and mourning play as we think and dream our future into being, otherwise a "thought of dust" could be our future if we cannot recover an intimate tragic sense of life.

Apart from natural catastrophes like hurricanes or the rare meteor that wiped out the dinosaurs, which human beings can do nothing to prevent, tragedy is generated by human beings. If we look at tragedy and attempt to find its causes, we come up with a simple answer. Tragedy has its roots in phantasy in the minds of humans.

We construe our exterior world on the basis of what is subjectively perceived by using our inner worlds. To repeat what was said in chapter one, human beings are continually misinterpreting what reality is because of their phantasy life that is interpreting their real external sensations and perceptions. To be sure, the salience of phantasy diminishes with maturity—but it is always present and never leaves us. External reality is brought into being and given meaning not only by the conscious mind but also by the inner world of phantasy. My final hypothesis is that tragedy is engendered at all levels of society, national and local, because of the narcissist who single-mindedly pursues his or her personal project irrespective of others.

Narcissism versus social-ism

When Bion wrote of the struggle between narcissism and "social-ism" in groups, he was pointing to a fundamental dynamic of human beings in groups. The narcissistic individual is so caught up in his/her inner world of phantasy that the common concerns, which are the fundamentals of social-ism, cannot be engaged with. Truly narcissistic individuals, ruthless, selfish, will have no capability for empathy or compassion. And because of this they are condemned to live on the level of the trivial. For·them, issues of transcendence, the cosmos, and all the other major issues of being human—like the consideration of the relationship between life and death—are irrelevant, for they are only concerned with preserving the desires and ambitions of their inner world. The dream that they dream, which gives them their identity and place in the world, is narrow and proscribed by their narcissistic tendencies. But this is the extreme case of narcissism.

All narcissists have schizoid characteristics. Ronald Fairbairn, the Scottish psychoanalyst, who was a contemporary of Melanie Klein, adumbrated the schizoid personality. According to John Sutherland, the schizoid has three distinguishing characteristics: "They are (a) an attitude of omnipotence; (b) an attitude of isolation and detachment; and (c) a preoccupation with inner reality" (Sutherland, 1989, p. 97). Overall, the relationship of the mind is more salient emotionally with the inner world than with the outer world of other people. Sutherland says that such schizoid features arise from whole persons whose ego has functioned as a whole from the beginning. I submit that this can be recast as the ego operates *as if* it were a whole, as this has been learned, albeit painfully, in subsequent socialization. In actuality, everyone, with limited exceptions, is schizoid. As Winnicott wrote, "It is important that we find clinically *no sharp line* between health and the schizoid state or even between health and full blown schizophrenia" (Winnicott, 1971, p. 66, italics in original).

Underlying the schizoid state is a profound sense of futility. As I have already indicated, there is a close link between tragedy and the futility of the schizoid state. This sense of futility rests on the feeling that life has no meaning, is pointless, is useless. John of Salisbury [c. 1150–1180] captures the essence of futility when he writes:

> The brevity of our life, the dullness of our senses, the torpor of our indifference, the futility of our occupation, suffer us to know but little and that little is soon shaken and then torn

from the mind by that traitor to learning, that hostile and faithless stepmother to memory, oblivion.

In a sense, futility is the condition that comes about when we recognize that all will end in death. And no matter what we achieve in terms of learning and understanding, in the end it seems to be for nought. We spend our time attaining achievements to give us a sense of worth, but this sense of pride in oneself is also a defence against the horrors of futility. As Philip Larkin, the poet, pointed out somewhere, it is an achievement for people to get and go about their business without being crippled by the thought of encroaching death.

Human beings can work creatively with this sense of hopelessness and futility. It is always experienced at some point in life, even if only for moments. At the most profound levels of mood we capture the sense of being schizoid. If we wallow in it, we can become schizoid personalities bordering on being immature narcissists. If we entertain it and attempt to work with it—to recognize the meaning of futility (the meaning of meaninglessness)—we can achieve a mode of being that is life-enhancing, despite the bedrock of futility.

It would be convenient to demonize the narcissist by making him/her the bad object in thinking about groups. This I want to avoid as being too simplistic. It is necessary to see the narcissist in context. A simple continuum would have the narcissist and the socialist at the two ends, with the schizoid covering most of the space in the middle of the continuum. At the very centre of the continuum we can place the healthy individual, but this is an ideal state that is rarely achieved.

Narcissism when used appropriately can be the source of creativity that is generative. Essentially, this is when the ego learns to use the internal objects for conscious creativity. It is this working partnership that allows individuals to be creative. To be sure, the subtlety of the creative process on the part of the individual is such that the wish to be original is about the wish to make reparation for destructive impulses—to rework in a life-giving way the deathliness of life that continually surrounds human beings. This mature narcissism is positive for the most part, though doubtless it will be experienced as destructive at times.

There is, I believe, a state that we can call immature, even pathological, narcissism, which takes us into the realm of the dysfunctional personality. At the other extreme there would be some state that could be called immature socialism, which we have witnessed this century in the many totalitarian regimes in Europe and Africa, for instance. Most people, it can be assumed, oscillate between the mid-states of narcissism and social-ism—that is, towards the middle of the spectrum. This would comprise the great bulk of a population.

The narcissistic personality loves himself, or herself, only (Bollas, 1987, pp. 90ff.), seeking relationships with no objects in the environment for such objects he construes as being part of his own self system. The narcissist wants to seduce the other in passive ways as he wishes to transact only his image of himself to the other. He is, therefore, always in control, for there will be no relationship unless this wish is satisfied. Thus the narcissist can exercise power and authority over his object relations. "By inviting the other to fall in love with his image of himself. The narcissist aims to control the other's eventual effect upon him" (ibid., p. 93). This arises from the mother of the narcissist failing to enable the child in a "good-enough" fashion to establish a version of himself. Because of early conflicts with mother resulting in frustration and rage, he decides what the fate of the child will be. He consequently "mothers himself in an intense and rigid manner" (ibid., p. 93). In assuming his own care of himself, the narcissist feels a sense of triumph at gaining power and control over the senses of self-esteem. So he comes to control the image of himself as a way of experiencing power over the objects he wishes to control in his environment.

Immature narcissistic individuals have a capacity for attaining a position that ensures that they are able not only to satisfy their own needs but also to provide conditions for others to cope with their anxieties. Nowhere is this more apparent than in the development by leaders/managers of the totalitarian state of mind. In a state of business flux, where there is anxiety held by everyone that they could be made redundant, there is the wish for a leader/manager who will deliver the whole enterprise and its people from this anxiety. Consequently, a leader/manager is selected who will fulfil this promise.

This works for a time, but gradually the role-holders realize that they are in the grip of the totalitarian state of mind in the organization. Aggression and bullying become more apparent. In time, the leader/manager may be made redundant. It begins as a collusive process: the leader/manager has sanction for his behaviour in that, initially, he/she is supported. Gradually, role-holders are able to recuperate their ego function and to search for a way of creatively living in the workplace (Lawrence, 1995a, 1995b, 1998).

It is the immature narcissist who pursues his/her own course of action, paying no attention to their inner world of objects and any pairing of their sense of self with them, but only attempting to satisfy their "I want" wishes and desires, who is the truly destructive member of any society or group. For them "social-ism" has no place in their thinking. By this kind of social-ism I am referring to the kind of community one could have in a religious community of monks or nuns, for instance. As, however, these may well cease to exist in some 20 to 30 years, we will have no model in society of a community sharing the ideals of social-ism.

My contention is that narcissistic people beget tragedy, for they enter into a course of action without considering the consequences except on their own terms. Unlike the drama of tragedy there seems to be no recognition of *hubris*, or ultimate self-knowledge. As was said in chapter five when discussing the case for Ba Me-ness, we apparently live in societies where the wish to survive, which is a basic instinct, is increasingly pre-eminent. I sometimes see the narcissistic person as being like a greedy baby, anxious that the food will be taken away. How we can reverse this trend towards narcissism and retain some ideals of social-ism in the personality rests primarily on understanding the nature of the unconscious life of groups by revivifying our capacity to think.

The issue becomes more complicated when considering that form of immature narcissism which pervades much of human life. When Bion introduced the idea that the great struggle in groups is between narcissism and social-ism, between the tendency to be ego-centric or socio-centric, he could not have anticipated the import of what he said as being so long-lasting in its effect. As he put it, in a passage describing the impulsive drives (ego-centric and socio-centric) in the personality:

They are equal in amount and opposite in sign. Thus, if the
love impulses are narcissistic at any time, then the hate impulses are social-istic, i.e. directed towards the group, and,
vice versa: if the hate is directed towards an individual as a
part of narcissistic tendency, then the group will be loved
narcissistically. That is to say, if A hates B, as an expression of
narcissism, then he will love the society. "I hate B because he
is so harmful to the society that I love", might be an assertion
symptomatic of what I would call a state of narcissistic hate of
A for B. I maintain that in a narcissistic statement there is
always implied a social-istic statement. The *two* must go together; if one is operating, so is the other. [Bion, 1992, p. 122]

The immature narcissist always tries to operate in, and construct, a
closed society, or group, or organization. In this way they know
that their chances of survival are that much more enhanced. For
them, the survival of the individual is more important than the
survival of the group. In a sense, they need the group in order to
survive in so far as it serves their individual project. At the same
time there is a hint that fundamentally they despise the group, and
whatever work it may represent. But this is difficult to detect and
observe.

A closed society is a tribal society. The narcissist tends to behave as if the group were a tribe. As Karl Popper puts it:

civilization has not yet fully recovered from the shock of its
birth—the transition from the tribal or "closed society", with
its submission to magical forces, to the "open society" which
sets free the critical powers of man.

He continues on the subject of *The Open Society and Its Enemies*
that it

attempts to show that the shock of this transition is one of the
factors that have made possible the rise of those reactionary
movements which have tried, and still try, to overthrow civilization and to return to tribalism. And it suggests that what we
call nowadays totalitarianism belongs to a tradition which is
just as old or just as young as our civilization itself. [Popper,
1945, p. 1]

The narcissist treats the group, organization, or society as if it were
a closed society. In tribal groups the use of a meritocracy is lim-

ited, for it is the family and kinship that are the important status-giving institutions. History—particularly ancient history—is littered with examples of the distaff side getting status through judicious marriages. This could equally apply to the British aristocracy. Although there are exceptions, this seems to be a perennial truth.

From such arrangements, it is but a short step to nepotism or, to use the current term, "cronyism". These are all attempts to recreate cumulatively the tribal feeling, which is the sure condition for the survival of the narcissist. Narcissists are such because of their inner feelings of insecurity, which they compensate for in sometimes bizarre ways. What is, for me, important is that once that nexus of sponsored mobility and nepotism are in place—as opposed to contest mobility and the idea of meritocracy—there is created a matrix, so to speak, from which it is difficult to state what one thinks might be taking place unconsciously. The narcissist will not brook any interpretation of events in the terms I have described. And whoever voices it has to be converted into a bad object. There may have to be some fabrication of "gossip", or disinformation about envy, but the primary task is to survive, and if this means the destruction of the awkward one, so be it. The desired result is that the bad object is deemed not good enough to fulfil their role. By implication, only the narcissist can do so. And the narcissist can attain his or her desired ends, while apparently loving the group.

This description could well fit Milosovic in former Yugoslavia or any totalitarian/fascist head of state since the last World War, whether in Europe or Africa. Unlike any organization such narcissistic heads of state have the power of death over their adversaries. At another level—that of the ownership of ideas—F. R. Leavis would have his students of English Literature condemn and despise works that they had never read. Thus they, in parasitically following their leader, cut themselves off from expressions of human experience and ignore the diversity and complexity of human life. This is a necessary condition for the hegemony of one man's ideas to survive.

This is further complicated by the narcissistic tendency in one person evoking the anti-narcissistic qualities in others. To be sure, both are flawed categories of human beings, caught as they are in a dynamic that drives them inexorably to its denouement. The anti-narcissist, Bollas suggests, has to convert him or herself into a fated person. This is done by systematically destroying any thoughts of destiny. The anti-narcissist can thus preserve his or her "old, apparently stable internal chemistry . . . but only in the way a dead thing is" (Rayner, 1990, p. 164). This, I am suggesting, is as much a product of the social situation as it is of character. There is a real sense in which the attacks of the narcissist on what he or she identifies as an enemy, who then becomes the enemy of the whole group and its political position, becomes a self-fulfilling prophecy.

The nexus of sponsored mobility, nepotism, narcissism, anti-narcissism, and tribal, closed society is further complicated by the fact that these all become part of the unthought known of the group, which has to be held always in thralldom to tribalism and the closed society. If the unthought known is present in transference–countertransference feelings, according to Bollas (1987, pp. 210–213), such evidence has to be discarded, for they would cause the authority of the narcissists to be questioned. Any attempt at interpretation will be met with the demand on the part of the narcissist that the projections be taken back. No discussion can be allowed of the interpretation, which the narcissist has defined as a projection. So the *status quo* of the Establishment is maintained, and the deadlock of the collusive, parasitic matrix continues—at least as long as the narcissistic leader lives and has power.

But, as I am attempting to sketch, the roots of tragedy always have their origins in narcissism and its *hubris* (pride), repeating a drama that is as old as time itself.

An open society, on the other hand, is democratic, which I take Bion to mean when he writes of being socio-centric in groups. In such a group or organization the narcissist has a limited life because the democratic forces ensure the rise of a meritocracy. Whereas a closed society has as one of its defining features being like "a herd or a tribe in being a semi-organic unit whose members are held together by semi-biological ties—kinship, living together, sharing common efforts, common joys and common distress (Popper, 1945, p. 173), an open society has, as its defining characteristic, "competition for status among its members" (p. 174). Popper, admitting an exaggeration, points to the ultimate form of society, which is an "abstract society". With the advent of the Information Society, such a society becomes more real.

Holding to the ego-centric and socio-centric argument, there is a real sense in which the socio-centric ideals of the group can be subverted by the narcissist, for these ideals have to be confined within the narrow limits that the narcissist determines. This narrow prescription of the aims, visions, and ideals of the group or enterprise means that the major reality issues of living in a complex society that are outside the boundary of the group come to be denied, or sabotaged, by being held "off-stage", or out of mind. The external reality of the group comes to be hated because it demands new thinking.

The narcissist leads an anti-intellectual posture of not taking into account that the society in which the group is located is subject to continual change. The narcissist is able, because of his or her power in the tribal society, to define continually the ideals of the group in terms he or she is familiar with. No new idea can be tolerated, and anyone showing evidence of this will not be in the group. The last thing a narcissistic leader wants is anyone who will question his or her authority. It, therefore, becomes a situation that mirrors what Bion says about the mystic/genius and the Establishment. Bion writes that the mystic is both creative and destructive. There are two types that coexist in the same person. There is the "creative" mystic, and there is the mystic nihilist who destroys his or her own creations. It seems to me that these two forces will be present at any one time in the mystic, but he/she has to win through to the positive dimension, which may take years, by interpreting the situation, including the psychopathology in which he or she finds themselves.

The group in this context has to be seen as an Establishment that has become institutionalized through the establishment of a work group (Bion, 1961). It is essential for the development of all the individuals, including the mystic, who are associated with it. What the group as institution has to represent is the work that is institutionalized in the Word. This may be psychoanalysis, which is the example that Bion gives. The mystic holds some version of what the Truth might be. (Bion writes of God, in this context.) The mystic is also *explosive.* As part of this explosiveness, the mystic will hold an interpretation.

Here, I am pointing to the interpretation of the mystic/genius, which has to be traduced and discarded by the narcissists with power in the Establishment, for it would be death to the state of mind that exists in the Establishment. More particularly, Bion writes of the relationship between the narcissistic leader and his or her Establishment and the mystic/genius, who has had to be excluded and kept outside the group: "The problem posed by the relationship between the mystic and the institution has an emotional pattern that repeats itself in history and in a variety of forms" (Bion, 1970, p. 74). According to Bion, the group and the mystic can have a relationship that is of three kinds: commensal, symbiotic, or parasitic. The commensal relationship is where the two coexist and neither harms the other. Whereas the symbiotic relationship produces growth in both parties, in the parasitic relationship the outcome is the destruction of both the host and the parasite. This is because the group–individual relationship is one that is dominated by envy. The envy cannot be ascribed to one party or the other, for it is a function of the relationship. Since the narcissistic leader, through the closed, tribal society, heads a parasitic Establishment, operating through nepotism and cronyism, the mystic has to be destroyed and never allowed to be in a potentially symbiotic relationship with the Establishment; he, or she, is never to be in a position where they are acknowledged to exist. That the Establishment loses out in the long term is obvious. All that is required is that the Establishment last as long as the narcissist requires his or her position in the short term.

Thus it is that human beings are precluded from thinking of the nature of the society in which the group is embedded. So, for example, the issues that Mary Catherine Bateson (1985) puts before us have to be disregarded. She writes, with passion, to the effect that we have to replace competition with interdependence. She makes the point that we are depleting our planet of resources and creating poverty in the Southern Hemisphere.

The bedrock, or matrix, from which such thinking could emerge will be an open democratic society that is internalized by the majority of a particular population and expressed through their behaviour. The population may compose a group, enterprise, or nation. In a paper of 1950, "Thoughts on the Meaning of the word Democracy", Winnicott defines a democracy as being an achievement when it can be said:

> In this society at this time there is sufficient maturity in the emotional development of a sufficient proportion of the individuals that comprise it for there to exist an innate tendency towards the creation, recreation and maintenance of the democratic machinery. [Winnicott, 1950, p. 548]

The tone of this definition makes it clear that the reality of a democratic society is always in a process of becoming, is never attained absolutely, and is rarely in a state of being. This comes from the phrase "creation and recreation". Winnicott goes on to say that a democratic society depends on there being a majority who are mature and who can absorb the anti-socials. The anti-socials are of two types: those who are against society and those who identify with authority as a way of coping with their inner insecurity. This is aside from the "indeterminates", who can be persuaded to move either for or against society. What Winnicott calls the "hidden anti-socials" are not "whole persons", in much the same fashion as are "manifest anti-socials", for they are always projecting their inner conflicts onto the external reality of the society. In my terms, these are the immature narcissists. Such people subscribe to a type of leadership that is never sociologically mature. They, therefore, always follow the kind of leadership that is of a totalitarian or fascist state of mind as a way of protecting their fragile inner state of mind. This is the method of defending themselves from the anxieties that go with being in an uncertain and surprising world that is characterized both by synchronicity and by causal relationships.

Winnicott relies on the "ordinary good home" to provide the nurturing experiences that will lead to the innate democratic factor. While not disagreeing with this, one wonders about the families who cannot provide this. Where such conditions have been impaired, there is the possibility of learning in other contexts.

Education is the subject of this book on group relations. There is a necessity to scrutinize how enterprises that provide such an education are organized and what values they explicitly and implicitly subscribe to. Vigilance, at the profoundest psychological depth, which implies psychoanalytic understanding, needs to be exercised unremittingly. By this, I mean that the institutions that provide such education always have to be striving to be open societies, never taking on the characteristics of closed, tribal ones. This must mean addressing the unthought known that is always present in the transference and countertransference between participants and consultant staff. To deny this evidence is to enter into the Lie. No matter how distinguished the protagonists, the Lie(s) have to be addressed, for it is the nexus of nepotism (cronyism), sponsored mobility (as opposed to contest mobility), and narcissism that is the enemy of the democratic ideal, which provides the conditions for thinking about the socio-centric impulse in groups.

By mobilizing our innate socio-centric tendencies, except possibly for the psychopath, we could *start* to think in the way that Bateson and other writers are indicating. As it is, in groups, in organizations, and in society there is always the wish to revert to the ego-centric, the finite, the well-known. It is then but a short step to attempting to recreate the tribal closed society. Governments, for example, do this when they convene quangos, which is an unconscious example of the wish for political control and, therefore, of the closed society. A truly open society presents the individual with challenges to their personal authority, with the trials of having merit or not, as it is based on democratic ideals. Furthermore, the open society presents us with the unknown, the unexpected, and the surprising. Overall, the closed society, with its narcissistic preoccupations and its propensity for generating tragedy, will never allow for the conditions to be fostered that would allow us the hope to celebrate the sacredness of that which is still to be brought into being through the group, the organization, the enterprise, and the society.

REFERENCES

Adams, A. (1992). *Bullying at Work*. London: Virago.

Alex, W. (1971). *When Old Gods Die . . .* San Francisco, CA: C. G. Jung Institute.

Alford, C. F. (1989). *Melanie Klein and Critical Social Theory*. New Haven/London: Yale University Press.

Alvarez, A. (1974). *The Savage God*. Harmondsworth: Penguin Books.

Armstrong, D. (1991). Thinking aloud: contributions to three dialogues. In: W. G. Lawrence (Ed.), *Social Dreaming @ Work*. London: Karnac Books, 1989.

Back, K. (1973). *Beyond Words*. Harmondsworth: Pelican Books.

Bain, A., Long, S., & Ross, S. (1992). *Paper Houses: The Authority Vacuum in a Government School*. Melbourne: Collins Dove.

Barham, P., & Lawrence, W. G. (1974). Some notes on Tavistock working conferences. *Group Analysis, 11* (2).

Barnaby, F. (1988). *The Gaia Peace Atlas*. London: Pan Books.

Bateson, M. C. (1985). *With a Daughter's Eye*. New York: Washington Square Press.

Becker, E. (1972). *The Birth and Death of Meaning*. Harmondsworth: Penguin Books.

Becker, E. (1973). *The Denial of Death*. New York: Free Press.

Bellah, R. N. (1985). *Habits of the Heart*. London: University of California Press.

Bennis, W. (1971). Beyond bureaucracy. In: I. L. Horowitz & M. S. Strong (Eds.), *Sociological Realities*. New York: Harper & Row.

Beradt, C. (1968). *The Third Reich of Dreams*. Chicago, IL: Quadrangle Books.

Berger, P. (1971). *A Rumor of Angels*. Harmondsworth: Penguin.

Berry, A. J. (1979). Policy, accounting and the problem of order. *Personnel Review, 8* (2).

Bettelheim, B. (1983). *Freud and Man's Soul*. London: Hogarth Press.

Bion, W. R. (1946). The leaderless group project. *Bulletin of the Menninger Clinic, 10* (May).

Bion, W. R. (1961). *Experiences in Groups*. London: Tavistock Publications.

Bion, W. R. (1962). *Learning from Experience*. London: Heinemann.

Bion, W. R. (1970). *Attention and Interpretation*. London: Tavistock Publications.

Bion, W. R. (1974). *Brazilian Lectures*. Rio de Janeiro: Imago Editora.

Bion, W. R. (1976). Interview. *Group and Organizational Studies, 1* (3).

Bion, W. R. (1984). *Second Thoughts*. London: Karnac Books.

Bion, W. R. (1992). *Cogitations*. London: Karnac Books.

Biran, H. (1997). Myths, memories and roles—how they live again in the group process. *Free Associations, 7* (Part 1, No. 41): 31–48.

Bleakley, A. (1989). *Earth's Embrace*. Bath: Gateway.

Bléandonu, G. (1994). *Wilfred Bion*. London: Free Association.

Bohm, D. (1992). *Thought as a System*. London: Routledge.

Bohm, D., & Edwards, M. (1991). *Changing Consciousness*. San Francisco, CA: Harper.

Bollas, C. (1987). *The Shadow of the Object*. London: Free Association.

Bollas, C. (1989). *Forces of Destiny*. North Vale, NJ: Jason Aronson.

Broadbent, J. (1979). Darkness. In W. G. Lawrence (Ed.), *Exploring Individual and Organizational Boundaries* (pp. 193–203). Chichester: John Wiley.

Cahoone, L. E. (1988). *The Dilemmas of Modernity*. New York: State University of New York Press.

Camporesi, P. (1990). *The Fear of Hell*. Cambridge: Polity Press.

Canetti, E. (1973). *Crowds and Power*. Harmondsworth: Penguin.

Carey, J. (1992). *The Intellectuals and the Masses.* London: Faber and Faber.

Cohen, J., & Stewart, I. (1995). *The Collapse of Chaos.* Harmondsworth: Penguin.

Colman, A. D., & Bexton, W. H. (Eds.) (1975). *Group Relations Reader.* Washington, DC: A. K. Rice Institute.

Colman, A. D., & Geller, M. H. (Eds.) (1985). *Group Relations Reader II.* Washington, DC: A. K. Rice Institute.

Davies, P., & Gribbin, J. (1991). *The Matter Myth.* London: Viking.

Day, D. (1973). *Malcolm Lowry.* Oxford: Oxford University Press.

Dubbane, E., & Lee, A. P. N. (1980). "Countertransference and the Rescue Phantasy." Unpublished paper presented to the Canadian Psychoanalytic Society, Montreal.

Duve, C. de (1995). *Vital Dust.* New York: Basic Books.

Eliade, M. (1978). *No Souvenirs, Journal, 1957–69.* London: Routledge & Kegan Paul.

Elias, N. (1987). *Die Gesellschaft der Individuen.* Frankfurt: Suhrkamp.

Eliot, T. S. (1943). *Four Quartets.* New York: Harcourt Brace & Company.

Eliot, T. S. (1953). *Selected Prose.* Harmondsworth: Penguin.

Eliot, T. S. (1963). *Collected Poems.* London: Faber & Faber.

Elliot, G. (1972). *Twentieth Century Book of the Dead.* London: Penguin.

Fairbairn, W. R. D. (1952). *Psychoanalytic Studies of the Personality.* London: Tavistock Publications.

Frankl, V. E. (1964). *Man's Search for Meaning.* London: Hodder & Stoughton.

Frankl, V. E. (1967). *Psychotherapy and Existentialism: Selected Papers on Logotherapy.* New York: Pelican.

Freud, S. (1908e [1907]). Creative writers and day-dreaming. *The Standard Edition of the Complete Psychological Works of Sigmund Freud, 14.* London: Hogarth Press.

Freud, S. (1915b). Thoughts for the times on war and death. *S.E., 18.*

Freud, S. (1921c). *Group Psychology and the Analysis of the Ego. S.E., 18.*

Freud, S. (1930a). *Civilization and Its Discontents. S.E., 21.*

Friedenberg, E. Z. (1973). *Laing.* Glasgow: Fontana/Collins.

Fromm, E. (1976). *To Have or to Be.* London: Cape.

Fromm, E. (1977). *The Anatomy of Human Destructiveness.* Harmondsworth: Penguin.

Fulton, R. (1971). *The Spaces between the Stones*. New York: New Rivers Press.

Gilmore, T. N. (1988). *Making a Leadership Change*. San Francisco, CA: Jossey-Bass.

Gorer, G. (1955). The pornography of death. *Encounter, 5:* 49–52.

Gramsci, A. (1977). *The Selections from the Prison Notebooks of Antonio Gramsci*. London: Lawrence & Wishart.

Greene, G. (1992). *A World of My Own*. London: Viking.

Greenstein, G. (1988). *The Symbiotic Universe*. New York: William Morrow.

Grinberg, L., Sor, D., & Tabak Bianchedi, E. (1972). *Introduction to the Work of Bion*. London: Karnac Books.

Grotstein, J. S. (Ed.) (1981). *Do I Dare Disturb the Universe? A Memorial to Wilfred R. Bion*. Beverly Hills, CA: Caesura Press [reprinted London: Karnac Books, 1986].

Guntrip, H. (1961). *Personality structure and Human Interaction*. London: Hogarth Press.

Guntrip, H. (1968). *Schizoid Phenomena, Object Relations and the Self*. London: Hogarth Press.

Hampden-Turner, C. M. (1973). Radical man and the hidden moralities of social science. *Interpersonal Development, 2* (4).

Harman, W. (1992). Shifting assumptions and extended science. *ICIS Forum, 22* (3).

Hay, D. (1982). *Exploring Inner Space*. Harmondsworth: Penguin.

Hay, D. (1990). The bearing of empirical studies of religious experience on education. *Research Papers in Education*. Nottingham: Nottingham University Press.

Heidegger, M. (1953). *Being and Time*. Oxford: Blackwells.

Higgin, G., & Bridger, H. (1965). The psychodynamics of an intergroup exercise. *Tavistock Pamphlet No. 10*.

Hillman, J. (1991). *A Blue Fire*. New York: Harper Perennial.

Hobsbawm, E. (1994). *The Age of Extremes*. London: Michael Joseph.

Howe, I. (1971). *Decline of the New*. London: Gollancz.

Jaques, E. (1955). Social systems as a defence against persecutory and depressive anxiety. In: M. Klein, P. Heimann, & R. E. Money-Kyrle (Eds.), *New Directions in Psycho-Analysis* (pp. 478–498). London: Tavistock, 1955 [reprinted London: Karnac Books, 1985].

Joyce, J. (1939). *Finnegan's Wake*. Harmondsworth: Penguin, 1992.

Kellogg, R. T. (1994). *The Psychology of Writing*. Oxford: Oxford University Press.

Klein, M. (1921). The development of a child. In: *The Writings of Melanie Klein, Vol. I: Love Guilt and Reparation* (pp. 1–53). London: Hogarth Press, 1975 [reprinted London: Karnac Books, 1992].

Klein, M. (1928). Early stages of the Oedipus conflict. In: *The Writings of Melanie Klein, Vol. I: Love Guilt and Reparation* (pp. 186–198). London: Hogarth Press, 1975 [reprinted London: Karnac Books, 1992].

Klein, M. (1963). *Our Adult World and Other Essays*. London: Heinemann Medical.

Knights, L. C. (1959). *Some Shakespearian Themes*. London: Chatto and Windus.

Kristeva, J. (1987). *In the Beginning Was Love: Psychoanalysis and Faith*. New York: Columbia University Press.

Laplanche, J., & Pontalis, J.-B. (1973). *The Language of Psycho-Analysis*. London: Hogarth Press and the Institute of Psycho-Analysis [reprinted London: Karnac Books, 1996].

Lasch, C. (1978). *The Culture of Narcissism*. New York: W. W. Norton.

Lawrence, W. G. (1977). Management development: ideals, images and realities. *Journal of European Industrial Training, 1* (2): 21–25. [Also in: A. D. Colman & M. H. Geller (Eds.), *Group Relations Reader, 2*. Washington, DC: A. K. Rice Institute, 1985.]

Lawrence, W. G. (Ed.) (1979a). *Exploring Individual and Organizational Boundaries*. Chichester: John Wiley.

Lawrence, W. G. (1979b). Introductory essay: exploring boundaries. In: W. G. Lawrence (Ed.), *Exploring Individual and Organizational Boundaries* (pp. 1–19). Chichester: John Wiley.

Lawrence, W. G. (1980). Citizenship and the work place: a current case study. In B. Sievers & W. Slessina (Eds.), *Arbeitspapier des Fachbereichs Wirtschaftswissen der Gesamthochschule* (Wuppertal), No. 44.

Lawrence, W. G. (1982). *Some Psychic and Political Dimensions of Work Experience*. London: Tavistock Institute, Occasional Paper.

Lawrence, W. G. (1985). Beyond the frames. In: M. Pines (Ed.), *Bion and Group Psychotherapy*. London: Routledge and Kegan Paul.

Lawrence, W. G. (1986). A psycho-analytic perspective for understanding organizational life. In: G. Chattopadhyay, Z. Gangee, L. Hunt, & W. G. Lawrence (Eds.), *When the Twain Meet*. Allahabad: A. H. Wheeler.

Lawrence, W. G. (1993). Signals of transcendence in large groups as systems. *Group, 17* (4): 254–266.

Lawrence, W. G. (1995a). Exiles. In: I. A. Olson (Ed.), *No Other Place.* East Lothian: Tuckwell Press.

Lawrence, W. G. (1995b). Totalitaere sinsdstilstande i insitutioner. Copenhagen: *Aggrippa—Psykiatriske Tekster., 16* (1–2).

Lawrence, W. G. (Ed.) (1998). *Social Dreaming @ Work.* London: Karnac Books.

Lawrence, W. G., Bain, A., & Gould, L. J. (1966). The Fifth Basic Assumption. *Free Associations, 6* (37): 28–55.

Lawrence, W. G., & Hakim-Goldsbrough, C. (1973). *The Schools Reception Centre of the Commonwealth Institute.* London: Tavistock Institute of Human Relations, Document No. 871.

Lawrence, W. G., & Miller, E. J. (1976). Epilogie. In: E. J. Miller (Ed.), *Task and Organization* (pp. 361–366). Chichester: John Wiley.

Lawrence, W. G., & Robinson, P. (1974). *Development Project on Syndicate Methods Teaching.* London: Tavistock Institute of Human Relations, Document No. 970.

Lawrence, W. G., & Robinson, P. (1975). *An Innovation and Its Implementation: Issues of Evaluation.* London: Tavistock Institute of Human Relations, Document No. 1069.

Le Bon, G. (1896). *The Crowd: A Study of the Popular Mind.* London: Benn.

Lomas, H. D. (1979). Institutional transference revisited. *Bulletin of the Menninger Clinic:* 547–551.

McDannell, C., & Lang, B. (1988). *Heaven: A History.* New Haven/London: Yale University Press.

McDonagh, S. (1980). *The Eden Blueprint.* Manila, Philippines: Columban Fathers.

McDougall, W. (1920). *The Group Mind.* Cambridge: Cambridge University Press.

McKellar, P. (1957). *Imagination and Thinking.* New York: Basic Books.

McKellar, P. (1968). *Experience and Behaviour.* Harmondsworth: Penguin.

McLuhan, M., & Nevitt, B. (1972). *Take Today: the Executive as Dropout.* New York: Harcourt Brace Jovanovich.

Mennell, S. (1992). *Norbert Elias: An Introduction.* Oxford: Blackwell.

Menninger, R. (1972). The impact of group relations conferences on organizational growth. *International Journal of Psychotherapy*, 22.

Menzies Lyth, I. E. P. (1960). Nurses under stress. *International Nursing Review*, 7 (5): 9–16.

Menzies Lyth, I. E. P. (1965). Some mutual interactions between organizations and their members. *Psychotherapy and Psychosomatics*, 13: 194–200.

Menzies Lyth, I. E. P. (1975). Thoughts on the maternal role in contemporary society. *Journal of Child Psychotherapy*, 4 (1): 5–14.

Menzies Lyth, I. E. P. (1981). Bion's contribution to thinking about groups. In J. S. Grotstein (Ed.), *Do I Dare Disturb the Universe?* (pp. 661–665). Beverly Hills, CA: Caesura Press.

Menzies Lyth, I. E. P. (1988). *Containing Anxiety in Institutions*. London: Free Association Books.

Miller, E. J. (1976). Introductory essay: role perspectives and the understanding of organisational behaviour. In: E. J. Miller (Ed.), *Task and Organization* (pp. 1–16). Chichester: John Wiley.

Miller, E. J. (1977). Organisational development and industrial democracy: a current case study. In: C. Cooper (Ed.), *Organisational Development in the UK and USA: A Joint Evaluation* (pp. 31–63). London: Macmillan.

Miller, E. J. (1990). Experiential learning in groups. In: E. Trist & H. Murray (Eds.), *The Social Engagement of Social Science*. London: Free Association Books.

Miller, E. J. (1993). *From Dependency to Autonomy*. London: Free Association Books

Miller, E. J., & Gwynne, G. V. (1972). *A Life Apart*. London: Tavistock Publications.

Miller, E. J., & Rice, A. K. (1967). *Systems of Organization*. London: Tavistock.

Mills, C. W. (1970). *The Sociological Imagination*. Harmondsworth: Penguin.

Novak, M. (1971). *The Experience of Nothingness*. New York: Harper Colophon.

O'Neill, J. (1972). *Sociology as a Skin Trade*. New York: Harper Torchbooks.

Pederson-Krag, G. (1951). A psychoanalytic approach to mass production. *Psychoanalytic Quarterly*, 20: 434–451.

Polkinghorne, J. (1996). *Beyond Science*. Cambridge: Canto.

Popper, K. (1945). *The Open Society and Its Enemies* (2 vols.). London: Routledge.

Poulantzas, N. (1969). Capitalism and the state. *New Left Review* (58).

Rayner, E. (1990). *The Independent Mind in British Psychoanalysis*. London: Free Association Books.

Rayner, E. (1995). *Unconscious Logic*. London: Routledge.

Reid, L. (1962). *The Sociology of Nature*. Harmondsworth: Penguin.

Rice, A. K. (1951). The use of unrecognised cultural mechanisms in an expanding machine shop. *Human Relations, 4* (2): 143–160.

Rice, A. K. (1958). *Productivity and Social Organization: The Ahmedabad Experiment*. London: Tavistock Publications.

Rice, A. K. (1965). *Learning for Leadership*. London: Tavistock Publications.

Rice, A. K. (1970). *The Modern University: A Model Organization*. London: Tavistock Publications.

Richardson, E. (1973). *The Teacher, the School and the Task of Management*. London: Heinemann.

Rioch, M. J. (1970). The work of Wilfred Bion. *Psychiatry, 33*: 56–66.

Riviere, J. (1936). A contribution to the analysis of the negative therapeutic reaction. *International Journal of Psycho-Analysis, 17*: 304–320.

Schwartz, E. (1971). *Overskill*. New York: Ballantine Books.

Schwartz, P. (1991). *The Art of the Long View*. London: Century Business.

Senge, P. (1990). *The Fifth Dimensions; The Art and Practice of the Learning Organization*. New York: Doubleday.

Sievers, B., & Armstrong, D. (Eds.) (in preparation). *Discovering Social Meanings and Social Dreaming: Essays in Honour of Gordon Lawrence* (2 vols.). London: Karnac Books.

Steiner, G. (1961). *The Death of Tragedy*. London: Faber and Faber.

Steiner, G. (1971). *In Bluebeard's Castle*. London: Faber and Faber.

Sutherland, J. D. (1989). *Fairbairn's Journey into the Interior*. London: Free Association Books.

Symington, J. , & Symington, N. (1996). *The Clinical Thinking of Wilfred Bion*. London: Routledge.

Symington, N. (1986). *The Analytic Experience*. New York: St Martin's Press.

Tanner, T. (1971). *City of Words*. London: Jonathan Cape.

Tarnas, R. (1991). *The Passion of the Western Mind*. London: Pimlico.

Tecglen, E. H. (1992). *The Anguish of Abundance: Leonardo*. London: The Independent.

Thompson, E. P. (1968). *The Making of the English Working Class*. Harmondsworth: Penguin Books.

Toch, H. (1966). *The Social Psychology of Social Movements*. London: Methuen.

Trist, E. (1985). Working with Bion in the 1940s. In M. Pines (Ed.), *Bion and Group Psychotherapy*. London: Routledge.

Trist, E. L., & Bamforth, K. (1951). Some social and psychological consequences of the long-wall method of coal-getting. *Human Relations*, 4: 3–38.

Trist, E. L., & Sofer, C. (1959). *Exploration in Group Relations*. Leicester: Leicester University Press.

Trotter, W. (1916). *Instincts of the Herd in Peace and War*. London: T. Fisher Unwin.

Turquet, P. M. (1974). Leadership—the individual in the group. In: G. S. Gibbard, J. J. Hartman, & R. D. Mann (Eds.), *Analysis of Groups*. San Francisco, CA: Jossey-Bass.

Turquet, P. M. (1975). Threats to identity in the large group. In L. Kreeger (Ed.), *The Large Group*. London: Constable.

Ullman, M. (1975). The transformation process in dreams. *The American Academy of Psychoanalysis*, 19 (2): 8–10.

Unamuno, M. de (1921). *Tragic Sense of Life*. New York: Dover.

Weber, A. (1947). *Farewell to European History*. London: Kegan Paul, Trench, Trubner.

Whitehead, A. N. (1926). *Science and the Modern World*. Cambridge: Cambridge University Press.

Wijers, L., & Pijnappel, J. (1990). *Art Meets Science and Spirituality*. London: Academy Editions.

Williams, R. (1974). *The English Novel from Dickens to Lawrence*. St Albans: Paladin.

Wilson, A. T. M. (1951). Some aspects of social process. *Journal of Social Issues* (Supplementary Series, No. 5).

Winnicott, D. M. (1950). Some thoughts on the meaning of the word "democracy". *Human Relations*, 3 (2): 171–185. Reprinted in: E. Trist & H. Murray, *The Engagement of Social Science*. London: Free Association Books, 1990.

Winnicott, D. M. (1971). *Playing and Reality*. London: Tavistock Publications.

Winnicott, D. M. (1980). *Human Nature:* New York, NY: Schocken Books.

Zweig, A. (1937). *Insulted and Exiled*. London: John Miles.

INDEX

Miller, E. J., xvii, 32, 45, 51, 54, 200–202, 207
  empowerment, 173–174
  primary task, 128, 202
  sentient group, 130–131
Mills, C. W., 41, 42, 101
Mills, J., xix
Milton, J., 24
mind:
  and body, 18
  and brain, 16, 19
  and the text, 78
mob:
  power of, 83–84
  Self and Other, 85–87, 90
model, usage and danger of concept, 53–54
Moment, 143
mother–infant relationship:
  phantasy, 27–28
  potential space, 205–206
  thinking and language, 3
Murdoch, I., 5
mutative interpretations, 204, 214
mystic, 228–229
mystical, 190
myth, 63–64, 217

narcissism:
  basic assumption groups, 85
  large groups, 65
  social-ism, 4–5, 63, 220–231
narrative, and picaresque mode, 213–214
nationalism, 98–99
Nazism, xvi
  Self and Other, 90
Negative Capability, 150, 159
neonate:
  phantasy, 27–28
  unthought known, 11
nepotism, and narcissism, 226, 229
neuroscience, 15
Nevitt, B., exposition and exploration, 33, 138–139
Newton, I., 169
no-imago, and imago of cosmos, 81–82

non-work, basic assumption states, 127
normative primary task, 128, 202
no-thought, and thought, 80
not-known, 79
noumenon, 56
Novak, M., objectivity and subjectivity, 57
nursing, 198–199

objectivity:
  social sciences, 37–40
  and subjectivity, 20–21, 32, 57, 175
  see also reality; science; subjectivity
observer and observed, 173
Oedipal myth, and Sphinx myth, 3–5, 28–29
Oedipus complex, and dreaming, 10
Olson, xii
omnipotence:
  basic assumption groups, 63–64
  membership of the mob, 84
O'Neill, J., objectivity of sociologists, 38
oneness: *see* basic assumption oneness
open society, and narcissism, 227
open systems, 71, 76, 81
  see also socio-technical systems
order, 88, 136
  and bureaucracy, 126–127
organizational forms, as reflection of our imago/no-imago of cosmos, 81–82
organizations:
  impact of information technology, 176–177
  political relatedness and psyche, 192–207
originality, and tradition, 140
Other:
  and chaos, 82–83
  and ecology, 91
  and self, 74–76, 79, 82–86, 89, 90

pairing: *see* basic assumption pairing
paranoid–schizoid position, 26, 27, 211